DATE DUE

DEMCO 38-296

Textbooks for Learning

Textbooks for Learning
Nurturing Children's Minds

Marilyn J. Chambliss

Robert C. Calfee

BLACKWELL
Publishers

ublished 1998

8 10 9 7 5 3 1

l Publishers Inc.
Main Street
assachusetts 02148
USA

l Publishers Ltd
108 Cowley Road
Oxford OX4 1JF
UK

Library of Congress Cataloging-in-Publication Data

Chambliss, Marilyn J.
    Textbooks for learning : nurturing children's minds / Marilyn J.
Chambliss, Robert C. Calfee.
        p.   cm.
    Includes bibliographical references (p.   ) and index.
    ISBN 1–55786–411-X (hdbk : alk. paper). — ISBN 1–55786–412–8
(alk. : alk. paper)
    1. Textbooks—United States. 2. Textbooks—United States—
Authorship. 3. Textbooks—Publishing—United States. I. Calfee,
Robert C. II. Title.
LB3047.C49   1998
371.3'2'0973—dc21
                                                                                97–51454
                                                                                CIP

British Library Cataloguing in Publication Data

A CIP catalogue record for this book is available from the British Library

Typeset in 10.5/12 pt Ehrhardt
by York House Typographic Ltd, London
Printed in Great Britain by MPG Books Ltd, Bodmin, Cornwall

This book is printed on acid-free paper

CONTENTS

FIGURES

TABLES

FOREWORD

At long last, a comprehensive pastime report on the design, selection, and adoption of non-narrative, expository textbooks. Drawing whenever appropriate on the studies of others but largely focusing on their own analysis, the authors have fashioned not only a comprehensive report on what makes textbooks in the content areas more readable but the steps that designers and adopters may take to apply the recommendations.

One of the unique values of the report is that it recognizes the continuing significance of textbooks in the classrooms of most American teachers. The authors do not then seek to replace the present textbook-oriented curriculum with a completely different support system. Rather, they seek to improve approaches that are presently in place throughout this country. Thus the report seems more practical than the many well-intentioned but critical analyses that have become the norm for reform.

In focusing on comprehensibility and on the relationship between textbooks and curriculum and instruction, the authors pinpoint the problems of greatest concern in improving materials for use in American instruction, but they do not ignore recommendations from earlier reform. Ralph Tyler, Albert North Whitehead, Ernest Boyer, Joseph Schwab, Courtney Cazden, Bonnie Armbruster, and Dianne Ravich are among those quoted. But these authors conclude that the design of textbooks is the key, not the content factors alone.

Designers will find here clear-cut guidelines for creating and revising instructional material. Those selecting textbooks have now at their disposal a framework to suport the analysis of expository texts as well as a procedure to consider for training teachers. Future studies of textbooks will necessarily have to start with this book.

James R. Squire

PREFACE

The interest in textbooks waxes and wanes. When interest is high, newspaper and magazine articles draw public attention to problems with textbook content, writing, and instructional activities. States and districts develop "systems" for controlling the characteristics of the books that they choose. University researchers (and the foundations that fund the research) direct their efforts toward studying what textbooks are like and how they came to be that way. Publishers and adoption states tend to be identified as the "villains." When interest is low, textbooks receive scant attention. Newspaper articles, public interest, research funds, and finger pointing fade away. Through it all, textbooks remain remarkably unchanged, a central feature in most classrooms across the country.

The purpose of this book is to try to transcend the pendulum swings by embedding the analysis of textbooks in the larger concerns of curriculum, comprehension, and instruction, issues that are more consistently in the foreground than textbooks *per se*. Consequently, we identify no villains. Instead, this book presents tools for evaluating the curriculum present in a textbook, for judging how comprehensible the textbook would be, and for determining the calibre of the available instructional support. It envisions a future where teacher materials are at the core, supporting student-centered education that nurtures children as they construct for themselves important models, theories, and understandings. It describes current textbook publishing, state adoption, and district selection, and suggests tools for redesigning each of these enterprises. Finally, the book proposes leadership roles for publishers, states, districts, professional organizations, and university researchers that could transform the instructional materials used by children and their teachers.

This book has been written for the textbook publishers, state adoption committees, district selection committees, classroom teachers, parents, professional organizations, and university researchers who share responsibility for the textbooks that children read. We have tried to craft a coherent book, and we believe that each chapter builds on what has come before. However, because the intended audience is varied, certain chapters may hold more interest for one group of readers than for another group. In this Preface we synopsize the chapters to aid readers in choosing how to approach the book – which chapters to read closely and which to give a more cursory look.

- Chapter 1, "Today's textbooks, tomorrow's minds: The importance of textbooks," sets the stage. It claims that focusing on textbooks is important for three reasons. First, textbooks have the power to either nurture or stifle children's minds by the ideas that they present, their comprehensibility, and the instruction that they support. Second, textbooks are the repository for the closest thing that the United States has to a national curriculum. In a country of fiercely independent states and districts, textbooks prepared for a national market provide a coherence to what US citizens know and believe, for better or for worse. Third, textbook selection is one of the only forums in the United States for discussing and choosing curricula and instruction for the nation as a whole. While many states and districts choose textbooks haphazardly, others design a system that brings practitioners, academics, the news media, politicians, and parents together to choose the content that children are to cover, how it is to be organized, and how it is to be presented. The mechanisms are in place for transformational change.

Part I, *"The characteristics of well-designed textbooks"*

- Chapter 2, "Designing the ideal text," introduces notions of design that reappear throughout the rest of the book. This chapter claims that to nurture children's minds and enhance learning, textbooks must be carefully designed to be comprehensible, to represent an exemplary curriculum, and to support student-centered instruction. Most of the chapter focuses on the first of these requirements, comprehensibility. It reviews research on the characteristics of comprehensible text, applying research findings to the analysis of a passage on earthquakes and volcanoes from a sixth-grade science textbook.
- Chapter 3, "The design of curriculum and instruction," turns away from textbooks briefly to consider the features of an exemplary curriculum and student-centered instruction. This chapter claims that a major purpose of curriculum is to expose children to the domain-based ideas, understand-ings, models, and so on that experts have developed to make sense of experience. Student-centered instruction ensures that children who most likely will never become experts in any academic domain will nonetheless learn to use expert lenses. Such instruction connects the experts' lenses to

the experience of children, helps them organize what they are learning, gives them opportunities to reflect (or think about) what they are doing and learning, and prods them to extend (or transfer) their new understandings to other situations. The chapter concludes by presenting a rewrite on earthquakes and volcanoes that models how a textbook passage can be designed to be comprehensible, to convey the lens of experts, and to support student-centered instruction.

- Chapter 4, "Designing the ideal textbook," extends the claims in chapters 2 and 3 to entire textbooks of several hundred pages. It analyzes a curriculum framework and two social studies textbooks to demonstrate the usefulness of the ideas developed in these two earlier chapters. Chapter 4 concludes by presenting two tables of contents for US social studies books that model how an entire book could be designed to be comprehensible, to convey the lens of either a geographer or an historian, and to sustain student-centered instruction.
- Chapter 5, "Finding the design in textbook materials," introduces a set of tools, or rubrics, to use to describe the design in a passage or a table of contents, to represent it graphically for ease of analysis, and subsequently to evaluate its curriculum, comprehensibility, and instruction. The chapter presents many examples of both tables of contents and passages to model the rubrics and give the reader an opportunity to try out the approach.

Part II, *"Well-designed textbook publishing, state adoption, and district selection"*

- Chapter 6, "Current practices: publishers, states, and districts," describes two models of current textbook publishing, adopting, and selecting. In the *Responder* stance, those responsible for textbook materials primarily respond to outside influences. *Designers*, on the other hand, act customarily according to their own design decisions. The chapter fleshes out these models with examples from textbook publishers, state adoption staff, and district administrators. The chapter claims that only Designers are in a position to bring about fundamental change to US textbooks.
- Chapter 7, "Creating a design for publishing, adopting, and selecting," demonstrates how the same design rubrics that are useful for evaluating textbook materials can be used to improve how textbooks are published, adopted, and selected. The chapter introduces an "improved" model, and describes how textbook publishers, state adopters, and district selectors would complete their work according to the model. Most of the chapter demonstrates the value of the model by imagining how a fictitious district would complete its tasks from establishing curricular, comprehensibility, and instructional goals to selecting a social studies series that indeed matches the goals as closely as possible.

Part III, "*Stepping into the future*"

- Chapter 8, "A new approach to textbook design: Instructional Support Systems," proposes an evolution of textbooks into entire instructional systems centered around a Teacher's Guide that would link student books, electronic media, and assessment into a well-designed coherent whole, with curricular integrity, comprehensibility, and student-centeredness. The chapter presents examples to model well-designed curriculum plans, including one that spans several years of schooling, instructional plans that last from a few days to several months, and a year-long plan for student assessment.
- Chapter 9, "Bringing about the ideal: Leaders and collaborators," claims that Instructional Support Systems will not come about without substantial changes to textbook publishing, state adoption, and district selection. It describes leadership roles that publishers, states, districts, professional and trade groups, and university researchers could assume to transform the entire system. The chapter concludes by explaining that all of these participants will have to collaborate as well in order to bring about the requisite changes and describes a model that could support such collaboration.

This book has benefitted from the input of many people. The initial impetus for the volume is a project funded by the Carnegie Corporation of New York to the Text Analysis Project at Stanford University, Stanford, California. During spring 1989, Dr Mary Kiely, then a program officer at Carnegie, and excited by the possibility of using California textbook adoption as a case study of textbook reform, approached the two of us. Soon after, Dr Anthony Jackson became the program officer for the Text Analysis Project, providing us with valuable guidance and support. Subsequently, we and a staff of Stanford graduate students reviewed the work of other researchers; studied the documents of several states and interviewed staff at the California Department of Education; shadowed district selection committees and read the documents and interviewed the members of other committees; and interviewed editors and consultants at several textbook publishers, both large and small. We continued our work by developing rubrics for analyzing textbook materials; applying the rubrics to textbooks in science and social studies; conducting workshops to teach the rubrics to district administrators, classroom teachers, and textbook editors; and conducting research to explore how well our passage rewrites enhance comprehensibility. What we learned from the Text Analysis Project became the well-spring for this book. While we could list many names, we are particularly grateful to the following research assistants at Stanford, district administrators, and publishing executives: Anne Beauford, Research Assistant;

Elizabeth Burris, Research Assistant; Donald Eklund, Association of American Publishers (retired); Colleen Halverson, Research Assistant; John Hathaway, Eastside Union High School District, San Jose, California; Robert Hull, Addison-Wesley; Melissa Beretz Miller, Research Assistant; Carol Moran, Research Assistant; Bernie Mulvaney, Silver-Burdett Ginn; Barbara Schweiger, Omaha City Schools, Omaha, Nebraska; and Margaret Watt, Research Assistant.

During the writing of this book, a willing group of colleagues read early drafts and gave us valuable feedback. These colleagues included researchers at other universities, graduate students at Stanford University, executives at textbook publishers with whom we had worked, and a director of the Office of Curriculum Framework and Textbook Development, California Department of Education. We list their names below, fearful that, despite our best intentions, we may have omitted a name: Roger Bruning, University of Nebraska; Rosemarie Fontana, Stanford University; Michael Graves, University of Minnesota; Scott Paris, University of Michigan; Cynthia Patrick, Stanford University; John Ridley, Houghton Mifflin; Joseph Rios, Stanford University; James Squire, Silver-Burdett Ginn (retired); and Glen Thomas, California Department of Education.

Finally, this book would not have been possible without the help of several staff members. Bruce Templeton and Renée Christensen helped to design early drafts of the many graphics in the book and to complete copy editing. Our most heartfelt appreciation goes to Jay Thorp, who magically transformed our scribbles into elegant figures and patiently revised and revised as we changed our minds.

We conclude this preface by acknowledging the help and support of all those listed above as well as our families and friends. The accuracy of our observations and the value of our recommendations are due in large measure to our collaboration with others. However, we assume sole responsibility for inaccuracies and suggestions that appear ill-conceived.

Marilyn J. Chambliss and Robert C. Calfee

ACKNOWLEDGMENTS

The authors would like to thank the following organizations that have kindly given permission to reproduce copyright figures and tables.

Table 2.1 adapted with permission from *Strategies of Discourse Comprehension* (p. 256), by T. A. van Dijk and W. Kintsch, 1983, New York: Academic Press. © 1983 Academic Press, Inc.: adapted with permission. Table 2.2 adapted from Chou Hare, Victoria; Rabinowitz, Mitchell; and Schieble, Karen Magnus. (1989, Winter). Text effects on main idea comprehension. Reading Research Quarterly, *24*(1), 72–88. Reprinted with permission of Victoria Chou and the International Reading Association. All rights reserved. Figure 2.1 adapted with permission from *Discover Science/Grade 6* (pp. 302–304), by M. R. Cohen, T. M. Cooney, and C. M. Hawthorne, 1989, Glenview, IL: Scott Foresman and Company. © 1989 Scott Foresman and Company. Figure 4.6 adapted with permission from *The World and its People/The United States and its Neighbors*, 1986, Morristown, NJ: Silver Burdett Company. © 1986 Silver Burdett Company, a Division of Simon and Schuster, Inc. Figure 5.2 reprinted with permission from *Our United States/Grade 5*, by S. Klein, 1983, Madison, NJ: Steck–Vaughn Company. © 1983 Steck–Vaughn Company. Figure 5.5 adapted and figure 5.13 reprinted, with permission from *Our World/Grade 6*, by J. Canjemi (ed.), 1987, Orlando, FL: Holt, Rinehart, and Winston, Inc. © 1987 Holt, Rinehart, and Winston, Inc. Figure 5.7 – Houghton Mifflin for table of contents from 'A message of ancient days' in Armento et al., *Houghton Mifflin Social Studies*. Copyright © 1991 by Houghton Mifflin Company. Reprinted by permission of Houghton Mifflin Company. All rights reserved. Figure 5.9 reprinted with permission from *Legacy of Freedom Volume 1: United States History Through Reconstruction*, by G. M. Linden, D. C. Brink, and R. H. Huntington. 1986, River Forest, IL: Laidlaw Brothers Publishers. © 1986 Laidlaw Brothers Publishers, a Division of Macmillan Publishing Company, Inc. Figure 5.11 adapted with permission from *Silver Burdett Science/Grade 5* (pp. 63–66), by G. G. Mallinson. J. B. Mallinson, and W. L. Smallwood, 1985,

Morristown, NJ: Silver Burdett Company. © 1985 Silver Burdett Company, a Division of Simon and Schuster, Inc. Figure 5.15 adapted with permission from *All About Birds*, by R. S. Lemon, 1955, New York: Ransom House. © 1955 Random House. Figure 5.17 adapted with permission from *HBJ Science/Grade 5* (pp. 83–84), by E. K. Cooper, P E. Blackwood, and J. A. Boeschen, 1985, Orlando FL: Harcourt Brace Jovanovich, Inc. © 1985 Harcourt Brace Jovanovich, Inc. Figure 5.19 adapted with permission from *HBJ Science/Grade 6* (p. 152), by E. K. Cooper, P. E. Blackwood, and J. A. Boeschen, 1985, Orlando FL: Harcourt Brace Jovanovich, Inc. © 1985 Harcourt Brace Jovanovich, Inc. Figure 5.21 adapted with permission from *Silver Burdett Science/Grade 4* (pp. 139–141), by G. G. Mallinson, J. B. Mallinson, and W. L. Smallwood, 1985, Morristown, NJ: Silver Burdett Company. © 1985 Silver Burdett Company, A Division of Simon and Schuster, Inc.

The publishers apologize for any errors or omissions in the above list and would be grateful to be notified of any corrections that should be incorporated in the next edition or reprint of this book.

1

TODAY'S TEXTBOOKS, TOMORROW'S MINDS: THE IMPORTANCE OF TEXTBOOKS

The reading specialist listened quietly while we laid out our case. We had presented the litany many times before. "Textbooks can be improved . . . . A book's organization influences how students understand and learn from what they read . . . . What's in a book affects what students know about the world." Finally unable to restrain herself, the specialist burst out: 'Why are you spending all this effort on a dinosaur? Textbooks will soon be completely replaced by trade books, video disks, and computers. You're wasting my time and yours!"

Many educators agree that textbooks will soon become extinct – and should. Current textbooks can make for dismal reading. The best science programs keep children curious and their minds' turning ". . . with no textbooks at all," says physicist Jerome Pine of the California Institute of Technology. Students should learn from real experiments rather than books.[1] The 1988 California History–Social Science framework encouraged publishers to prepare short booklets with original materials rather than old-fashioned tomes.[2]

"Wait a minute!" cry voices on the other side of the issue. Textbooks may have problems, but they are the foundation for public education in the United States, the surrogate for a national curriculum.[3] Estimates show that textbooks determine 75–90 per cent of instructional content and activities in schools throughout the nation. Many teachers lack either the subject matter expertise or time to construct their own curriculum, particularly in the elementary grades. The textbook is both the subject-matter authority and the heart of the instructional program. Whatever shared vision we have about what should be taught and how it should be presented currently depends on textbooks.[4]

Proponents also point out that the machinery for producing and selecting textbooks is in place. Changing textbooks is the most economical and efficient way to improve the content and instruction in our classrooms.[5] Rather than tossing out textbooks, we should improve them. California has relied on textbook adoptions as an important lever in bringing about significant educational change.[6] Ernest L. Boyer, former president of the Carnegie Foundation for the Advancement of Teaching and a former United States Commissioner of Education, suggests that choosing textbooks "is the closest thing that we have to systematic debate over what our schools should be teaching."[7]

We propose that the potential of textbooks has yet to be fully exploited. The ideal book would be well-written and clearly organized, bridging the gap between student experience and expert knowledge. It would guide students in developing a lens for viewing and interacting with the world. It would expand student experience throughout time and space. It would support the teacher in designing flexible, student-centered instruction. This image is an ideal, to be sure, but one that, if realized, could be a powerful tool for nurturing our children's minds.

Our purpose in writing this book is to explore this ideal image – to present a design for textbooks of the future, and to suggest concrete steps that could be taken now to improve what we have. We are not the first to address these issues, and we build on previous work wherever possible. It is tempting to bash current practice or transport ourselves to a dazzling technocratic future. Our window is the next decade, and our question is what to do with what we have during a time of tumultuous change. While the nation is wiring its schools and figuring out what to do with the most recent kindergarten "bubble," while the talk is about higher standards and fewer dollars, while the emphases are on professional development and increased class sizes, we think it likely that textbooks will continue to be the primary technology in many classrooms across the grades. Our focus will be on three goals – "big ideas" rather than encyclopedic content coverage, instructional adaptability and flexibility rather than tightly prescriptive activities, and coherent organization rather than never-ending shipping lists.

This chapter explores the potential of the textbook to nurture minds, describes the strengths and weaknesses of current textbooks, and assesses the gap between where we are and where we might be. Chapters 2–4 lay out a vision of comprehensible instructional materials that support effective curriculum and student-centered instruction. Chapter 5 describes tools for analyzing and evaluating the comprehensibility, curriculum, and instructional support in textbook materials. Chapters 6 and 7 cover the publication, adoption, and selection systems that undergird current textbook offerings. Chapter 8 presents a vision of instructional support systems that could revolutionize instructional materials, while chapter 9 describes a parallel strategy for publication and selection, in which publishers and educators work together in the design of instructional support systems.

The Power of Textbooks to Nurture Minds

Textbooks can transform our children's minds. What a revolutionary idea! We often think of textbooks as repositories of information to be pushed into students' skulls, rather than as resources that provide opportunities for exploration and enjoyment. The power of the textbook to influence what children know, can do, and value is an assumption that undergirds most textbook reform. Bill Honig, former Superintendent for Public Instruction in California, relied heavily on textbook policies as a lever for changing schools, and for influencing children's values, knowledge, and skills – a strategy that has been adopted in many other states. Nor are state superintendents the only ones who believe in the power of print. Special-interest groups and concerned parent groups routinely picket, pack, and address school board hearings to protest the content of to-be-adopted textbooks. Ethnic minorities worry about materials that may negatively affect how students view their group. Parents with strong religious beliefs have asked courts to excuse their children from exposure to books that go against their convictions. An assumption driving these activities is the belief that a child's mind is malleable, and that textbooks have the power to affect minds – for better or worse.

What are the distinctive features of an educated mind, and how do these features develop? Surprisingly, notions from philosophers, psychologists, and educators all converge on the same two-part answer. First, a relatively small number of critical ideas have the power to organize much of experience. Education is not so much "knowing more" as "knowing differently." To be sure, experts know more than novices, but sheer bulk is not the key. The expert's knowledge is organized around principles, models, and ideas.[8] When students first attempt physics problems, they focus on surface features. They see hammers, screwdrivers, crowbars, and pliers as falling into one category, while nails, screws, and springs fall into another cluster. Such practical knowledge works well for many purposes. Expert physicists group the same objects differently, based on the mechanical principles at work – leverage, for instance. These principles are important for theoretical purposes. One can calculate the relation between force and length of a lever in ways that apply equally to hammers, crowbars, and pliers (although, when the physicist replaces a screen door, he or she probably relies on practical ways of thinking). The educated mind is a relatively orderly place – or at least it has some orderly areas.

The philosopher, Alfred North Whitehead, described eloquently the relations between actual experience and the educated mind, likening experience to a chaotic stream of events – messy and fragmentary – the mind searching for patterns wherever they can be found. He saw in schooling the potential "to impart an intimate sense for the power of ideas, for the beauty of ideas, and for the structure of ideas . . . ."[9] He warned educators, "Do not teach too many subjects, [and] what you teach, teach thoroughly, seizing on the few general ideas which illuminate the whole, and persistently marshalling subsidiary facts round them."[10]

Second, these ideas must be reconstructed by the knower, not merely absorbed. To be useful, the ideas must be used. Learning abstract ideas divorced from concrete experience was viewed by Whitehead as ineffective.[11] He was a philosopher, but recent psychological research has shown that empty generalizations are indeed quickly forgotten or misplaced in memory. Children need lots of examples that bring principles to life, concrete and familiar examples that they can work through thoroughly; that they can twist and turn; with which they can play. These findings are the basis for recommending depth over breadth in the school curriculum; for proposing the sustained study of a given topic rather than brief exposure to a myriad of factoids.[12]

Such an educated mind is not restricted to the bright or exceptional student, but is within the reach of virtually all students. Expertise is found in every field of endeavor. Years ago one of us overheard a conversation between two moving men as they took the furniture from her parents' house. The boss was in his early fifties, hefty and calloused. He had obviously spent years in the business. His helper was younger, taller, and thinner, and clearly less experienced. As they worked, they discussed the pros and cons of two models for moving furniture. During the discussion, the job proceeded according to the boss's model.

According to the boss, furniture should be removed from a house and packed into the van room by room, saving steps at both ends of the move. People organized by rooms in the new house the same way as in the old one, he explained. The helper held to a different model, in which furniture was organized by size. Bulky, heavy pieces were collected first and placed on the floor of the van, and smaller pieces then placed on the top. This method packed the van more economically and made for a more stable load.

This example suggests that each mover had a "mental model" when it came to moving furniture. Each operated according to a small number of principles that he could explain and justify. Furniture movers learn their craft not from books, but through apprenticeships with more experienced colleagues. And because they actually move furniture while they are learning, they attend the "school of hard knocks"; they learn by doing. Book learning, learning by knowing, often amounts to little more than memorizing meaningless statements. But if a book is properly designed, then book learning can lead to expertise more efficiently than randomly "knocking around" in an area. Some educators recommend that textbooks be tossed out and replaced with hands-on activities. We disagree; a well-crafted textbook offers the best of both worlds, serving as a wise "master" while leading children through richly informative exercises.

Today's Textbooks

It's first day in fifth grade. The teacher hands each student a science textbook, his or hers for the whole year. The book is new and smells fresh. A scarlet apple is emblazoned on the cover's dark brown background. Students flip through the pages. This is a *big*, grown-up book. They are impressed and overwhelmed. How can they ever learn everything in it? But the pictures draw the students in. A dramatic picture of the eruption of Mount St. Helens; satellite photos of Mars in shades of orange and red; students conducting laboratory experiments; brightly colored charts and graphs. This is a book anyone would want to read!

Not every child encounters this experience, to be sure. Many teachers manage with out-of-date and dilapidated textbooks, more often teachers whose students come from poor or isolated communities. Other teachers prefer "real books" to textbooks, relying on libraries and book stores for the riches that they have to offer. The bottom line, however, is that the textbook materials available to most US students are the envy of many other countries.

What Makes our Textbooks the Best?

Given the generally negative tone of most press reports about American education, you may be surprised by talk about the quality of our instructional materials. But the World Bank, as just one instance, in recommending reforms to other countries, often places improved textbooks near the top of the list, and points to our materials as examples. Some of the positive features were sketched above. For instance, the books are visually captivating. Arthur Woodward, in his analysis of textbooks, describes them as worthy of anyone's coffee table.[13] Equally important, they are durable. The covers are hard and waterproof. The glossy pages are tear-resistant, and the bindings sturdy. The books can survive rough treatment, short of being run over by a car, dropped into a water puddle, or defacement with graffiti.

The books contain enormous amounts of information. A fifth-grade science book runs to about 350 pages, and eighth-grade books to more than double this number. Many pages, especially in the early grades, have extensive photographic coverage, but the printed material is still substantial. The books include a variety of supplemental features: a detailed table of contents, glossary, and index; worksheets and tests; boxed sections describing occupations; scientific contributions by ethnic minorities and women; student exercises; and so on. The books have something for everyone.

The student textbook does not stand alone, but is part of a larger system. The hefty teacher's manual guides the teacher through the school year with a detailed script. The manual, a spiral binder or loose-leaf notebook, is carefully designed to fit lap or lectern. Activities are color-coded by type (direct instruction, small-group activity, individual practice). The manual is organized around weekly segments, with specific information about how to begin, conduct, and end each lesson. There are suggestions for adapting lessons and materials to students with special needs, those for whom English is a second language or who have been identified as learning disabled. The front section of the manual includes a scope-and-sequence chart that shows how program content and activities meet various curriculum outcomes. For a school administrator challenged by the community to show that students are being taught phonics, the scope-and-sequence chart offers a ready answer. And all of this material is presented in a colorful and practical design. The teacher manual is every bit as appealing as the student's textbook.

The textbook package includes many other supplemental components. Student workbooks accompany each lesson to ensure opportunities for practicing skills. "Project packets" offer photographs, video cassettes, audio cassettes, or even puppets to keep students busy. There are end-of-unit tests, "masters" for preparing transparencies to help with lectures, and computer software for instruction and assessment. You name it, and the system has it.

Finally, it is worth noting that, in the United States, textbooks belong to the people. They are either free or cost a small fee for children in the public schools. Children in many other countries are not as fortunate. Not only are textbooks readily available, but they reflect the influence of the citizens. True to the democratic spirit, parents, children, and community spokepersons, as well as teachers, administrators, and professors, all have a say about school books. For better or worse, today's texts reflect society's interests, beliefs, and values.

What's Wrong with our Textbooks?

While today's instructional materials have much to recommend them, some of the strengths also lead to problems, and criticisms are legion. The debate sometimes centers around beliefs and values, a natural part of the democratic enterprise. But some of the very features with greatest appeal also spark the loudest protests.

For instance, the books are noteworthy for their attractiveness. The pictures, charts, and boxes are captivating, but often unrelated to the text. They can be seductive distractors, peaking interest rather than instructing, decorative more than substantive. Boxed vignettes, tacked on to cover special objectives and topics, intrude on the flow of the text. Each page is full of busy-ness. Wide margins are sprinkled with notes, definitions, questions, and mini-photos. The text is interrupted by bold-faced pronunciation guides [e.g., Tuskeegee (**tuss-kee'-jee**)], presumably to help students when reading the material aloud. Imagine reading an encyclopedia aloud. The four-color graphics grab the eye, but seldom are explained in the text. Instead, separate "skills" sections train the student to "read a figure," but disconnected from any real purpose: "Five presidents were born in Ohio. Look at the atlas map for the town of Delaware, OH, where Rutherford B. Hayes was born, and find the coordinates."

The books are comprehensive. The hefty size, especially in science and social studies, arises from the emphasis on comprehensive coverage. Science books in grades 6–9 contain four to five thousand specialized or technical words, at least half of them new and unfamiliar.[14] The result is that even major topics receive skimpy treatment. A sixth-grade social studies book in our sample devotes one chapter to the continent of Africa and a short paragraph to North and South Korea. Harriet Tyson-Bernstein, a persuasive and persistent critic, concludes that ". . . skimpy coverage of important topics heads the list of faults."[15] The encyclopedic quality results because every interested party wants to get in their two cents' worth, and so publishers "mention" everything that anyone asks to be covered. As a consequence, the books lack depth, and important principles – big ideas – are lost in the shuffle.

Textbooks offer students a rich array of new and potentially interesting facts, and open the door to a world of fantastic experiences. Unfortunately, they seldom link this new content with students' prior knowledge. These materials, by definition, are read by novices. The typical reader will not know the topic, but will probably have a variety of beliefs (misconceptions) arising from common-sense perceptions based on everyday experience. These beliefs are likely to be quite at odds with the "expert" understanding presented in the book.

People's misconceptions about the seasons illustrate the problem. Surveys show that a sizeable percentage of adults think that summer and winter are caused by annual variations in the distance between the sun and earth. Summer comes when the earth is closer to the sun, and winter when the planet swings away into outer space. Social studies and science textbooks at several grade levels describe the Copernican model, and explain how the tilt of the earth on its axis causes the seasonal changes. Along with the prose explanation come pictures and diagrams, as well as activities in which children play the roles of sun and earth, using a flashlight to concretize the principles. The efforts clearly do not work. While it is unfair to place all of the blame for misunderstandings on textbooks, we have not found a single instance in which the textbook or teacher's manual begins by asking the student, "What do you [the student] think causes the seasons – what makes winter cold and summer hot?" Rather, they launch into a largely counter-intuitive explanation; students may remember what the book says, but it does not displace their original beliefs.

Connecting does not require fancy technology, nor are more words and pictures needed. To illustrate, consider what happens when adults are asked to imagine the setting sun. Virtually everyone reports that they see the sun sinking below the horizon, even though they have learned many times (in school and out) that the sun does not move across the sky, but the earth turns. To "connect" adults with their book learning, ask them to imagine that they are watching the "setting" sun while grown to the size of a ten-mile-high giant. They look out into space, their feet rooted on the ground while their eyes peer toward the sun from the stratosphere. The scene goes into motion as they imagine the Earth rotating backward, away from the sun, which is gradually covered by the far horizon. We have tried this scenario repeatedly in workshops, and a substantial proportion of the adults "get it," to the degree that they experience dizziness!

Finally, and despite extensive editorial investment, textbooks are often just poorly written. Part of the problem comes from the encyclopedic quality, and difficulties also arise because the books are written by committees and consultants rather than authors. As we will illustrate in later chapters, the organization is often weak, all the way from the table of contents, introductions, and conclusions to the design of individual paragraphs. Interest is carried by the graphics; the prose makes little reliance on vivid vocabulary, metaphors, or examples. Compare library books on similar topics, and we think most readers will conclude that textbooks come out second best by these criteria. Of course, library books meet a different criterion – librarians purchase them because they think readers will want to read them, whereas textbooks are "adopted" by adults, and students have little say in the matter. Teachers can play a major role in textbook selection, but we have not encountered an instance in which student opinions have been surveyed.

Reasons for Optimism

We began this chapter by outlining the potential of textbooks, and we will end on a positive note. First, there are no villains in this piece. Educators need resources as a foundation for curriculum and instruction. Administrators confront many pressures in the selection process. Publishers must respond to the marketplace.

We can also point to several instances of positive responses by publishers and others to opportunities for improving textbook materials. Recent changes in reading textbooks, for instance, mean that students are reading higher-quality literature from top-ranked authors. A broad range of multi-cultural stories appear in today's anthologies, much changed from the "Dick and Jane" of earlier decades. Science books include more opportunities for students to do "hands-on" science. But the basic problems sketched above – especially the prevailing emphasis on content coverage – continue to challenge both educators and publishers, as we shall see in the chapters that follow. Many of today's sharpest critics continue to beat the coverage drum; teachers don't teach enough and students don't learn enough. For example, Diane Ravitch charges that "[Today's students] are culturally illiterate. They can read the words put in front of them, but they have no "furniture" in their minds, no vocabulary of historical persons or events to draw upon, no reference to the ordinary literary images that fifth graders once imbibed in every common school in the nation."[16] In fact, studies suggest that today's students know as much as previous generations, and probably a good deal more.[17] We are not suggesting that students should not experience the canons of the various subject matters. But given what we know about learning, and looking ahead toward what it will mean to "know" in the future, schools need to move from exposure to engagement, from memorization of factoids toward understanding – not only of important ideas, but also of how to access and manage information.

Whatever the shape of school reforms in the next several years, textbooks will be part of the action. The themes sketched above thread their way through the rest of this volume: a focus on big ideas, coherent organization, connections with student experience and interest, and high-quality writing. In our reviews of textbook materials, we have been struck by "missed opportunities": opening and closing sections that, with a small amount of rewriting, could introduce and conclude more effectively; weak organizational structures that with modest reordering could become strong; pictures and graphics that could be linked to the text in a few sentences; unrelated modules that with carefully considered redesign could be joined thematically, while still retaining important flexibility. Some of these problems require substantial redesign, but many do not.

Textbooks certainly are not the only issue in school improvement, but we intend to show that improving these materials can be a powerful and possible action. We will focus in this volume on social science, science, and language textbooks for grades 4–9. Starting with grade 4, textbooks in social science and science present significant amounts of expository prose from which youngsters are expected to learn. These are formative years, during which students must be able to handle the challenge of comprehending expository passages dealing with novel and complex topics. The calibre of these materials contributes substantially to youngsters" success, either nurturing or stifling their minds. We are convinced – and hope to be convincing – that substantial improvements are possible even in the short run.

Notes

1   Begley et al. (1990), p. 56.
2   California State Board of Education (1988).
3   Carus (1990).
4   Apple (1985) and Tyson and Woodward (1989), but see Freeman and Porter (1989) and Stodolsky (1989).
5   Komoski (1985).
6   California State Board of Education (1988, 1990).
7   Fiske (1987) p. 20.
8   Nickerson (1985).
9   Whitehead (1974), p. 23.
10 Ibid., p. 3.
11 Whitehead (1929, 1974).
12 Nickerson (1985) and Newmann (1988).
13 Woodward (1989).
14 Yager (1983).
15 Bernstein (1985).
16 Ravitch (1985).
17 Berliner and Biddle (1996).

Part I

THE CHARACTERISTICS OF WELL-DESIGNED TEXTBOOKS

2

DESIGNING THE IDEAL TEXT

The USA is moving rapidly into a high-tech, information age: pico-computers, virtual realities, compact-disk encyclopedias. Each day brings new breakthroughs, and tomorrow's students need to be prepared for change and challenge. At the same time, the student population is becoming more diverse. Can books really compete any more? We think so. As we argued in the previous chapter, books may be uniquely suited to support learning and nurture children's minds. A simple technology, textbooks are the closest thing in the United States to a national curriculum. Teachers rely heavily on textbook packages to guide their instruction. Most of the experience that students have with reading in school centers around textbooks. While today's textbooks provide integrated instructional packages, appealingly illustrated, and bolstered with diverse supplements, they also tend to present bits and pieces of content rather than a coherent curriculum. The rigid linear format of many series does not lend itself to student-centered instruction, while the booklet design of other series can be too fragmented to support effective pedagogy. Typically, textbook materials present needless comprehension challenges to young readers. These materials, prepared for inexperienced readers, exhibit the hallmarks of poor writing and consequently can be difficult to understand. Textbooks redesigned to correct these deficiencies have the potential to nurture the minds of our children.

This chapter and the two that follow explore the capacity of this simple technology to improve student learning. The chapters are based on several claims. To support learning, textbooks must be carefully designed to be *comprehensible*, to represent an exemplary *curriculum*, and to support *student-centered instruction*. The minimum requirement for written materials is comprehensibility. Readers more easily understand text when it is familiar, interesting, and well-organized rather than obscure, boring, and chaotic. Textbooks must also convey an exemplary curriculum of intellectual ideas and support student-centered instruction. Comprehensibility is a necessary but not a sufficient characteristic of well-designed textbooks. An exemplary curriculum reflects important topics, explanatory models and theories, and critical ways of knowing from the minds of domain experts. Student-centered instruction connects with the knowledge, interests, and skills of students; helps them to organize the content; encourages them to reflect on their learning; and enables them to extend what they have learned to other contexts.

For a concrete image of what we are talking about, look at "How Does Plate Tectonics Explain Earthquakes and Volcanoes?" in figure 2.1, a typical sixth-grade science text. The figure includes graphics from the original, but we have dropped marginal items that did not appear to be of central importance to the text. We have changed the beginning of the passage by picking up two paragraphs from an earlier section in the book, to give background knowledge on plate tectonics.

Scan the material and ask yourself the following questions:

- Which parts of the passage connect with what you already know?
- What are the most interesting features of the passage?
- How would you summarize or outline the passage?
- What do you think you learned from the passage? What will you remember a month from now?
- If you were going to discuss plate tectonics with someone, how might this passage make you "look smart?"

The first three questions address the comprehensibility of the passage: Is it reasonably familiar? Does it engage your attention? Is it coherently organized? The last two questions touch on curriculum and instruction: What does the passage teach? Does it teach the content in a way that allows you to use the information in other settings? You will want to keep this textbook example in mind, because we return to it repeatedly.

A textbook that is comprehensible, reflects an exemplary curriculum, and supports student-centered instruction will not occur by happenstance. Some-one, an author or editor, must design the book by choosing content and organizational structures that meet these criteria. The notion of design is perhaps the most important touchstone in this book. We call upon principles of design throughout the following chapters and discuss how these principles can shape textbooks for the future.

Chapters 2–4 support and explain our claims. Chapter 2 lays out a set of design principles and applies them to text comprehensibility. Chapter 3 focuses on the design of exemplary curriculum and student-centered instruction. Throughout both chapters, we refer repeatedly to examples of text, including the one that you have already read. We conclude chapter 3 with a rewrite of "Volcanoes and Earthquakes" that is comprehensible and exemplifies sound curricular and instructional design.

Figure 2.1   An example of a typical passage from a sixth-grade science textbook (Cohen et al., 1989).

How Does Plate Tectonics Explain Earthquakes and Volcanoes?

Scientists have formed a new theory--called **plate tectonics**--to explain how continents move. According to this theory, both the continents and the ocean floors are located on **plates** that move over the earth. Each plate is a huge block of rock. Notice in the picture that a plate is made up of crust and the upper part of the mantle. The plates float on the partly melted rock in the mantle. Currents in the melted rock move the plates. These currents are called **convection currents**. They are caused by heat from within the earth.

Most changes on the earth's surface are due to plate tectonics. Some changes happen very slowly--usually over millions of years. Other changes occur quickly--sometimes without warning! Earthquakes and volcanoes are two sudden changes on the earth's surface that are caused by plate tectonics.

Changes at Plate Boundaries

Most earthquakes occur at plate boundaries. An earthquake is a release of energy caused by the breaking or moving of rock layers within a plate. The release of energy causes the ground to shake.

Many earthquakes take place along **fracture boundaries**. A fracture boundary is an area where two plates are sliding past one another. A **fault** is a crack in the earth's crust along which rock layers move. The San Andreas Fault is a fracture boundary that is really a series of many faults. Energy from within the earth moves the two plates along a fracture boundary. Sometimes, rock layers near the edges of the plates do not move. Energy builds up in the rocks as the plates continue to move. Eventually, the energy overcomes the strength of the rocks. Suddenly this energy is released as the rock layers slip past one another.

The release of energy is greatest at the **focus** of an earthquake. The focus is the point along the fault where the rock layers moved. The focus is usually far below the surface of the earth. If you were standing directly above the focus of an earthquake, you would be the first person to feel the ground shake.

Volcanoes also are common at plate boundaries. Volcanoes are found on both the continents and the ocean floor. A volcano is an opening on the surface of a plate through which magma rises. The magma comes from the melted layer of the mantle on which the plate moves.

Most volcanoes are found along **colliding boundaries** and **spreading boundaries.** At colliding boundaries two plates are moving toward one another. At spreading boundaries two plates are moving away from one another. Volcanoes at colliding boundaries are generally explosive. Look at the picture of a colliding boundary. Notice that as the crust moves into the mantle, it melts into magma. Hot magma is less dense than the solid rock that makes up the plates. As a result, magma drifts upwards through openings in the plates. Gases become trapped within this thick magma. The trapped gases and the heat cause pressure to build up in the openings. When the pressure becomes very great, the magma explodes out of the openings through the volcano. Magma that reaches the surface is called lava.

Volcanoes at spreading boundaries do not explode when they erupt. Instead, magma flows out onto the surface of the plate, adding new crust to the ocean floor. As the hot magma reaches the cold ocean water, it cools and forms pillows of hard lava.

Figure 2.1 contd.

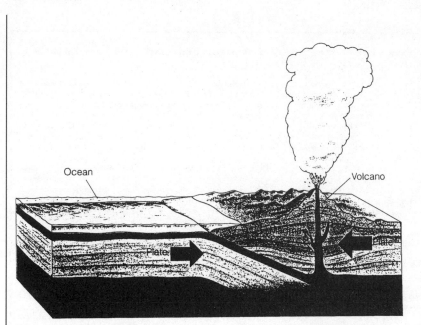

Volcano at a colliding boundary

Types of Volcanic Cones

As a volcano erupts, it builds a mountain called a volcano cone. Some cones are steep mountains. Others are smooth domes. The way a volcano erupts and the kind of matter that is erupted determine the shape of a volcano's cone.

Volcanoes that erupt explosively form **cinder cones**. Notice that this kind of cone has steep sides. Cinders-- small pieces of hard lava-- are thrown out of the volcano. Large amounts of ash also are thrown out. The cinders and ash form the cone as they fall back to the ground. Most cinder cones look like the Paricutin Volcano in Mexico.

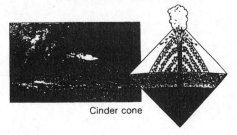

Cinder cone

Volcanoes that do not erupt form **shield cones**. Hot lava flows from the volcano's large opening as well as through cracks elsewhere on the ground. When the lava hardens, it forms a cone with gentle slopes. The Hawaiian Islands are shield cones. Notice the gentle slope of the Mauna Loa Volcano on the island of Hawaii.

Figure 2.1 contd.

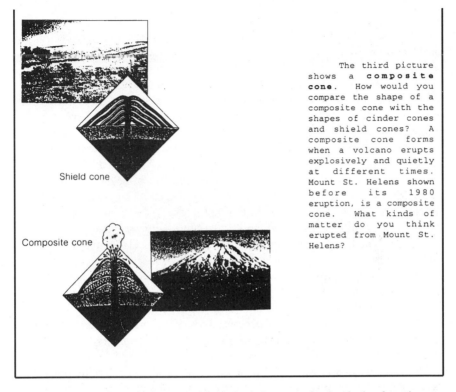

The third picture shows a **composite cone**. How would you compare the shape of a composite cone with the shapes of cinder cones and shield cones? A composite cone forms when a volcano erupts explosively and quietly at different times. Mount St. Helens shown before its 1980 eruption, is a composite cone. What kinds of matter do you think erupted from Mount St. Helens?

Shield cone

Composite cone

Chapter 4 applies the same design principles to entire books by focusing on tables of contents. Textbooks come in layers, something like an onion. The entire book, the outer husk, as signalled in the table of contents (TOC), seldom receives the attention it deserves. Next come units and chapters, relatively large and often difficult to digest. While chapter 4 focuses on TOCs, the approach to understanding the design of units and chapters as signalled by titles, headings, and subheadings is similar. Chapter 4 concludes with table of contents rewrites analogous to the final passage rewrite of chapter 3.

Textbooks can do only so much. Our vision of a well-designed textbook is set against an image of schooling in which teachers act as professionals in adapting curriculum to the diversities of students now entering the nation's classrooms. The question remains: What is the best we can do in textbook design and development given existing knowledge and resources and given that textbook reform is part of a larger vision of educational reform?

The Concept of Design

For a passage to be comprehensible, for an argument to persuade, for an explanation to lead to understanding, each must be constructed in a principled fashion. Designs exist at different levels and styles. A passage is inherently linear. What is to go first? Last? In the middle? A passage is necessarily limited. What is essential and what is decorative? Art is important, but these and related questions suggest the importance of planfulness, of design, in creating the passages that are the basic building blocks of a textbook.

A coherent design starts with a small set of distinctive elements, and uses linkages to mold the elements into a thematic whole. The elements in today's texts are too often lists of specific topics (earthquakes, volcanoes, plate tectonics, dinosaurs, stages in the life cycle, magnets, the solar system) and skills (learning vocabulary definitions, finding main ideas). Textbooks keep expanding because nothing is discarded, and the result is understandably chaotic and confusing. The linkages are topical; chunks of content elaborated with examples, facts, and activities. The theme is a form of cultural literacy, education as coverage of the minutiae of our heritage. This ever-increasing list of topics often leads to what Harriet Tyson-Bernstein has called the "mentioning" effect.[1] The present approach is what cognitive psychologists label "bottom-up."[2] A mass of information is presented for the reader to integrate into a coherent whole; a reasonable task for the expert, but an overwhelming challenge for the novice student – or teacher.

The obvious alternative is a "top-down" approach[3] – the development of an overarching "big picture" and a commitment to "keep it simple" – in short, a design. The Golden Gate Bridge, Picasso's *Guernica*, Shakespeare's *Hamlet*, the *US Constitution* – all are marvelous designs, as may be a young child's Lego creation. Nobel laureate Herbert Simon describes design as the difference between happenstance and artifice, between chaos and planfulness.[4]

How does one create a design? The previous examples combine art and technology, and may seem beyond the reach of the publisher struggling to prepare a few pages of text that say something significant about earthquakes and volcanoes. And so we will fall back on a couple of metaphors – bicycles and turkeys – to illustrate the concept of a coherent design, and to indicate how things can go awry. The elements of a bicycle include handlebars, saddles, and wheels (figure 2.2). Linking these elements are welds, bolts, and chains. The theme, in this instance the function, is to propel a person efficiently from one place to another to another. The bicycle in the top panel of Figure 2.2 is well designed; elements and linkages support the theme coherently with no extra parts or cluttered connections. The middle panel shows what happens with the right elements but strange linkages. The bottom panel has reasonable linkages,

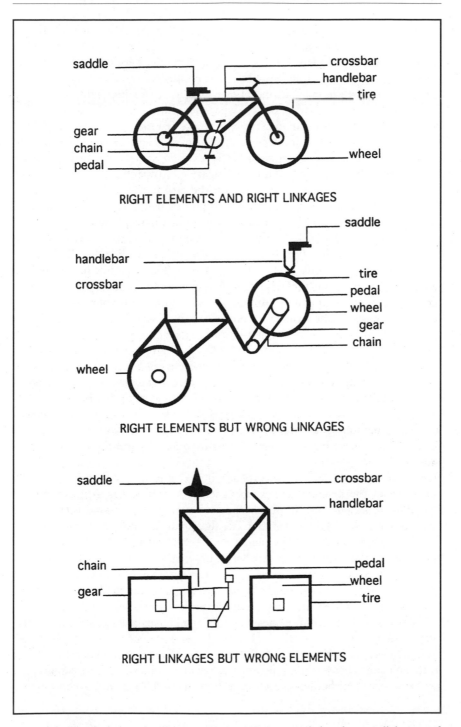

RIGHT ELEMENTS AND RIGHT LINKAGES

RIGHT ELEMENTS BUT WRONG LINKAGES

RIGHT LINKAGES BUT WRONG ELEMENTS

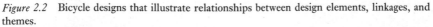

Figure 2.2 Bicycle designs that illustrate relationships between design elements, linkages, and themes.

but the elements are peculiar. Neither plan satisfies the basic function. If this example strikes you as untoward, think about the ornate gas-guzzlers offered to US car buyers in the 1960's and 1970's. The elements were fuzzy, the linkages weak, and the functional themes lost in the confusion.

While turkeys are not human artifacts, their design highlights two other design features – separability and transparency. Simon argued that any viable system, no matter how complex, comprises a few distinctive components.[5] Infinitely complicated systems fall of their own weight. Some systems, like bicycles, are relatively transparent; it is easy to see the "chunks." Other systems, like roast turkeys (and textbooks), are more opaque. The expert carver possesses an X-ray vision, seeing through the bird to the underlying joints. A few swift strokes and the gobbler is divided into a small number of large chunks that are easily sliced and laid on the platter. The novice, lacking the expert's vision, produces turkey hash. To be sure, poultry producers might tattoo a diagram on the outside of the bird ("Cut here first; then slice there"), but this ruse is a feeble alternative to the expert's image. Transparency lies in the eye (actually, the mind) of the beholder. When we asked you to summarize or outline the passage on plate tectonics, we were calling up your X-ray vision: What do you see as the structural "bones" of the text?

The concept of theme is the most subtle facet of a design, and we will look at it from several perspectives. We begin by discussing what we do not mean. The term "theme" has lately become quite popular among educators. Teachers are encouraged (or directed) to "do" thematic projects; publishers are expected to support these endeavors. The results can be rather silly, as when a second-grade class spends a week on "green": Dr Seuss' *Green Eggs and Ham* as literature, fractions by cutting up green pickles, and so on. Nothing wrong with some of the pieces, but the theme is inconsequential, and the lessons fail to mesh.

For our purposes, theme has a broader, deeper meaning. A theme reflects the substance of the problem and is purposeful. A bicycle has a transportation theme, as does a boat, car, or plane. *The United States Constitution* establishes a new government. The Golden Gate Bridge spans a strait. A theme can also have more than one facet. The theme for a bicycle can also be recreational or competitive: the Golden Gate Bridge spans a strait in a particularly elegant manner; *The Constitution* proposes a certain relationship between citizens and their government – and so on. In a good design, a theme guides the choice of elements and how they are linked into a meaningful whole.

Elements, linkages, and themes – this design concept will guide our discussion in the remainder of the book. Figure 2.3 provides a road map through the territory covered in chapters 2–4. We will proceed from top to bottom, looking in this chapter at how the elements in a passage – the sentences, paragraphs, and sections – can be linked according to a purposeful theme: comprehensi-

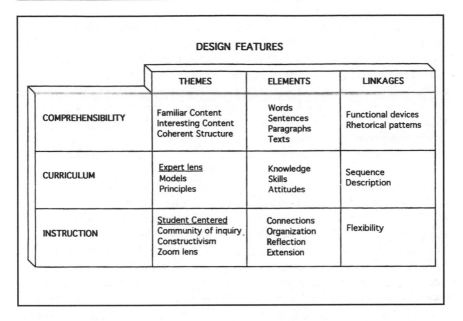

DESIGN FEATURES			
	THEMES	ELEMENTS	LINKAGES
COMPREHENSIBILITY	Familiar Content Interesting Content Coherent Structure	Words Sentences Paragraphs Texts	Functional devices Rhetorical patterns
CURRICULUM	Expert lens Models Principles	Knowledge Skills Attitudes	Sequence Description
INSTRUCTION	Student Centered Community of inquiry Constructivism Zoom lens	Connections Organization Reflection Extension	Flexibility

Figure 2.3 The elements, linkages, and themes in comprehensibility, curriculum, and instruction designs.

bility. The chapter summarizes the research on comprehensibility, which has identified the sub-themes of familiarity, interest, and coherent organization. It also introduces rhetorical patterns and functional devices, two types of linkages that authors use to connect the elements in a comprehensible text.

Chapter 3 turns to the elements, linkages, and themes in exemplary curriculum and student-centered instruction. In today's objectives-based curriculum, individual passages are convenient repositories for conveying factoids. In tomorrow's curriculum, individual passages will carry some information – but of equal or greater importance – they will impel students to think and reflect, to understand and to feel, to go beyond the information given. In chapter 4, where we consider the design of an entire textbook, we look again at comprehensibility, curriculum, and instruction from a slightly different perspective.

Designing a Comprehensible Text

We have all enjoyed friendly pieces of writing, and growled at passages that made no sense despite repeated efforts. What makes the difference? What makes one text easy to read and another one an absolute horror?

Early answers to this question relied on simplistic readability formulas;[6] commonplace words and short sentences make for a readable text, while uncommon words and longer sentences lead to greater difficulty. At one level, it is clear why these formulas predict reading time and performance on multiple-choice tests. Short words and sentences are easy to read and remember. In contrast, the writer who calls upon a more extensive lexicon and embeds these entries in complicated syntactical constructions challenges both comprehension and retrieval. These two preceding sentences illustrate the point; the first is sixth-grade material, while the second is more appropriate to doctoral students.

Nonetheless, anyone who has read "Dick and Jane" stories knows that readability formulas tell only part of the story. Government efforts to ensure that public documents are comprehensible by mandating readability formulas can produce results that are actually less comprehensible. Comprehensibility is more than words and sentences. For instance, consider these instructions for a new drug: "If you become nauseous or perspire, then you should stop the treatment and inform your physician." A more "readable" version based on readability formulas would go something like this: "You become sick to your stomach. You sweat. Stop taking the pills. Call your doctor." The two versions are equally long, and the vocabulary is clearly plainer in the second version. But chopping up the first version into several short sentences obliterates the *if–then* relation that is explicit in the first text.

Comprehensibility is the preeminent hallmark of well-designed written material for young readers. The sixth-grader who cannot understand a three-paragraph discussion of electric motors will fail to learn from the text. Fortunately, during the past two decades educational researchers have concentrated on identifying text features that enhance the comprehension of young readers. Researchers gave texts that differed according to a particular feature (e.g., familiarity of content) to school-age children with various levels of reading skills. After reading they completed comprehension tests, writing down everything that they could remember, creating a summary, answering multiple-choice comprehension questions, or choosing sentences consistent with the text. Three general features consistently affected their answers: familiarity, personal interest, and text structure.

Consider the sample passage "How Does Plate Tectonics Explain Earthquakes and Volcanoes?" How does this example match up against the criteria of familiarity, interest, and structure? First, familiarity – review the passage and ask yourself about connections with what students know about the world around them. Second, interest – geology might not appeal to students, but earthquakes and volcanoes are certainly attention grabbers. Third, structure – we will not assess your passage summary, but you might ask how you think sixth-graders would handle this task. The remainder of the chapter discusses each of these criteria and applies it to "How Does Plate Tectonics Explain Earthquakes and Volcanoes?"

Familiarity: Connecting with Student Knowledge

The relationship between a reader's background knowledge and his or her success in comprehending a text is well established. A student who already knows a lot about a topic performs better on comprehension tests than one with less prior knowledge. Select a text in an area about which you know little. No matter how competent you may be in your own field, you will struggle to remember bits and pieces of what you read. Background knowledge varies with the reader, of course. For a passage to connect with everyone, it must include words, examples, and analogies that touch base with a wide range of everyday experiences.

A leader in reading research, Richard Anderson, along with his colleagues, has clearly demonstrated the relationship between familiarity of both vocabulary and text topic and school-age children's comprehension.[7] In a seminal study, sixth-graders read a passage with either familiar vocabulary or a more difficult synonym substituted for every fourth word. Students who read the familiar version recalled and summarized it more accurately than those who read the less familiar text. Another group of sixth-graders was even more strongly affected by their familiarity with a text's topic. They read a text about either a visit to a supermarket or the game of horseshoes, both familiar topics, and another text about either a visit to a Niugini Sing-Sing (an intervillage musical ceremony) or an American Indian game called huta, both unfamiliar topics. After reading each passage, students wrote down whatever they could remember. They also read a list of sentences that were both consistent and inconsistent with the passage's topic and marked sentences that they thought fitted with the passage. The students performed far more accurately on both tasks for familiar than for unfamiliar topics.

Vocabulary familiarity is an attribute of individual words. Topic familiarity is a characteristic of entire texts. Unfamiliar topics can cause readers more problems than unfamiliar vocabulary. Readers can use dictionaries and context to decipher word meanings. They have no readily available tools or strategies to understand an entire topic that is unfamiliar.

You have probably wrestled with unfamiliarity of both vocabulary and topics in your own reading. Government documents often pose a challenge for this reason. Connecting is the key to familiarity. No matter how abstruse the topic of a passage, most of us know something that can help us to understand it, if only we can make the link. On the other hand, a writer can confuse the reader, even when the passage is about a commonplace matter. Psychologists have tested comprehension with texts designed to obscure the familiar:[8]

> The procedure is actually quite simple. First you arrange the pieces into different groups. Of course, one pile may be sufficient, depending on how much there is to do, and how different the pieces are. If you have to go somewhere else due to lack of facilities, that is the next step. Otherwise, you are set. Do *not*, however, overload the unit.

Test results showed that college students could not understand these materials, not because the words or sentences were unknown, but because they could not relate the text to anything they knew. When told that the passage was about laundry, readers gasped and giggled.

Familiarity is more of a problem in passages about science and social studies than in basal reader stories. Millennia of human experience in a variety of cultures have generated a repository of life-like stories. As long as publishers tap into these stories from many cultures to match the cultural mix in many US classrooms, they can hardly go wrong. In contrast, the topics in science and social studies are genuinely new to most students. You may be familiar with concepts such as democracy and molecules, and sixth-graders may have heard the words. But genuine comprehension of these abstractions requires fundamental shifts in perspective. "My vote doesn't count" versus "E pluribus unum" is a giant step for most individuals.

In science and social studies, publishers confront a real challenge; they have to connect abstract topics such as plate tectonics with the varied range of backgrounds throughout the United States. Students in California neighborhoods have first-hand experience with earthquakes, and youngsters in the Hawaiian islands live atop active volcanoes; children in Iowa or Florida know more about tornadoes or hurricanes.

From the student's perspective, familiarity means more than "being there," however. Television ensures some degree of familiarity with virtually everything in the entire world – indeed, almost anything that can be imagined! Moreover, first-hand experience does not guarantee understanding. California children walk across earthquake fault lines without appreciating the experience, and Hawaiian youngsters play with volcanic rocks unaware that molten lava seethes beneath their feet.

From the writer's perspective, familiarity depends on sensitivity to the audience – a "familiar" challenge. In "How Does Plate Tectonics Explain Earthquakes and Volcanoes?", for instance, what is the likelihood that a student connects the concept of a plate ("a huge block of rock") with a continental expanse? Most of us associate rocks with boulders – maybe even granite precipices – but not entire continents. The writer needs to find a different route in order to link the reader to the idea of a plate as large as a continent!

The textbook writer must make certain assumptions about students, to be sure. Sometimes these suppositions will fail. Most US children spend a lot of time in front of television; the student newly arrived from the jungles of Southeast Asia will be an exception. Experience does not guarantee understanding. Most children have seen soup boil, but did not realize that they were viewing convection currents in action. Metaphor can bridge concrete experience and abstract concept. The textbook writer who employs this strategy can provide the teacher with models that can be extended in the classroom setting. In "How Does Plate Tectonics Explain Earthquakes and Volcanoes?", for example, the notion that convection currents cause plate movement may make little sense. A more comprehensible image comes from a pot of pea soup, simmering on the stove. The surface forms a crust, the soup burbles underneath, and the surface ripples and breaks into chunks. To be sure, metaphors are not complete in and of themselves. Care must be taken that the metaphor is linked to the phenomenon. Sixth-graders will not automatically see the connection between a pot of pea soup and continents floating on liquid magma. If crucial linkages are missing, metaphors may actually mislead rather than clarify. Reading that dinosaurs flooded across the ancient land bridge connecting Asia with North America, children may picture dinosaurs frantically swimming in a flood and drowning rather than migrating across land in large numbers. One of us knows a group of sixth-graders who made this "mistake."

How well does the writer of the plate tectonics passage connect unfamiliar topics with the knowledge that we could expect sixth graders to have? The challenge is significant: continent-sized rock plates; convection currents in semi-liquid magma beneath our feet; locked plates causing energy buildup. The writer appears to be relying heavily on graphics to make at least some of these notions concrete and, hopefully, familiar. We find the actual text to be less effective. In some ways, the passage has the character of a vocabulary lesson, introducing many new terms – "plate tectonics," "convection currents," "fracture boundaries," "fault," "focus," and so on. The definitions – for example, "These currents are called **convection currents**. They are caused by heat from within the earth" – typically do not connect with sixth-graders' experience.

Besides definitions, the passage contains two cause–effect events: the buildup of energy that causes an earthquake and the buildup of pressure that causes volcanic eruptions. The text does not explicitly link either event with typical student knowledge. It contains no metaphors and very little elaboration. The examples of the Paricutin Volcano in Mexico, the Hawaiian Islands, and Mount St. Helens would only be in the direct experience of a relatively small number of readers, and, as we have already explained, living on or near a volcano – even witnessing a volcanic eruption – would not suggest the theory of plate tectonics to anyone without the special lens of the geologist. This passage is typical textbook fare. We conclude that it could do a better job of connecting the scientific model of plate tectonics to the understandings of a sixth-grader.

Interest: Attracting Student Attention

A boring passage puts readers to sleep. While this comment may seem commonplace, research has both demonstrated the general principle and enlightened us about the details. As with reader knowledge, interest depends partly on the reader and partly on the text. You are intrigued by an article about investment tips if you are in the stock market, but not if you have just lost your job. Certain topics – death, danger, sex – create "absolute interest."[9]

Dramatic verbs, personal pronouns, character identification, fast action, concrete detail, and novelty are other text characteristics that enhance reader interest and recall.[10] We will not bore you with the original version, but think about your reaction to this revision of a recent message that one of us received from the Internal Revenue Service:

HEY! YOU MAY HAVE A PROBLEM! We checked your tax return, and guess what – no, you don't owe us anything. But the other person named on the return does not match our records. You may have gotten married (congratulations!) or changed your name (it happens). Please check the form, and be sure that everything is kopesetic – after all, YOU DON'T WANT THE IRS ON YOUR CASE!

The research on text interest is not always as exciting as this example, but you get the point. Interest is greater when the text establishes a personal relation with the reader. Stories are more interesting than expository texts because we can empathize with people more easily than with objects or facts. Vivid language and engaging illustrations capture and sustain attention. Conflict and surprise keep the reader involved.

Work by educational researchers Suzanne Hidi and William Baird focused on the effect that these characteristics have on the comprehension of school children in the middle years.[11] Fourth- and sixth-graders read a text about inventors: Edison inventing the light bulb, Morse inventing the telegraph, and Spenser inventing the thermostat. The researchers hypothesized that inventors would be inherently interesting to children. They added details about the inventors' lives to increase character identification. They used vivid verbs to increase the sense of action and excitement. A second version also included 19 additional sentences that added elaborative details (e.g., "Sometimes [these inventors] became so interested they would forget to go home to eat dinner." (p. 471)). The third version added questions that the text answered a paragraph later to create suspense and resolution. Students remembered significantly more of all three versions both immediately after reading them as well as one week later than did a comparable group of fourth- and sixth-graders who read typical textbook passages that lacked these features.

Tradebooks (those you find in the children's section of the library) employ the same devices.[12] For instance, imagine a passage on tectonics that begins:

> Join us in the Nautilus – you are about to take a trip to the middle of the earth! The entire history of the world will pass before your eyes as we descend – the bones of dinosaurs and the shells of prehistoric fish and birds, pools of oil and veins of gold and silver. We force our way through waves of molten lava as it rises toward the earth's surface, ready to burst forth as a volcano. The trip is dangerous; earthquakes will shake our vessel. Finally we reach the dark core, source of the intense gravitational power that holds everything on earth from flying into space.

The key, of course, is to engage without distracting. The relationship between interest and comprehension is far more complex than the relationship between familiarity and comprehension. If interest-creating text features are not selected carefully, an interesting text can actually disrupt comprehension. Readers remember and consider important whatever they deem to be interesting over whatever bores them, even if the interesting content is only an interesting tidbit. The developmental psychologist, Ruth Garner, and her colleagues found that interesting, or "seductive," details disrupted how well seventh graders remembered both the important ideas and other details in a passage.[13] Children read a passage on insects either with or without interesting details. For example, the first sentence of the first paragraph presented a topic sentence: "Some insects live alone and some live in large families." The remaining sentences offered examples of the two types of insects. The seductive detail sentence was interesting but irrelevant to the topic sentence: "When a Click Beetle is on its back, it flips itself into the air and lands right side up while it makes a clicking noise." Garner and her colleagues surmise that readers who confront an interesting detail tag it as important. Students who read a seductive details version recalled fewer passage main ideas and relevant details than children who read a version without these interesting but irrelevant sentences.

Seductive details can capture the reader's interest so that nothing is remembered except the decorations. Some tradebooks on earthquakes and volcanoes describe making a volcano out of vinegar, baking soda, and red food coloring. The project is totally engaging – but teaches nothing about the underlying causal model. In order to enhance comprehension, interest-enhancing features must be integral to the concepts.

As with familiarity, to write interesting science and social studies passages is a greater challenge than to compose interesting stories. Good children's stories are full of emotion, far-off places, suspense, and "once upon a time" adventures. Social studies and science topics (at least those in textbooks) are drier, "factual," and information-laden, not something that you would normally pick up to read for enjoyment.

How well does the author of the plate tectonics passage use dramatic verbs, personal pronouns, character identification, fast action, concrete detail, and novelty? To what extent does the topic involve death or danger and therefore have absolute interest? Do interesting features coincide with or support important passage generalizations? We have already noted that earthquakes and volcanoes should hold absolute interest for sixth-graders, who probably have seen on video the effects of both and may even have lived through one or the other. They know that people die during earthquakes and volcanic eruptions; that these natural phenomena are dangerous. Furthermore, the scientific model is dramatic and full of action. Under our feet is a bubbling cauldron of magma, churning because of convection currents. The plates on which we live can crash into one another or jerk apart, releasing massive amounts of energy. Pressure caused by gases under the plates can push molten magma out through cracks between the plates. This topic should lend itself to the use of dramatic verbs and novelty, not as seductive details but to communicate the characteristics of the model.

Sporadically, the author does use dramatic verbs: the plates *float* on the partly melted rock in the mantle; the release of energy causes the ground "to shake;" when the pressure becomes very great, the magma "explodes" out of the openings through the volcano; as a volcano "erupts," it builds a mountain called a volcano cone; cinders – small pieces of hard lava – "are thrown" out of the volcano; hot lava "flows" from the volcano's large opening. More often, the author uses the innocuous, unexciting verb "to move" to depict what is happening. In the following examples, we have suggested synonyms enclosed in brackets. The theory, plate tectonics, explains how continents "move" [shift around]; currents in the melted rock "move" [propel] the plates [against each other]; a fault is a crack in the earth's crust along which rock layers "move" [slide]; energy from within the earth "moves" [pushes] the two plates along a fracture boundary; at colliding boundaries two plates "are moving" [glide] toward one another; and so on. Word choice fails to communicate the drama.

The text also uses the pronoun "you" three times: "If you were standing directly above the focus of an earthquake, you would be the first person to feel the ground shake"; and "What kinds of matter do you think erupted from Mount St. Helens?" We find these three examples to be weak efforts at personalization. Contrast them with the sentence that we presented earlier: "Imagine that you are tunneling to the earth's core!" The effect of this sentence is to draw the reader into a scenario that explains the underlying scientific model.

As is typical of textbook writing, the plate tectonics sample errs on the safe side, presenting facts and little more than facts. We conclude that the author could have done a better job of making the writing interesting. To be fair to the publisher, it is the type of writing that teachers expect in a textbook and with which they are likely to feel most comfortable.

Structure: Organizing for Students

Decades of research and centuries of experience suggest that text structure – the organization of sentences, paragraphs, and the total discourse – has a powerful effect on comprehensibility. This influence is strongest when the reader attempts to recall and apply the material, and can be almost negligible when the task is simply to recognize discrete facts. Organization matters less for a multiple-choice test than it does for an essay examination. When you prepare for your driver's license test, you skim the manual for facts. When studying for a job interview, it is often wiser to focus on conceptual insights, in which case a clearly structured text could make the job a lot easier.

The importance of organization reflects one of the strongest propensities of the human mind – to make order out of experience. The philosopher Alfred North Whitehead portrayed experience as a stream of events, untidy, fragmentary, and ill-adjusted, and admired the unique capacity of the human mind to create order from the chaos.[14] In fact, people have to organize to survive. Psychologist George Miller summarized research on the limitations of attentional memory in "The magical number seven, plus or minus two."[15] His point was that human beings can juggle only a handful of informational "chunks" at any given moment. Coherent structure is not only a propensity; it is mandatory for learning and thinking in all domains.

In particular, coherent structure is a critical feature for effective text design. Structure provides the linkages that hold the design together. Good writers employ a handful of structural patterns for organizing ideas and composing texts. Good readers know these patterns well and use them to comprehend a passage by making order out of it. This task is difficult if the reader cannot identify the text structure. Chaos in text is highly disruptive to the comprehension of readers. Communication is thwarted when either writers or readers fail to use the patterns; the writer composes by compilation, or the reader treats the text as a shopping list.

What types of linkages undergird the design of a text? The first and most fundamental distinction separates narrative from expository writing. Narratives (stories) tend to be the more natural forum; the author places characters in a setting, confronts them with a problem, and moves them toward a resolution. Story design employs the plot as the primary linkage that binds the various characters as they move from beginning to end. In contrast, expositions take shape as the reports and essays found in the worlds of business, government, and academe. Expository designs typically describe a topic or lay out a process, the linkages depending on whether the exposition is descriptive or sequential.[16]

Children, in particular, tend to find narrative linkages more comprehensible than expository types.[17] Virtually all children in the United States have had extensive experience with narrative plots. Even if they have seldom been taken up into an adult lap to hear a story, they have watched hours of television drama. Furthermore, narrative often occurs in informal conversation between children and adults – the tale a child recounts when asked, "What happened in school today?" or the yarn spun by a parent begged by several offspring to "Tell us a story." Children as young as four years old can tell a story with a rudamentary plot.[18]

Exposition is even more likely to have a formal structure. Good expository structures are seldom used in conversation. While children may ask their parents to explain or to give them information, they often also plead, "But keep it short." Rarely would a child ask, "Give me a complete report."

To be sure, children from homes where dinner-table conversations are valued and children's ideas are honored do experience rudimentary patterns for exposition in their natural conversations. Parents give their children information to increase their youngsters' knowledge about the world. They explain why the world works the way it does. They argue with their children to make a point. Even where natural expository patterns do appear, they are less well-formed and therefore less useful than the patterns in conversational narratives. These patterns have been labeled "tell all you know" and "mind dump" by researchers studying how young children form their expositions.[19] Virtually all children come to school far less experienced with well-formed exposition than with well-crafted narrative. If they learn them at all, children acquire most expository patterns in formal educational settings. School-age children asked to read and recall both narratives and expositions remember far more of the stories than of the reports.[20]

Since they are familiar with narrative linkages, young readers can "go with the flow" in reading a familiar, interesting story. With science or social studies texts, their reading must be more strategic. These texts often offer a triple whammy: unfamiliar and uninteresting content linked into an organizational pattern that the child does not recognize. Exposition, in brief, makes strong demands on the reader. Effective linkages are the key to making exposition work.

Even good adult readers recall little of the important content in an expository text that is poorly organized. Walter Kintsch, a preeminent cognitive psychologist who has focused on studying text comprehension, and his colleague, Y. Craig Yarbrough, asked college students to read a text that conformed closely to an established expository pattern, or a second version in which the

Table 2.1   Texts in good and poor rhetorical form (van Dijk and Kintsch (1983).

Good rhetorical form	*Poor rhetorical form*
In order to obtain an understanding of how man has evolved it is often helpful to analyze him in relation to the other primates. One major way of seeing this relationship is by examining locomotor patterns.	A developmentally rather advanced form is quadrupedalism. As the name suggests all four limbs are involved in this pattern. Macaques and howler monkeys typify this form.
The most developmentally constricted form of locomotion is called vertical clinging and leaping. All prosimians fall into this form. In this pattern the animal normally clings to the branch with its head above its limbs. In its predominant locomotive form the animal pushes off from the branch or tree with its hind limbs and springs or leaps to the next.	It should be noted that bipedalism is the characteristic locomotive form of man: bipedalism include standing, striding, and running. This form completes an adaptive developmental sequence which began sometime in the deep past with vertical clinging and leaping.
A developmentally more advanced form is quadrupendalism. As the name suggests all four limbs are involved in this pattern. Macaques and howler monkeys typify this form.	In order to obtain an understanding of how man has evolved it is often heipful to analyze him in relation to the other primates. One major way of seeing this relationship is by examining locomotor patterns.
Next is ape locomotion which is characterized by arm swinging and/or occasional linked branch-to-branch swinging, climbing, and knuckle walking. The gibbon, orangutan, and chimpanzee locomotive patterns are characterized by this form.	The most developmentally constricted form of locomotion is called vertical clinging and leaping. All prosimians fall into this form. In this pattern the animal normally clings to the branch with its head above its limbs. In its predominant locomotive form the animal pushes off from the branch or tree with its hind limbs and springs or leaps to the next.
Finally, we find bipedalism which is the characteristic locomotive form of man: bipedalism includes standing, striding, and running. This form completes an adaptive developmental sequence which began sometime in the deep past with vertical clinging and leaping.	Ape locomotion is usually characterized by arm swinging and/or occasional linked branch-to-branch swinging, climbing, and knuckle walking. The gibbon, orangutan, and chimpanzee locomotive patterns are characterized by this form.

paragraphs were disordered (table 2.1).[21]

After reading each text, the college students answered two questions: "What is this essay about?" and "What are the major points made?" Correct answers for the two example versions would have been "types of locomotion" or some paraphrase for the first question, and the four types of locomotion described in

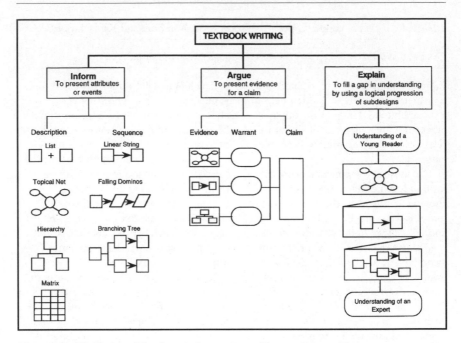

Figure 2.4   The design of the rhetorical patterns used in expository writing.

the article for the second question. Those who read the organized versions answered the questions far better (51 per cent correct) than students who read the poor versions (26 per cent correct).

Rhetorical Patterns

Because of the crucial importance of expository structure in comprehension, our work has concentrated on the linkages in well-designed exposition. Expository structures have been the focus of a good deal of research, and several structural systems have been proposed by researchers.[22] Most of these have their basis in linguistics, and are powerful tools for designing comprehension research using very short texts of a few sentences. The linkages that we propose come, instead, from the rhetorical patterns that are taught in composition courses; you probably remember the five-paragraph essay, the compare-contrast paper, and the cause-effect composition. Our scheme for representing these rhetorical patterns is displayed in figure 2.4. The system is designed to include a wide range of expository genre of any length, including newspapers and essays, book reports, and research papers, in addition to textbooks.

We will illustrate the application of these structures throughout the remainder of the book, but a quick trip through the graphics will help to introduce you to the scheme. The upper level in the figure identifies the author's purpose: to inform, to argue, to explain. Seven informational designs in the lower left-hand corner are basic building blocks for exposition. Information structures are classified as either descriptive or sequential. Description presents character-istics fixed in time, a snapshot (e.g., the population and landforms of the continents). Sequence presents events progressing over time, a motion picture (e.g., the stages in a life cycle). In the descriptive patterns, the list – great for taking to the grocery store but poor at organizing a text – provides the loosest linkages. The hierarchy and matrix have the tightest linkages and can coher-ently organize large amounts of content. In the sequential patterns, the linear string provides the least structure while the branching tree can link several sequences coherently.

These basic building blocks frame the overall structure of an exposition, and used in combination they generate structures of considerable complexity. The entries under Argue and Explain in figure 2.4 give two examples of the iterative possibilities. An argument presents evidence for a claim. In complex argu-ments, these two parts are further linked by an explicit warrant. If you have studied formal logic, you can think of the warrant as analogous to the major premise in a syllogism. An explanation "fills the gap" between a young reader's understanding of a phenomenon and the scientific explanation by presenting important information, metaphors, and analogies in tiers, or layers, of sub-explanations. In both of these examples, icons within each of the structures illustrate how the basic informational structures operate much as the parts of a Lego set or a Tinker Toy.

Are any of these structures "real?" Exposition is an invention, an artifact, a construction. It does not emerge naturally in human development, but is a result of schooling. The taxonomy presented above organizes the jumble of "writing prompts" taught by composition teachers (but seldom by science or social studies teachers).[23] These graphic structures provide authors with a foundation for linking ideas in complex subject matters, and they equip readers with plans for organizing information – whether or not a passage is well-organized to begin with.

The graphics are just one part of the puzzle, of course. Research shows that even young readers can tell the difference among some of the structures. Carol Sue Englert and Elfrieda Hiebert, educational psychologists interested in the literacy of children, gave third and sixth graders a task to measure their awareness of text structure.[24] Children read pairs of sentences structured as a linear string, a matrix, and a topical net. Note that we are using our taxonomy to describe these tasks, not the one used by Englert and Hiebert.[25] For example, children read the following two sentences to test their awareness of the matrix structure comparing cats and people:

"Cats have colds just as people do."
"Cats sneeze when they have colds."

After each pair, they read four target sentences. The four targets for this example item are:

"Cats' noses run just like people's."
"Cats' eyes become watery, just as the eyes of people who have colds."
"You can find cats with many different colors of fur."
"A calico cat has golden fur."

After reading each target, children rated its "degree of fit" with the original two sentences by choosing one of four possibilities: "YES! – the sentence definitely belonged in the paragraph," "yes? – the sentence 'sort of' belonged in the paragraph," "no? – the sentence 'sort of' did not belong in the paragraph," and "NO! – the sentence definitely did not belong in that paragraph." While all children were more accurate at selecting YES! for a consistent target sentence than NO! for a distractor sentence, sixth-graders typically distinguished among the two, while fourth-graders tended to answer YES! or yes? for all sentences. In other words, sixth graders seemed aware of the distinguishing features of these structures, while third-graders at times seemed almost oblivious to them. Perhaps not surprisingly, children scoring higher on a standardized reading test were more proficient at both grade levels than those with low scores.

Apparently, young readers find some rhetorical patterns more comprehensible than others. Victoria Chou Hare, a researcher interested in the effects of different types of text structure, and her colleagues measured how four rhetorical patterns influence the comprehension of fourth- and sixth-graders.[26] She used short texts linked as topical nets, linear strings, matrices, and falling dominoes, again using our taxonomy to characterize the different structures. In addition, each of these building-block patterns was also presented in an argument version, with a claim statement appearing as a topic sentence. Table 2.2 displays examples.

The children read a short passage, and underlined the "main idea" if they could find it, or made up an appropriate main idea sentence. Note that none of the building-block patterns explicitly stated the main idea, while all of the argument texts presented it as the claim. Children performed far more accurately when the text stated the answer than when they had to make one up. Their average score for arguments was 3.11, while they scored an average of 0.63 for the four building-block texts. While differences were less striking among the building-block structures themselves, these young readers comprehended the topical net version best, followed by the linear string, matrix, and falling dominoes structures. Their performance was particularly poor with the

Table 2.2 Example paragraphs linked according to five rhetorical patterns (Chou Hare et al., 1989).

	Building block	*Argument*
Topical net	The reindeer supply meat and milk. The Lapps make warm clothing, boats, and tents from reindeer hides. Some of the small leg bones are used as needles. Strong thread to sew tents and clothing is made from the sinews or tendons.	Reindeer give the Lapps almost everything they need to live in their cold land. The reindeer supply meat and milk. The Lapps make warm clothing, boats, and tents from reindeer hides. Some of the small leg bones are used as needles. Strong thread to sew tents and clothing is made from the sinews or tendons.
Matrix	Most of the people of the world live on smooth level lands that are called plains. People like to live on plains because the land is easy to farm. Roads and railroads, towns and cities are easy to build where the land is level. Fewer people live on hilly land than on plains. Hilly land is harder to farm than level land. If the hills are steep. the farmers can't use tractors or other machinery.	It seems easier to live on plains than on hilly land. Most of the people of the world live on smooth level lands that are called plains. People like to live on plains because the land is easy to farm. Roads and railroads, towns and cities are easy to build where the land is level. Fewer people live on hilly land than on plains. Hilly land is harder to farm than level land. If the hills are steep, the farmers can't use tractors or other machinery.
Linear string	A maple tree is bare during the winter, but if you look closely, you can find tiny buds on the tree. These buds begin to grow in the spring and slowly open up to become broad green leaves. Late in the summer, some of the green leaves turn bright red or orange. By autumn the whole tree is covered with brightly colored leaves. As winter approaches, all the leaves fall off the tree.	A maple tree is one kind of tree that changes with each season. A maple tree is bare during the winter, but if you look closely, you can find tiny buds on the tree. These buds begin to grow in the spring and slowly open up to become broad green leaves. Late in the summer, some of the green leaves turn bright red or orange. By autumn the whole tree is covered with brightly colored leaves. As winter approaches, all the leaves fall off the tree.

Falling dominos	Once-healthy pineapple plants became sick and turned yellow. Everyone had thought that the soil was good. It was formed from red lava, and had iron and other minerals in it. It was true that the soil was good, but it was the kind that could not be used by the pineapple plants. So, a fertilizer with another type of iron in it was sprayed on the plants. Almost at once, the plants became healthy again.	A special kind of fertilizer saved a pineapple crop. Once-healthy pineapple plants became sick and turned yellow. Everyone had thought that the soil was good. It was formed from red lava, and had iron and other minerals in it. It was true that the soil was good, but it was the kind that could not be used by the pineapple plants. So, a fertilizer with another type of iron in it was sprayed on the plants. Almost at once, the plants became healthy again.

last two structures, where virtually no fourth-graders and only a few sixth-graders accurately identified the main idea.

Quite consistently across studies, fourth-, fifth-, and sixth-graders summarized in a single sentence or phrase and recalled some structures better than other structures. A set of linkages that young readers handle quite well is the topical net, which connects a topic (e.g., the many ways Lapps use their reindeer) with subtopics of details to flesh it out. In contrast, falling dominoes, which links causes and their effects, gives readers in the middle grades significant problems. They customarily fail either to come up with a single-sentence summary or to recall cause–effect texts accurately. Children's performance on the matrix, which compares and contrasts characteristics, is inconsistent. Young readers in some studies perform better than readers in other studies. The differences seem to be more in the young readers than in the text structures; many children seem unaware of cause–effect and compare–contrast linkages, approaching them as if the text followed no organizational pattern. On the other hand, they can make use of the argument structure quite well. The additional layer of structure in an argument tends to render it the most comprehensible, particularly if young readers are asked to summarize the text in a single "main idea" sentence.

Adults also find some rhetorical patterns more comprehensible than others.[27] However, results for children and adults differ. Adults recall matrix and domino patterns better than topical nets. Apparently, they capitalize on the additional linkages afforded by compare–contrast and causal relationships. Children seem to comprehend topical nets better than either falling dominoes or matrices. Topical nets are probably more natural than matrices or falling dominoes; far more likely to structure conversations. Furthermore, our review of social studies and science textbooks for the middle grades revealed a heavy preponderance of topical nets.[28] Children apparently have little experience with more tightly linked structures outside of research studies!

At first glance, these results might suggest that all exposition written for children be organized as either arguments or topical nets. We argue otherwise. While argument linkages are powerful and children can benefit from increasing proficiency in this text structure, good writers have at their fingertips other powerful structures as well – particularly explanation, and the matrix, hierarchy, branching tree, and falling domino informational patterns. While the topical net pattern is useful in some circumstances, the more children read well-designed exemplars of a variety of rhetorical patterns, the more familiar the patterns will become.

Functional Devices

A second set of linkages joins the sentences, paragraphs, sections, and so on of an exposition into a coherent whole and affects the comprehension of young readers powerfully. We have labeled these linkages "functional devices," because they function to provide the reader with cues to the text structure. We speculate that functional devices may derive from the structure of conversations;[29] that they may be essential for smooth communication between an author and a reader, particularly a young reader. Conversations have explicit openings consisting of a summons ("Hello"), a response ("Hi. How are you?"), and a statement of the topic ("You'll never guess what happened to me yesterday."). Conversational middles follow turn-taking rules to ensure orderly transitions from one speaker to another. (Think about how impatient we become listening to someone who talks way too long or, conversely, how irritating the constant interrupter is.) And conversations have distinct endings that signal to all participants that a topic has been completed ("Well, I've got to go now. See you tomorrow.").

Well-known college composition books universally recommend similar divisions for written exposition. For example, Cleanth Brooks and Robert Penn Warren's popular *Modern Rhetoric* proposes that all exposition be divided into three parts: an introduction, a discussion, and a conclusion.[30] The well-written introduction states the topic and provides a brief road map to the text. The discussion section adheres to a rhetorical pattern. An effective ending reiterates the thrust of the piece. Brooks and Warren admonish the writer to, "Put your finger on your main point, on what you want to bring into focus. Then write your conclusion on that point."

We have extended functional devices to include transitions and headings' in addition to introductions and conclusions. The author who has a potential reader clearly in mind uses appropriate functional devices to help this reader comprehend the text.

Our own work has demonstrated that explicit introductions and summaries help, while misleading beginnings and endings can confuse. In her dissertation, Andrea Whittaker, one of our colleagues, gave sixth-graders topical net and matrix passages to read either with or without introductions and conclusions that synopsized the text.[31] Subsequently, these children recalled the texts with good functional devices better than texts with missing introductions and conclusions. Interestingly, by signaling the matrix structure in text openings and closings the text apparently gave the young readers help in comprehending a structure that caused other children of the same grade level in other research studies to flounder.[32] In another study, one of us gave twelfth grade good readers lengthy arguments to read with either accurate or misleading introductions and conclusions.[33] Some of these readers were so confused by the misleading functional devices that they were unable to remember the author's argument. They performed flawlessly for arguments with well-crafted functional devices.

Other research has shown that readers rely heavily on titles, subtitles, and paragraph topic sentences.[34] Rewriting passages to have these functional devices improves the comprehension of children in the middle grades.[35]

As the length of this section suggests, research on text structure has been plentiful. Results demonstrate that a text's linkages have a powerful effect on how well even good readers will understand and remember what they read. Both the rhetorical patterns that link the substance of the text and the functional devices that join the parts of the text into a whole influence readers for better or for worse.

Looking back on "How Does Plate Tectonics Explain Earthquakes and Volcanoes?", how adequate are the linkages? Skimming the passage reveals that it has three major elements, each with two or more subelements: an opening section and two middle sections. It also has several functional devices, which should link it into a whole and signal the rhetorical pattern: a title, two introductory paragraphs, two subheadings, and a concluding question. We study the functional devices to discover which rhetorical pattern links the substance of the passage.

The message that the functional devices convey is mixed. The word "Explain" in the title and opening sentence suggests an explanation. The concluding sentence of the second paragraph ("Earthquakes and volcanoes are two sudden changes on the earth's surface that are caused by plate tectonics.") foreshadows a cause–effect sequence. As signaled by these first two functional devices, we could expect a text structured as an explanation that presents the scientific causal model and whatever examples, analogies, and background information that a typical sixth-grader would need to understand the model.

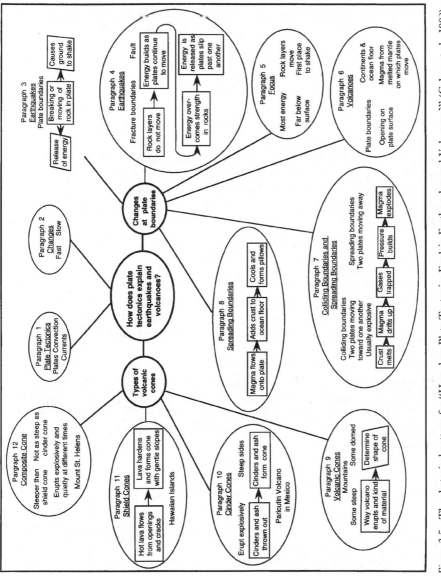

Figure 2.5 The rhetorical pattern for "How does Plate Tectonics Explain Earthquakes and Volcanoes?" (Cohen et al., 1983).

"Changes at Plate Boundaries," the first heading, seems to refer to a sequence of some type and fits this expectation. The second heading, "Types of Volcanic Cones," is descriptive and veers off in a new direction. The final concluding question, "What kinds of matter do you think erupted from Mount St. Helens?" seems to us to be too specific to fit the other functional devices and to relate only minimally to the opening of the passage.

The graphic in figure 2.4 depicts the actual pattern: a topical net with both descriptive and sequential linkages imbedded within some of the paragraphs – quite a complex structure. While we show how to discover and diagram text patterns in chapter 5, you may want to take a few minutes to compare the structure displayed in the figure with the passage itself. To find this structure, we approached the passage as if it were an onion, looking for the top-most layer by focusing on the large chunks – the introduction and two subsections – to determine how they related to one another. The subheadings do not suggest that the elements fill a gap by moving the young reader from current under-standings to the model of the scientist, the signs of an explanation. The subheadings are not related by time, the hallmarks of a sequence. They indicate quite different content, but are both about the main topic of earthquakes and volcanoes, strong indicators of the topical net structure. Having identified the overall pattern, we looked at how paragraphs within sections and sentences within paragraphs were linked to flesh out the net.

As with familiarity and interest, creating well-structured text is a challenge for a publisher. Anecdotes and examples take up valuable space. States and large districts make competing demands on publishers. California may insist that earthquakes be covered; Washington may demand the mention of Mount St. Helens; Hawaii would be pleased with the inclusion of the Hawaiian Islands; North Carolina might want to reduce the coverage on earthquakes and volcanoes altogether, while increasing the treatment of another earth science topic such as weather. The rhetorical pattern that best accommodates mention-ing different types of content under the same major topic without gobbling up too much space is the topical net, which also happens to be the most readily comprehended by young readers.

Nonetheless, "How Does Plate Tectonics Explain Earthquakes and Volca-noes?" could have more comprehensible linkages. The functional devices are misleading. The text does not explain the relationship between plate tectonics and earthquakes and volcanoes. The resulting rhetorical pattern is a mishmash: a topical net overall, linking a conglomeration of sequential causal models and descriptive characteristics, often within the same paragraph. Not surprisingly, most of these paragraphs have no topic sentence. No one sentence could capture the different linkages.

Concluding Thoughts About Passage Design

The hallmarks of comprehensible text are well-known. The elements (words, sentences, paragraphs, sections, and so on) present content that is familiar and interesting to the reader. These elements are linked together by functional devices and a coherent rhetorical pattern. "How Does Plate Tectonics Explain Earthquakes and Volcanoes?" demonstrates that these design characteristics are not so easy to achieve in a real-world textbook passage of several paragraphs. Textbook publishers experience strong market pressures to produce writing that does not match many of the principles of good writing taught in composition courses and verified by educational research. Furthermore, as Bonnie Armbruster and Tom Anderson noted in the title of an article on textbook design, "Good writing is damned hard!"[36]

Comprehensibility is not the only hallmark of effective textbook design, however. Textbooks are intended to teach a curriculum. In chapter 3, we describe the characteristics of powerful curricular and instructional designs.

Notes

1   Tyson-Bernstein (1988).
2   See Rayner and Pollatsek (1989).
3   Idem.
4   Simon (1981).
5   Idem.
6   Chall and Dale (1995).
7   Freebody and Anderson (1983).
8   Bransford and Johnson (1972).
9   Schank (1979).
10 Hidi and Baird (1988); Wade and Adams (1990).
11 Graves et al. (1991) and Hidi and Baird (1988).
12 Wong and Calfee (1988).
13 Garner, Gillingham, and White (1989).
14 Whitehead (1974).
15 Miller (1956).
16 Calfee and Chambliss (1987).
17 Langer (1986).
18 Applebee (1978) and Orsolini and DiGiacinto (1996).
19 Bereiter and Scardamalia (1987).
20 Langer (1986).
21 Kintsch and Yarbrough (1982).
22 Cook and Mayer (1988); Meyer (1985), and van Dijk and Kintsch (1983).
23 Calfee and Chambliss (1987).
24 Englert and Hiebert (1984).

25 Idem.
26 Chou Hare, Rabinowitz, and Schieble (1989).
27 Meyer and Freedle (1984).
28 Calfee and Chambliss (1988) and Chambliss, Calfee, and Wong (1990).
29 Sacks, Schegloff, and Jefferson (1974), Schegloff (1968) and Schegloff and Sacks (1973).
30 Brooks and Warren (1972).
31 Whittaker (1992).
32 Richgels et al. (1987).
33 Chambliss (1995).
34 Doctorow, Wittrock, and Marks (1978), Chou Hare, Rabinowitz, and Schieble (1989) and Richgels et al. (1987).
35 Baumann (1986).
36 Armbruster and Anderson (1985).

3

THE DESIGN OF CURRICULUM
AND INSTRUCTION

Despite pico-computers, virtual realities, or compact-disk encyclopedias, text-books can play a unique role in enhancing learning and nurturing children's minds, or so we claimed at the beginning of chapter 2 – but, we explained, only if those textbooks are comprehensible, convey an exemplary curriculum, and support student-centered instruction. Design is the key. Textbooks for learning will not occur by happenstance but must be carefully crafted. The elements – words, sentences, paragraphs, and entire texts – must be linked according to comprehensibility, curricular, and instructional themes. The last chapter focused on passage designs that are comprehensible. In the well-designed text functional devices and rhetorical patterns link words, sentences, paragraphs, and entire passages that are familiar and interesting into a comprehensible whole. Comprehensibility serves as a gatekeeper. Readers who comprehend the text have a chance at learning from it; without substantial intervention from the teacher, those who fail to comprehend will be left out.

Ideal textbook materials are far more than comprehensible, however. Comprehensibility does not address what students will learn or how they will be taught. We see textbooks as a device for conveying intellectual ideas. The ideas are the curriculum; the conveyor is instruction. The textbook writer faces a challenging task – designing materials that are true to the comprehensibility themes of familiarity, interest, and structural coherence, while conveying an exemplary curriculum in an instructionally effective manner. As the writing challenge increases, heeding the elements, linkages, and themes in the text becomes essential. Otherwise, writers tend to lose control over the text, resulting in written equivalents of the strange bicycles that we portrayed earlier: important elements with crazy linkages or trivial elements linked wondrously. This chapter simultaneously adds to the complexity by focusing on curriculum and instruction, while simplifying the task by considering the elements, linkages, and themes in a text's design.

The chapter has three major divisions: (a) curriculum, (b) instruction, and (c) implications for text design. The first two divisions turn, briefly, away from textbook materials to address the questions "What is important to teach?" and "What are powerful instructional strategies?" The third division returns specifically to textbooks and considers "What are the implications for textbook design?" Throughout, our discussion relies heavily on design. Curriculum and instruction can both be understood according to elements, linkages, and themes. Figure 2.2 in chapter 2 provides an overview of the curricular and instructional designs that we elaborate in this chapter. We suggest you take a moment to refresh your memory by reexamining it. You may also want to consider again what you learned from reading "How Does Plate Tectonics Explain Earthquakes and Volcanoes?," and how this passage could make you "look smart" if you wanted to discuss plate tectonics with a friend. Answers to this question address issues of curriculum and instruction. They suggest what the passage teaches and how it accomplishes the task.

Curriculum: The Expert's Lens

What is worth teaching? We propose that the best answer to this question comes from the design of the knowledge domains themselves. Other answers are certainly possible. Ralph Tyler, in his classic, *Basic Principles of Curriculum and Instruction*, proposes five responses to this question.[1] He classifies our answer as the one given by "essentialists" or "subject specialists." According to Tyler, progressives and child psychologists answer that student needs should guide curriculum decisions; that the goal of education is to produce well-adjusted adults. Sociologists, aware of the needs of society, argue that curriculum should be based on whatever the pressing societal problems are; that the goal of schooling is to produce good citizens. Educational philosophers point to important basic life values as a guide, because they see that the goal of education is to produce an ethical populace. Educational psychologists answer that curriculum must be developmentally appropriate; that the goal of schooling is to teach something. Tyler proposes that a well-designed curriculum must contain all five. Noting that no curriculum could effectively incorporate everything worthwhile, he suggests that curriculum designers use their philosophy of education and what they know about educational psychology to decide what to include among student needs, society needs, and the domain.

It is difficult to quarrel with arguments for designing a curriculum to meet student and society needs – somewhat analogous to denying the value of motherhood or truthfulness. Nonetheless, we argue that the unique contribution of the school is to transmit from one generation to the next the major ideas in the content domains, ideas that in some cases have been evolving for thousands of years.[2] If schools do not make this contribution, no other institution is prepared to take up the slack. This is not to say that schooling should ignore student and society needs or basic life values. We repeatedly explain throughout chapters 2, 3, and 4 that unfamiliar ideas must be linked firmly to the real-life experiences and problems of all students to be understood by all students. How classrooms are structured and whether the relationship between teachers and students is truly student-centered influence both whether student needs are met and the values that students come to hold. The design of the curriculum must come from an established content domain, however, so that schools can fulfill their unique mission.

Turning to the domains does not completely solve the problem. Traditionally, curriculum has been domain based. Since the 1950s, curriculum design has relied on task analysis: the developer divides a domain (e.g., history, language arts, or geology) into a large number of specific subtasks or objectives (the elements), and arranges these in a sequence (the linkages).[3] The underlying theme is the gradual accumulation of a body of skills and knowledge through continual exposure.

Our ideal curriculum begins not with tasks or topics but concepts, relying on Whitehead's[4] advice to teach a few things well, echoed by Tyler.[5] Tyler advises curriculum designers to choose a small number of objectives because it takes so long to learn anything, and to be sure that the objectives are coherent so that students will not become confused by contradictions. This counsel echoes both cognitive psychology and the KISS principle – "Keep it simple, sweetheart."[6] The difficulty, of course, arises in choosing the few understandings to teach. Complexity is easy; simplicity is hard won. As we have already explained, Tyler advises curriculum designers to use philosophy and psychology to make the choices. We focus on the design of the domain: the major elements, linkages, and themes that provide coherence to the subject-matter.

Domain Design

Joseph Schwab, in his essay "Education and the structure of the disciplines," argues that subject-matter disciplines (what we have been calling "domains") have a design.[7] He builds on the ideas of Auguste Comte, whom Schwab describes as a relatively modern student of discipline structure (Comte lived from 1798 to 1857). Schwab explains that, according to Comte, there are "roughly" two kinds of knowledge: *ad hoc* knowledge, the practical knowledge that fills a need literally thrust upon a person, and subject-matter knowledge, systematic knowledge of the properties and behaviors of a subject-matter. Schwab uses feeling cold and feeling hungry as examples of how the two types of knowledge develop and differ. In the beginning, people feel hungry, so they look for food. When they feel cold, they search for ways to warm themselves.

Such searches lead to bits and pieces of commonsense knowledge, which people use whenever they feel hungry or cold. Schwab explains,

> As time goes on, however, human culture discovers that there are many overlaps among the many entries in its catalogue of know hows. A way to keep warm, a way to get light, a way to tenderize tough meat, all turn on matters of fire and combustibles, for example. Someone sees, perhaps in a flash of inspiration, that we might better serve our practical needs by being not quite so practical, so immediate, so *ad hoc*. For, surely, if we turned our attention to fire itself, to the question of what will burn and what will not, how burning starts and what it does, we would be achieving knowledge of far greater scope and usefulness than by limiting ourselves only to trying to solve practical problems as they arise.
>
> In short, the idea of *subject matter*, of a something-to-be-studied, instead of a need-to-be-filled, is born.[8]

In chapter 1, we presented a different version of Schwab's argument. We proposed that the educated mind is organized around a relatively small number of LARGE ideas or concepts; that the educated person can employ these concepts to make sense of the seemingly chaotic world. The geologist can use a single concept – the theory of plate tectonics – to understand such diverse phenomena as earthquakes, volcanoes, ocean trenches, and the shape of continents. The furniture mover with a theory for how best to load furniture can employ this theory when packing either several moving vans with office furniture from a complex of buildings or one rental trailer with the few belongings of an apartment dweller. The harried parent can apply a theory of child development to negotiate the changing moods of a rambunctious two-year-old or acknowledge the fears of a sensitive five-year-old. Each of these cases demonstrates the effect of subject-matter knowledge.

According to Schwab, subject-matter knowledge is vastly superior to *ad hoc* practical knowledge.[9] Because it is systematic, it allows people to anticipate problems before they happen: to ponder, to plan, to alter, and to modify. And, we would add, because it is systematic, subject-matter knowledge has a design.

Although he frames the problem as a search for discipline structure, Schwab turns his attention to the hallmarks of a subject-matter design.[10] He explains that all subject-matters have components and organization, analogous to design elements and linkages. As a subject-matter develops, he notes, it first identifies the elements and then figures out the organization. You will notice that the design characteristic missing in Schwab's characterization is the theme. We propose that the theme comes from the models, theories, and principles that people in the discipline construct to explain the elements and the linkages.

What is important to teach? Schwab's essay implies an answer: the major elements, linkages, and themes in well-established, traditional subject-matters.

Both Tyler and Schwab raise a valid concern about this answer. Most children will not become experts in any subject-matter, and even exceptional children will not become experts in more than one or two. Indeed, this rubric was applied without widespread success in the 1960s and abandoned accordingly in the 1970s.[11] Furthermore, domains are combining and recombining so rapidly today (e.g., biophysics, psychobiology, and chemical engineering) that the traditional divisions among subject-matters often seem outdated and useless.

Tyler suggests that subject-matter specialists address the following question: "What can your subject contribute to the education of young people who are not going to be specialists in your field?"[12] Schwab proposes that schools need to impart subject-matter knowledge in such a way that laymen will be able to make use of it.[13] He acknowledges that it is unrealistic to expect the lay public to extract, unaided, useful knowledge from a discipline. Therefore, Schwab explains, the curriculum must use practical examples and activities carefully chosen according to the discipline's structure (or design) for at least the early years of schooling and models and analogies thereafter. The layperson must learn the kind of knowledge that each discipline produces, how that knowledge is verified, and where the growth points in the discipline are. Ignorance of the growth points will cause what students learned about a discipline to collapse around their ears, Schwab explains, quickly out-of-date.[14]

The "what to teach" conumdrum, then, turns on being able to identify the barebones design in a domain, which guides the choice of practical examples and activities, models, and analogies. One approach to this problem is to delineate the special lens of the expert. What does the expert know? What can the expert do? What is the expert's attitude toward the domain? How are the knowledge, skills, and attitudes of the expert linked? In other words, what is the design of the expert's subject-matter knowledge? A second method is to look for the themes, elements, and linkages in published curriculum frameworks. We focus on the expert's knowledge in this chapter and examine a curriculum framework in chapter 4.

Conversing with Experts

Experts see the world quite differently than novices. We propose that the goal of a course of study should be not the accumulation of facts, but the acquisition of a lens for viewing experience. The chess master looks at a board placement and sees a game. The novice sees a bunch of chess men. Most of us watch the sun sinking below the horizon. Copernicus was able to see the earth spinning in space, eclipsing the sun. The novice strolls through a botanical garden, delighted by the decorative diversity. The biologist observes plants adapting to variations in soil conditions. Education in this perspective is more than a trip to Disneyland (or a museum); instead, it means acquiring the expert's X-ray vision, the connoisseur's sense of taste, the scholar's capacity to appraise, the scientist's ability to analyze.

As part of our studies of curriculum design, we invited three Stanford University professors and one scientist from the nearby US Geological Survey (USGS), renowned for their work in physics, chemistry, geophysics, and biology, to sketch the design of their discipline on a single sheet of paper. To further complicate the task, we asked that the answer make sense to middle-school students – adolescents! All four experts protested that the task was virtually impossible. Nonetheless, we invited each one to lunch and posed the following questions:

- If you were to draw a picture of your discipline, what would it look like?
- What linkages connect the major topics in your discipline?
- What models, explanatory principles, and theories define your field?
- How do you think and work within your domain? What skills and knowledge are important in your work?

The lunches were fascinating, unveiling the mind of an expert struggling to deal with Tyler's question: "What can your subject contribute to the education of young people who are not going to be specialists in your field?" To be sure, experts are not always easy to talk with. When we first asked Brent Darwympel of the USGS to discuss elementary and middle school science curricula, he explained that he did not know how fruitful the conversation would be. He added that he did find the issues intriguing because of discussions he had had with his wife, an elementary school teacher. As background to our conversation, we sent him text samples from a few of the best-selling textbooks, our attempts as novices to sketch out the design of his discipline, and our four questions.

As he talked and sketched, it became increasingly clear that Darwympel saw the world around us in a different way – through a different lens – than the rest of us at the table (figure 3.1). The USGS is a news-maker in the San Francisco Bay Area because of our frequent earthquakes, and (like most kids) we were most interested in what he had to say about the sporadic jerkings of the ground around us. Darwympel placed these in the historical context of the evolution of our solar system, and the specific features of planet earth that make it unique in the system.

Darwympel began with a historical perspective – the origins of the earth when a molten mass of the sun spun off into space. The ball of fire that became the earth was rather special in size and makeup – large enough to remain molten at its core, but small enough to cool on the surface. We who live on the outer crust are largely unaware of the raging cauldron below, unless we live near an active fault or volcano. Even then, we take a local perspective. Darwympel,

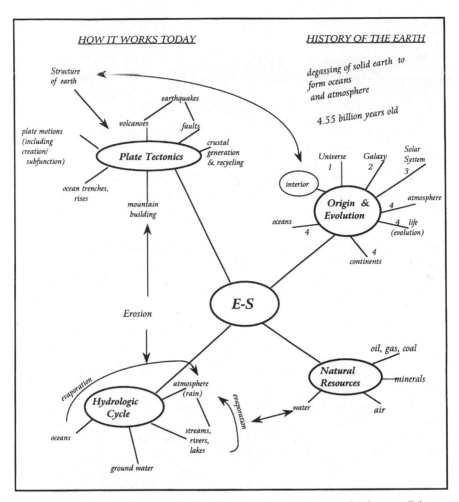

Figure 3.1   The picture that a geophysicist drew when asked to represent the elements, linkages, and themes in the design of his domain.

whose specialty is plate tectonics, viewed the earth's dynamics very differently. The basic elements in his account were the large plates into which the thin surface is broken, the underlying mantle of viscous lava, and the solid core. We had heard about plates, and had simple ways of understanding them. If you live near a crack, as we do, then every once in a while there is slippage and the ground shakes. If the crack goes too deep, lava comes out as a volcano.

A lot more was happening under foot when seen through Darwympel's lens.

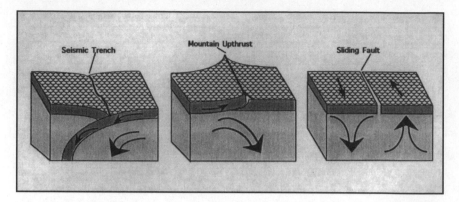

Figure 3.2   Pictures that represent our understanding of some of the effects of plate tectonics.

His ways of linking the elements explained several phenomena that we saw as unrelated. In tectonic theory, the core, pressured by gravity, generates enormous heat that keeps the mantle not only liquid but simmering in giant currents that rise to the surface and drift downward as they cool. These currents cause the breaks between plates, much like the crust that forms patterns in a pot of simmering pea soup. Plates move in different directions under the force of the currents, sometimes sliding past one another, other times spreading apart, and often pushing against one another. Mountain ranges, ocean trenches, as well as earthquakes and volcanoes, are all signs that our planet is still recycling itself even after billions of years. Not geophysicists, we subsequently studied several accounts to increase our knowledge of these phenomena. Our understanding of some of the effects of plate tectonics is depicted in figure 3.2.

The theme that emerged from Darwympel's account was one of renewal. Tectonic cycles, like the water and oxygen/carbon dioxide cycles, showed how natural processes tended toward continuous regeneration. Viewed against a time scale measured in millions of years, the Earth's surface was continuously drawn into the interior and replaced by new material, including minerals and other natural resources. For a species the life of which was measured in a few decades, of course, the message is quite clear: if the human race uses up the resources too quickly, or damages the thin surface that is our home, then we may not survive to enjoy the replacements that are currently being thrust up to the surface.

Darwympel contrasted his picture with the text samples that we had sent to him. The texts discouraged him, greatly overcomplicating the important ideas in his field, missing altogether what he saw as the major themes, and failing to show the relevance of his work to everyday life. The theories of evolution and plate tectonics had transformed geology from a discipline that sorted rocks and

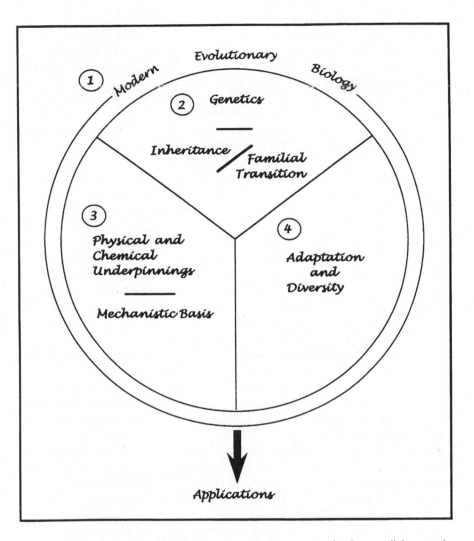

Figure 3.3 The picture that a biologist drew when asked to represent the elements, linkages, and themes in the design of his domain.

classified landforms to an explanatory science that could support predictions and hypotheses, he explained. These text samples presented a view of the earth as static (or descriptive) rather than dynamic (or sequential), highlighting factoids such as the three types of volcanic cones instead of the dynamic forces that lead to evolution and recycling.

Our conversation with Ward Watt from Stanford's Biology Department was amazingly similar. His "picture" also emphasized the theme of evolution, but from a very different perspective (figure 3.3). He took for granted the diversity in the natural environment brought about by forces both underground and on the surface. For Watt, the overarching theme in biology, the study of life, was the way in which living things adapted to diversity. Changing environments were a fact of life, from his viewpoint – a challenge but also an opportunity. He pointed through the window to a collection of potted plants: "Look at the leaves. See how they are different – some are thin and feathery, others are fat and leathery, and there are all kinds of gradations in between. Why do you think the leaves are different?" We puzzled over the question for a while, and finally a gardener in the group proposed that the variations had something to do with the soil and the amount of water. "Exactly. If you examine the soil, you'll find that the 'fat' leaves do best in hard clay soil that is quite dry. These plants have filled that niche with leaves that preserve water. The 'thin' leaves are in light soil, which needs to be kept moist. Water flows through them easily."

Watt's picture identified three elements linked into a whole by modern evolutionary theory: (1) physical and chemical underpinnings, (2) genetics, and (3) adaptation and diversity. Physical and chemical underpinnings – what he described as the mechanistic basis for evolution and genetics – provide both the possibilities for adaptation and the constraints. Plants and animals differ structurally and chemically, for example. Because of these differences, cacti and desert tortoises adapt to arid environments differently. The leaf structure that the cactus uses to capture and store water is not an option for the tortoise. Being able to move to a water source is an impossible solution for the cactus. Genetics, focusing on inheritance and familial transmission, provides the mechanism both for similarity and diversity among organisms. A "baby" cactus or tortoise shares similarities and differences with its "parents" that are not haphazard but are predictable. Physical and chemical underpinnings and genetics provide some important boundaries for how diverse living beings adapt to the environment, the third element. The linkages among the three elements are both causal and scaled. The underpinnings and genetics affect how organisms adapt to the environment in diverse ways. The elements also differ in scale from the atomic (physical and chemical underpinnings) to entire environments (adaptation and diversity). Like Darwympel, Watt found the textbook treatments to be turgid and far too detailed. "What is missing is the big picture," he complained. He pointed again to the plants outside the window: "Few people would walk past those plants and even notice the differences among the leaves. Even fewer would ask, 'Why?'." Focusing on the facts, what often ends up as a march through the phyla does not teach children to ask questions or seek answers, he explained.

And so, as the earth changes, whether naturally or unnaturally, new opportunities appear for life. We brought together the two perspectives, the geologist's and the biologist's, and made an imaginary trip around San Francisco Bay, thinking about the diversity of geologic features and the variety of life forms that have filled these niches – and thought as well about how the tinkering of human beings has changed the opportunities and the challenges.

From Expert's Lens to Curriculum Design

The starting point for a curriculum theme need not be sophisticated. For instance, fourth-grade science textbooks often cover dinosaurs and volcanoes, topics that are of clear-cut interest to preadolescents. These elements may accomplish little by themselves, but they open the way to explorations of a variety of important themes. The topic "Dinosaurs" can be linked to a wide range of contemporary topics, from the African veldt to ocean life (whales, dolphins, and salmon), but is also a natural way of introducing the theme of extinction and survival. Similarly, a passage on "Volcanoes" provides a springboard for thematic treatment of plate tectonics as "Spaceship Earth." Language arts curriculum themes often entail connections with human purposes, values, and commonalities. Most of us relate to the interplay of friendship and conflict in E. B. White's *Charlotte's Web* and Katherine Patterson's *Bridge to Terebithia*. Lukins' discussion of theme in children's literature supports this premise; she proposes that a genuine literary theme engages (a) the reader's personal world, (b) the world beyond the reader, (c) other texts, and (d) the author.[15]

Is this view of curriculum workable? We think that it is. Several professional organizations have advocated coherent designs that describe what should be taught.[16] The professional frameworks in mathematics and science have received applause for their clarity and cogency, although their impact on classroom practice remains less certain.

What about the "facts", the "objectives", the "skills" – the meat and potatoes of today's textbooks? We think that with a well designed text, we can have our cake and eat it too. Human beings have incredible capacity for information, if they find it engaging and organized. And so we propose a test for every textbook passage: Does it promote high-level objectives that move students toward significant curricular themes that illuminate expert lenses? A passage on earthquakes should do more than catalog a history of major quakes; a text on volcanoes should go beyond a description of conic forms. The aim should be to lead students to see their worlds of experience from a different perspective.

Instruction

How should instruction be designed so that students acquire an expert's lens? What elements, linkages, and themes undergird teaching practice in the ideal classroom? We propose that effective instruction has four elements, designated by the acronym CORE (see figure 3.4). Effective instruction *connects* to student knowledge, *organizes* new content for the student, provides opportunities for students to *reflect* strategically, and gives students occasions to *extend* what they have learned to new contexts. Note that the first two elements are hallmarks of comprehensibility. Not surprisingly, students must understand before they can reflect or extend. The four elements in effective instruction are linked flexibly. The linkages, in short, hinge on the dynamics of the lesson. If the teacher sees wrinkled frowns, then it may be time to reconnect; a wide-ranging discussion may call for organization. The linkages depend on the students' reactions rather than a fixed sequence.

The theme – student-centered – guides both the elements and linkages. Student-centered instruction is inherently social. It presumes a community of learners, working together to construct their own understandings. Student-centered instruction also must act as a zoom lens. Any lesson may entail several COREs, framing the overall activity, in a series, or embedded within one

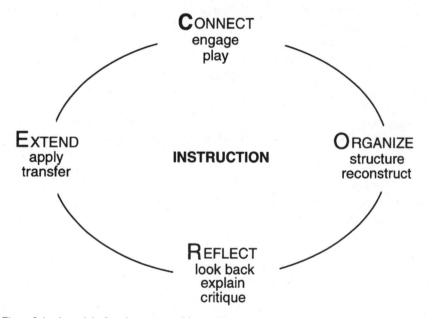

Figure 3.4   A model of student-centered instruction.

another. A CORE can be as short as a two-minute group interaction, or as long as a 30-minute "reading lesson" or a three-week class project. The theme, student-centered, renders the design infinitely capable of capitalizing on the moment; of building on the resources and responding to the interests and needs of the particular students in a classroom.

This design contrasts sharply with the teacher-directed instruction typical of today's elementary and middle-school classrooms. Current practice has been well-documented. The most prevalent design is the multi-step lesson plan. The teacher, guided by the textbook manual, opens by stating the objectives, presents information, leads a discussion, and closes with practice and assessment. The student's task is to follow instructions, which generally means reading the text material, answering teacher questions that call for regurgitation of the passage, and completing assignments and worksheets that are part of the textbook package.

Teacher-directed instruction emphasizes teacher control, correct answers, and practice as the primary basis for learning. Discussion is limited. Courtney Cazden, who is particularly interested in classroom discourse, describes an IRE sequence, in which the teacher Initiates the exchange by asking the student a question, the student called upon Responds with an answer, and the teacher then Evaluates the student's effort.[15] Questions are largely prescriptive; the teacher has a specific answer in mind.

The following "discussion" in a science class illustrates the model:

TEACHER: [Writes *vertebrate* on board] What does every vertebrate have in common?
STUDENT: A backbone.
TEACHER: Right. What are some examples of vertebrates?
STUDENT: Mammals and reptiles.
TEACHER: Good. What are some other examples?
STUDENT: Insects?
TEACHER: No. Insects do not have backbones. Any others?

And so on. The multi-step design is instructive; students acquire information, and many learn to play the academic game, particularly if they come from homes where parents practice IRE exchanges.

Where, however, do students acquire the expert's lens – the understanding that vertebrates evolved through a unique combination of physical and chemical underpinnings, genetics, and environmental responses? We speculate that underlying typical IRE exchanges is a fundamental belief. Present students with enough facts, and the facts will somehow coalesce into the important ideas in a domain as if by magic.

The Design of Student-Centered Instruction

To replace teacher-centered with student-centered instruction, one must focus on the special strengths and needs of a classroom of students in the middle grades. We make several assumptions about students and schooling: (a) any classroom of students knows a great deal relevant to virtually any topic; (b) this preexisting knowledge can easily remain unspoken, unanalyzed, and unconnected ("mind sharing" is a tough and unnatural task); and (c) instruction can resolve this paradox. The key to the riddle is to lead the class to activate "group knowledge," and to process, structure, and transform available data (both personal experience and the lesson content) into a construction, or concept, or understanding.

Designing student-centered instruction is not a trivial task. Even instruction that includes elements to connect, organize, reflect, and extend can lead to instruction that is actually sequential rather than flexible, and teacher-centered rather than student-centered. We have observed scenarios such as the following:

TEACHER: Today let's talk about EXTINCTION. I want to find out what you already know about the topic. How about some words? I'll write them down.

STUDENT A: Dead?

TEACHER: Good! Who else has a word?

STUDENT B: Dodo ...

TEACHER: Wonderful! Let's have a few more thoughts.

STUDENT C: Volcano?

TEACHER: Hm ... . Interesting, but it doesn't fit. Who else has a word?

As the lesson develops, the teacher begins to extract from the students words that match her own predetermined concept. She next directs them to cluster the words according to categories that she selected in advance to match the textbook. The lesson is more interactive than the standard IRE exchange to be sure, but still lacks a sense of genuine student involvement. Similarly, the reflection becomes a dry recital:

TEACHER: What was the lesson about?

STUDENT: We did a semantic map on *extinction*.

If the extension is "Read the chapter and answer the questions," then little has changed over other teacher-directed approaches. This lesson has not activated student knowledge (notice the rejection of "volcano"); nor has it presented data that students could process, structure, and transform – hence the development of CORE.

You may not agree with our assumptions about student capabilities or teacher responsibilities. Furthermore, the CORE strategy takes time and reduces the number of topics that can be covered – a strength rather than a weakness in our opinion. In-depth coverage of selected topics has several benefits, as we have noted previously. Now we turn to a depiction of the four elements.

Connect   Learning that is not connected to a person's experiences follows well-known patterns.[18] First, it is more difficult and time-consuming. Second, it has limited transferability: individuals fall back on what they "really know." For instance, you know the theory that the sun moving across the sky is actually an illusion caused by the daily rotation of the earth. Yet when you gaze at the horizon toward a gorgeous sunset, like most people you see the sun set, because the theory is not connected to your perceptions.

How can the teacher promote connections in the classroom? Our experience, and a meager research base, leads to two suggestions: (a) questioning strategies that elicit and articulate students' thoughts; and (b) genuine interest by the teacher in the substance of students' thoughts. The research suggests that more questions may be better than fewer, but the real key seems to be the character and quality of the questions.[19] Certain question types are more evocative than others; "yes–no" and "literal detail" requests generally lead nowhere, even when followed by "Why?" But asking the right question is easier said than done. For example, Suzanne Wilson, a teacher turned researcher, asked students, "What makes it hard to draw a good map?" Students responded with blank looks. She regrouped and asked, "What's the difference between a map and a picture?" They came to life.[20]

After the fact, you can probably generate several hypotheses about why the first question failed and the second one worked. "Picture" is more familiar than "map", and the contrast between the two jumpstarts students. The key may be that Wilson was genuinely interested in what students thought about the topic and was willing to experiment with different ways of posing the question. Cazden gives marvelous examples of real questions that engage elementary students in complex and unfamiliar topics, allowing them to use what they know while approaching an unknown.[21] She makes the critical distinction between answering and understanding, between "saying the secret word" and delving beneath the surface. Real questions entice the student to think a little further. What do you mean? Why did you say that? I don't understand; can you explain another way? Could you give me an example? Such questions connect the teacher to the student and the student to the topic.

Organize   Classroom conversations have a purpose that goes beyond the particular to the general. Instruction that only makes connections will not help the student to acquire the expert's lens. We suggested earlier that the expert's lens has a structure to it; that the expert uses the lens to make sense out of the world's chaos. If students and teachers are to use such a lens, coherence must permeate each lesson. We have already suggested two structural systems, which are also useful for organizing instruction: rhetorical patterns and domain design.

Particularly useful for instruction are the graphics that we introduced in chapter 2. Wilson's third-graders, while comparing maps and pictures, could fill in a matrix to organize their discussion and keep a permanent record of their thoughts. Sixth-graders wrestling with how plate tectonics explains earthquakes and volcanoes could complete two parallel falling domino sequences to organize the causal relationships in both sequences. Teachers can use domain design to choose one graphic over another. For example, a matrix could organize differences and similarities between earthquakes and volcanoes, but its static depiction is at odds with the dynamic plate tectonics theory of the geologist. Parallel falling dominoes allow for the same comparisons (How does each causal sequence begin? How do the intervening events differ? – and so on) while capitalizing on the structure in the domain.

Reflect   A conceptual advance springing from cognitive psychology has been the investigation of metacognition, the human capacity to think about thought. The idea has a long history under other names: for instance, Piaget's formal operational thought is a parallel concept.[22] During the past 25 years, psychologists have examined developmental changes and individual profiles, and have evaluated the impact of instructional programs designed to promote reflective thought.[23]

The bottom lines seem clear. Reflective thought fosters the transfer of learning from one situation to another. Moving to a metacognitive level is costly; it takes more time and effort. But the cost seems worth the long-term benefits. Some students, whether by predisposition or previous experience, are more inclined than others toward reflection. But virtually all students, including low achievers, can learn to metacognize, and their academic achievement improves as a result.[24] Finally, the reflective teacher is most effective in promoting high levels of student growth.[25]

What does reflection "look like"? How does it sound in the classroom? The key is the timing and placement of questions that lead students to back away from the task and talk about what has been done, the essential goals of the activity, and the potential for application in other settings. The individual capacity to introspect builds on reflective social experiences. The development of the reflective impulse seldom arises because we naturally look inside our minds, but through the process of explaining our thoughts to others.[26] In a sense, a teacher cannot teach metacognition, but can only promote it by modeling and by setting the stage for students to explain themselves to other youngsters.

Extend   Momentary reflection at the close of a lesson easily becomes an ineffective add-on. For an incident to become a habit of mind, practice is essential. For practice to have an effect, the exercises must be genuine, connected to previous experience, and purposeful – hence our suggestion that a lesson not simply end, but that it be extended to engage students in a larger activity, one in which they transfer the concepts and procedures to a new situation. Extension as we envision it involves both autonomy and cooperation where the teacher no longer instructs but acts instead as facilitator and assessor.

Imagine a text-based science lesson that leads students through a well-controlled experiment with a preset outcome. Assume that the students are connected, organized, and reflective. They have surveyed the relation between plant leaves and soil conditions; they have found that the leaves of plants growing in loose, moist soil differ noticeably from plants growing in packed, dry soil. They have created a matrix of leaf and soil characteristics to highlight the contrast. They have reflected on the possible cause–effect relations. How might they now extend the lesson? One possibility is an experiment in which they transplant several species, make predictions, and check it out. The aim is not only to confirm the ecological principle, but to reinforce the exploratory strategy as a habit of mind.

CORE in the Classroom

CORE is a dynamic design itself, created in response to the multiplicity of cultures and languages that are streaming into today's classrooms. In the CORE model, these variations become opportunities; creativity is joined with responsibility. How the four elements are linked flexibly according to the theme of student-centeredness can only be demonstrated in a story. Our story chronicles a demonstration lesson in a New York City school serving children from neighborhoods with large proportions of poor families. The lesson was conducted by one of us. [The story reads much more smoothly if we refer to him in the first person.]

Student background   It is late October, and I am visiting a third-grade class in the Bronx. Several teachers, the assistant principal, and I enter the room. The 32 students, recovering from lunch, are settling in for social studies. The youngsters are wiggly but well-behaved and curious about their visitors. This section of the borough has substantial migration from Puerto Rico and Central America. More than half of the students are Latino and recent arrivals to New York. The teacher describes them as "poor achievement, low test scores, not very interested in social studies." They all appear to understand English, and virtually every student has something to say during the 30-minute lesson. As the lesson begins, they sit quietly, curious, books open to Chapter 2.

Chapter 2 of their textbook spans 11 pages, eight with text and pictures, and three with activities and questions. The major headings – *Food, Homes, Working* – comprise a topical net. After a brief opening paragraph, the text introduces the Hopi Indians in the Southwestern USA. The three topics describe the practices of this agricultural tribe in each of the areas. Midway through the text, a "Study Help" page mentions the Apache, a hunting tribe from the same region, and briefly sketches how they handled the same three matters. The page suggests in passing that students might compare the two tribes. Then the text turns back to the Hopi. The Chapter Review includes short-answer questions and a suggestion to "Write a paragraph about why the Hopi cared about nature."

Connect   As a stranger to the class, how can I judge students' background experience and knowledge about the topic of deserts? The key to connecting is to reframe the question. What might I assume about the students, and how could I collect some "data" to test my hypotheses?

I need some information from the youngsters:

- What do you know about deserts?
- About the geography of the US?
- About Native Americans?
- About life on this continent four centuries ago?
- About basic necessities for life anywhere and anytime?

My starting assumptions are (a) that the students probably know the general meaning of "desert," (b) that they know a lot about the basics of life, (c) that they know relatively little about the other matters, but (d) that they could create an image of this situation with some guidance and support.

My opening question is simple: "*Where do you live?*" Noting the puzzled frowns, I explain, "*I'm a visitor from San Francisco, so I'm interested in where you're from.*" Hands go up. "New York," "The Bronx," "Tremont Avenue." "*Where's the Bronx? Where's New York City? Here's a map of the US.*" I circle my finger randomly, and ask, "*Getting warmer-colder?*" The class takes control of my finger, moving it to the northeast, and stopping when it reaches New York, the state name in large type. Several students object: "That's the name of the state. He hasn't got to New York City yet." They lead me home.

My next "big" question is equally simple: "*Where were you born? New York City?*" Voices call out: "Puerto Rico, Mississippi, El Salvador, Mexico, New Jersey." "*Where are those places?*" Again youngsters direct my moving finger, southward to the tropics. "*No deserts there – right?*" As I subtly insinuate the lesson topic, students prove me wrong. Many have lived in desert areas, on the western sides of the Central American countries. "*What are deserts like? Tell me some words that remind you of deserts.*" Words emerge; I scribble them on a butcher paper sheet next to the map.

A move to the text: "*Today we're going to read about Indians who lived in the Arizona desert hundreds of years ago. Let's use the map to go to Arizona slowly. Tell me when we pass places that you know about.*" My finger moves down the coast from New York to Florida, across Mississippi and Texas, and finally to Hopi country spreading from the Four Corners region down through Baja California. Children's voices mark the trail – "It's hot in Biloxi"; "Texas is a big state."

We reach Arizona. "*Before we read the chapter, tell me – for people to live somewhere, what do they need?*' – another big, simple question, leading to more words on the butcher paper: jobs, food, clothes, a place to live, water. "*OK, we're in the desert, four hundred years ago, you're an Indian – who knows something about Indians?*" The few responses to this question come mostly from television reruns of western movies. "*It's four hundred years ago. How would you get jobs, food, clothes, a place to live, water?*"

For the next five minutes, foreshortened because of schedule, the class constructs a dry, harsh environment lacking grocery stores or faucets, electricity or television, and apartments or subways. Youngsters connect by extending their personal experiences to create a situation through their capacity to imagine. First priority is water – where to find it, how to conserve and preserve it. Next is food. The desert seems dead, but they imagine edibles: cacti, rattlesnakes. A place to live is next in order, followed by clothes. They assume plenty of work.

We have described connecting in detail because a solid linkage to students' experiences and interests is critical to genuine learning. An effective connection engages the entire class. Genuine questions allow every student to generate a distinctive response; the intelligence of the entire group becomes available for public use. Also, a good connection builds the foundations for organization. As the children answer the questions, a possible structure begins to emerge. Students were urged at the outset to compare their situation with life in the desert a long time ago. As you will see, the compare–contrast or matrix structure effectively organizes an otherwise incoherent text.

Organize   In this lesson, students are guided toward two expository structures for classifying information about the topic. When I ask them to tell me what people need to live anywhere, I am not only encouraging them to connect with the topic, but I am also guiding them toward an organizational pattern – the topical net. This pattern builds on the natural inclination of the human mind to search for patterns, for commonalities, for collections. But a topical net does not have much form to it; it does not readily lead to comparisons, for example. The matrix is the ideal expository structure for organizing content so that it can be compared and contrasted. Using two different patterns for one lesson would not be sensible. However, I am able to set the stage for students to reorganize the topical net into a matrix during a subsequent lesson and use the matrix to compare two Native American cultures.

Following the 15 minutes of free-for-all discussion, I suggest, "*Let's see what chapter 2 says about deserts and Indians. Skim the pages, and tell me what you think it tells you.*" The students begin to read. Despite my entreaty to skim, the room is soon buzzing with sound; students are reading each word and sentence, many subvocalizing, and hence the buzz. After a couple of minutes I interrupt: "*Just look at the big headings, the words in big letters. See anything familiar?*" I flip through my book as a model. Hands begin to come up: "They are talking about food, and homes, and working." The students have discovered the pattern in the text and recognize it as virtually identical to their categories.

To complete the analysis of the text, I arrange students in four groups, each assigned to one segment of the text (including the Apache page). Their task is to review the segment, extract key facts, and prepare a list of questions about anything not covered in the text. Ten minutes later, each group gives a brief reportback, which I summarize on the butcher paper as a topical net with four subheadings: Food, Homes, Jobs, and Apaches.

Students spontaneously notice interesting differences between the Hopi (agricultural) and the Apache (hunting) styles. The text contains elements of a matrix, but these are scattered. I suggest to the class that in their next lesson they revise the messy topical net on the butcher paper into a matrix comparing the two adaptations to desert life covered in the chapter, but adding information from a previous chapter and from their own experience. These youngsters spring from various backgrounds, and could contribute richly to the theme of *adaptation*, a theme buried in textbook details, but clearly the most salient point.

Reflect and extend   These elements end the lesson. In this demonstration lesson I squeeze in more activities than is sensible. The guides to reflection are straightforward: "*What have we done in this lesson?*" "We created a topical net of the topic." "*What are some other topics that you could analyze this way – in this book; in science? What did you learn from the book? What did you already know?"* Students seem puzzled by the queries. On the one hand, the answers seem obvious. On the other hand, asking *"Why do you think it's worth studying this material?"* is unusual in most classroom discourse, and so the students seem wary.

Reflection connects naturally in this lesson to extension. By stepping back and pondering what they have done and why, students are ready to apply the same or similar approaches to new situations. The simplest extension would be for the class to restructure the topical net into a matrix. (Note that the same "activity" serves two functions in the model: organize and extend.) Once students have constructed their matrix, the domain theme should start to emerge. At that point, their teacher could ask, "In what ways were the Hopi and Apache styles alike? Why were they alike in these ways? How were they different? Why were they different?"

A far more elaborate extension would have several stages. The compare–contrast matrix actually provides a framework for integrating the first several chapters of the textbook. The teacher could introduce one chapter to illustrate the process of analysis and then divide the students into work teams, each assigned a chapter topic for analysis and further research, consummated by a report on environmental niches in their own neighborhood. Here the extension becomes a fully fledged thematic project, starting with one or two direct-instruction lessons, and then moving to team activities.

Before we leave extension, we want to note how well the rest of the model can support student writing. The creation of a graphic to organize information can be viewed as part of the prewriting stage of what has become known in recent years as "process writing."[27] The advantages of this approach are that it downplays the technical details of writing until they are needed, it gives students structures with which to organize their ideas while allowing substantial freedom for personal and creative framing of the topic, and it keeps the amount of actual writing to a minimum during the drafting stage. This last feature means that virtually every student can join in the composing activity, but it also mirrors effective practices by expert writers.

Relating CORE to Text Design

Our depiction of CORE may leave you wondering what implications student-centered instruction could have for textbook design. In many ways, CORE departs sharply from more traditional instruction where the teacher's primary task is to move students through the textbook. You might conclude that the most sensible approach would be to abandon textbooks altogether. We have already discussed and rejected this alternative. Instead, we propose a third test for a well-designed textbook passage. To what degree does the material provide connections to the wide variety of students (and teachers) who comprise the audience? How well and clearly organized is the presentation? What opportunities does the text advance for reflection? To what extent does the material open the way to go beyond the information presented?

Equally important, how flexible is the text design? Does it lend itself readily to group work, for example? Could the material be considered from different angles depending on the instructional goals of the teacher and students? Perhaps rather ironically, designs with tighter linkages (e.g., matrices, hierarchies, and branching trees) may also have the greatest potential for effective flexibility. Picture a text on the Hopi and Apache societies, linked as a matrix. To work with this text, a class could be divided into groups, each of which focuses on one row (or column) of the matrix, combining their work into a completed matrix by the end of the instruction. The class could focus on either the rows or columns of the matrix. If the teacher and students should be interested in comparing different desert dwellers, they could look for similarities and differences in the Hopi and Apache family life, culture, and livelihoods. Alternatively, if they should be intent on understanding the basic requirements for a society, they could focus on the need for a family life, culture, and livelihood, using the Hopi and Apache societies as examples.

Connect, Organize, Reflect, Extend – not only must the well-designed passage be comprehensible and reflect an expert's lens, but it must also support student-centered instruction.

Implications for Text Design

So far, we have been building a case for designing textbook passages to reflect comprehensibility, curricular, and instructional designs. We have described the themes, elements, and linkages for each of these designs at some length. In this section we pull comprehensibility, curriculum, and instruction together, explain how they can affect the design of a single textbook passage, look again at "How Does Plate Tectonics Explain Earthquakes and Volcanoes," and present a rewrite of this passage to demonstrate our notions.

Comprehensibility, Curriculum, Instruction, and Passage Design

The relationships among comprehensibility, curriculum, instruction, and passage designs are portrayed graphically in figure 3.5. According to the figure, the well-designed passage grows out of or is based on other designs. Another way to express the relationship is that comprehensibility, curricular, and instructional themes converge to guide the creation of a well-designed textbook

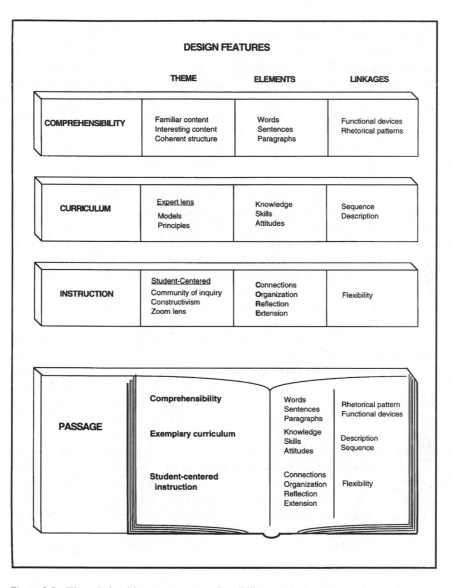

Figure 3.5   The relationships among comprehensibility, curriculum, instruction, and passage design.

passage. These three themes determine the elements – the content of the words, sentences, paragraphs, and sections in the passage – and how they are linked – both the rhetorical pattern and the functional devices. It is easy to say and to picture these notions in a graphic, probably challenging to understand them, and certainly difficult to bring them off.

How well do these three converge in the design of "How Does Plate Tectonics Explain Earthquakes and Volcanoes?" In chapter 2 we concluded that this passage would not be easily comprehensible to sixth-graders. Here we focus on curricular and instructional themes. What does the passage teach to readers? A skim of the passage (see figure 2.1) and a glance at the rhetorical pattern (figure 2.4) show content and linkages that reflect the lens of Dr Darwympel: plate tectonics and the causal models for earthquakes and volcanoes. However, we also notice content – types of volcanic cones in particular – that seems analogous to the rock sorting about which Darwympel despaired. And the overall static descriptive stucture is directly at odds with Darwympel's dynamic sequential model of the earth. The passage has not been crafted with a clear notion of the geologist's lens.

The problem with this passage is that it does not focus on a scientific principle that merits explanation, but exposes students to the factoids of cultural literacy. It does reflect a curricular theme: to become well-educated, students must learn a certain large repository of relatively isolated facts. Even the topical net rhetorical pattern reflects this theme. Nets loosely link large amounts of information within a limited amount of space.

How does this passage teach? Where would it fit in the CORE instructional model? How well does it connect, organize, reflect, and extend? We suspect that this passage would fail to connect with most sixth-grade readers. The loose rhetorical structure provides very little organization to the material. Because the expert's model is so embedded in the structure of the passage, it is hard to imagine how this text would promote either reflection or extension. Finally, the topical net linkages lack the flexibility of a matrix or a branching tree and would not enhance student-centered instruction. The adept teacher could help students to reorganize the passage to highlight the causal relationships. Students then could work in groups to reflect on what they have done and extend to other situations their new understanding – either about reorganizing loosely organized passages or about the plate tectonics model. Without significant teacher intervention, the content and linkages in the passage as written do not reflect CORE, and would promote rote-recitative instruction and right answers instead.

A Well-Designed Passage on Earthquakes and Volcanoes

In this section, we present our rewrite on earthquakes and volcanoes. It is easy to criticize an excerpt. It is another matter to revise a text to be comprehensible, reflect the lens of the expert, and support student-centered instruction. Given enough time and space, we are certain that textbook passages can be

understandable, can lead to a worthwhile curriculum outcome, and can promote sound instructional interaction. Achieving these goals means that the
writer begins not by writing, but by planning.

The model of plate tectonics was our starting point; our purpose was to
design a text that could help sixth-graders begin to understand this model and
use it to explain the causes of earthquakes and volcanoes. We asked ourselves
several questions as we began our design: What do sixth-graders probably think
about the interior of the earth? What background information would they need
to understand the model? According to plate tectonics, what causal sequences
lead to earthquakes and volcanoes? What analogies could we use that sixth-
graders would understand and that would map directly on to the causal
sequences? We read geology textbooks, reviewed our conversation with Darwympel, and checked articles in science magazines to understand plate
tectonics better ourselves. We held a discussion with a linguistically and
culturally heterogeneous class of upper-grade elementary school students to
assess their understanding and to try out several analogies. We put all of our
ideas together into a preliminary graphic representation that would guide our
writing in lieu of an outline. Figure 3.6 is a polished version of our original
graphic.

We built the text around an explanatory theme; our overriding purpose was
to link earthquakes and volcanoes to forces deep within the earth. The basic
elements are the same as the original – plate tectonics, earthquakes, and
volcanoes – with the addition of analogies and the elimination of types of
volcanic cones. These elements are linked together according to our depiction
of explanation presented in chapter 2. First, they gap-fill from the understanding of the typical reader (through the use of analogies) toward the
understanding of the expert (the application of the scientific model to common
phenomena). Second, the presentation of the tiers follows a logical order from
abstract to concrete. The design chronicles the abstract model of convection
currents in the mantle, which *no one* has seen. Next, it applies the model to the
slightly less abstract causal models first of earthquakes and then of volcanoes,
the effects of which children are likely to have either experienced or seen on
television or in movies. Finally, it presents concrete analogies, including a
simple children's game and a common kitchen experience.

Comprehensibility, curricular, and instructional designs guided our decisions. First, we chose an explanation as the rhetorical pattern most likely to lead
to scientific understanding (admittedly a rather lofty comprehension goal).
Many of the phenomena of importance for understanding the world from a
scientific perspective are either nonobservable or difficult to experience. Explanation as we have presented it is carefully designed to link the nonobservable to
the easily observable. In this case, the overarching structure is designed to
explain how mantle convection (nonobservable phenomenon) causes

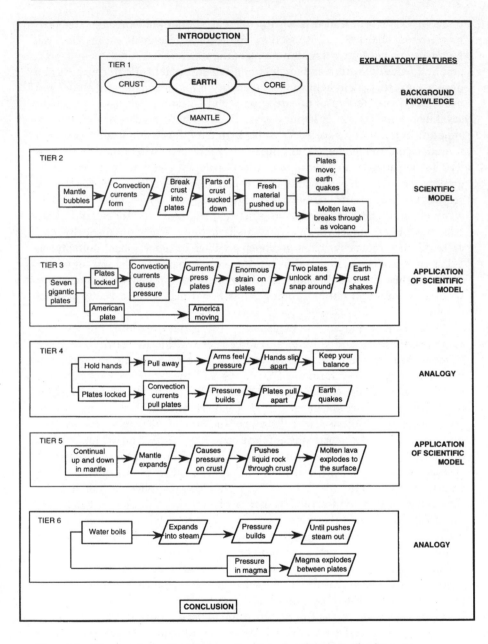

Figure 3.6   The rhetorical pattern for an explanation of earthquakes and volcanoes.

earthquakes and volcanoes (observable phenomena); to link earthquakes and volcanoes to forces deep within the earth. The pattern has several tiers, or subexplanations. The right-hand panel of the figure characterizes these elements of the design. The tiers present background information, chronicle the scientific model, apply the model to earthquakes and volcanoes, and offer two analogies.

Second, besides enhancing comprehension, explanation, as a rhetorical pattern, matches the geologist's lens well and therefore makes good curriculum sense. Geologists use the theory of plate tectonics to *explain*, to make sense of the world. According to Darwympel, before tectonics, geology was largely descriptive; the discipline had accumulated a rich array of information about how the earth was constructed. After tectonics, geology became a more dynamic discipline, showing how planet earth operates as an active and self-renewing system. A giant step, perhaps, but sixth grade is a time when students begin to look beyond family and neighborhood, to have a broader sense of community, to wonder how to "work the system." They have begun to enter Piaget's stage of formal operational thought, the capacity to handle abstract concepts.[28]

The basic building block patterns that we chose within all but one of the tiers also reflect the geologist's lens and differ significantly from the descriptive pattern in the original textbook version. From beginning to end, the revised design is a series of sequential, cause–effect structures, focusing on the reasons for earthquakes and volcanoes. Sequential patterns best match the dynamism of the scientific model, which is an important part of the geologist's lens.

Third, the design supports student-centered instruction well. It uses analogies to connect what the typical reader knows with the understanding of the geologist. The sequential linkages organize the elements consistently and coherently. This consistency provides opportunities for students to reflect about the expert's model; students could mentally manipulate the model by thinking about how different earth would be if it really were all hard rock to the core, or if the insides were icy cold. They could extend by researching how geologists predict earthquakes and volcanoes and making some reasonable predictions themselves. The design, with its parallel causal sequences, has the flexibility that is necessary to support student-centered instruction. For example, a class could be divided into groups, each group being given the task of becoming experts and teaching the rest of the class. Children in group 1, the experts on convection currents, could (carefully and safely) conduct experiments with boiling creamed soups or peas cooking in water. Groups 2 and 3, the experts on earthquakes and volcanoes, could construct models that depict the causal sequences. Students could then reconvene as a class to share their expertise with students from the other groups.

After developing the graphic in figure 3.5, we began to craft our passage (figure 3.7). Our task was to turn our design into text with accompanying figures, choosing the actual words, sentences, paragraphs, sections, and pictures that would become the passage. We realized that if we followed the graphical design closely, our overall text design would reflect the comprehensibility, curricular, and instructional themes that we had planned. You may want to compare figures 3.6 and 3.7 to verify the relationship between the graphic and the passage. Note that the content and organization of the sentences, paragraphs, sections, and figures in the passage closely match the elements and linkages in the design graphic. The functional devices – the introduction, transitions, and conclusion – link the three sections of the passage into a whole and provide both background information and signals to help the reader to comprehend the passage. For example, the first paragraph introduces tectonic theory, foreshadows that the passage will be an explanation, and brings to the surface the preconceptions that we assume are held by many students and on which the explanation builds. The final paragraph conveys the substantive theme of a "renewing earth"; wait around for a few million years and the junk being dropped everywhere will be drawn down into the mantle, and a fresh crust will be raised up to the surface.

As useful as the graphic was for designing the passage, it gave us little guidance in word choice. Mindful that differences in word familiarity and interest-value strongly affect comprehensibility, we chose our words with care. To enhance familiarity, we selected commonplace words that convey metaphorical images – eggshells, bubbling soup, holding hands. To render the material interesting, we chose vivid words and the personalizing pronoun "you." The attention-grabbing vocabulary includes "fire in the earth," "superhot," "jolt," "molten lava," and "exploding," to depict dramatic phenomena. The pronoun "you" appears in the text to draw the reader's attention to important prior conceptions and useful analogies. Since both types of interest enhancement are imbedded in central passage concepts, we were unconcerned that our vivid vocabulary and personalization might seduce young readers away from the scientific model and toward a trivial detail.

Admittedly, anecdotes are slim in this version, largely because of space limitations. Given another page, we might add narratives from Loma Prieta and Mount St. Helens, not as a diversion but to engage students and connect them to the substance to follow. For instance, imagine this opening paragraph:

> Janet gazed on Monterey Bay from her kitchen window, listening to the 1989 World Series, when suddenly the floor jerked beneath her feet. Fifty miles away on San Francisco's Bay Bridge, Tom saw the road ahead suddenly collapse before him. The Loma Prieta quake ruined Janet's dinner, canceled the World Series, and wrecked Tom's commute. In Oakland, dozens of drivers perished when the freeway collapsed on their cars.

Paragraphs take space, and connections come at a cost.

Figure 3.7   An explanation of earthquakes and volcanoes designed to be comprehensible, to apply the lens of the geophysicist (a curriculum theme), and to support student–centered instruction.

WHAT CAUSES EARTHQUAKES AND VOLCANOES?

If you could look beneath the earth's surface, what would you see? Probably lots of rock and dirt. But the earth is not as solid as you might think. We live on a thin surface, almost like the shell of an egg. Underneath this layer, scientists have discovered that the earth's inside is molten rock, bubbling like a pot of thick pea soup. They have developed a theory, plate tectonics, that explains how boiling lava inside the earth causes the earth to crack and quake and volcanoes to erupt. You will learn here about how the flowing rock causes earthquakes and volcanoes. You will learn how "fire in the earth" pushes and pulls the ground beneath your feet.

A Trip Beneath the Earth's Surface

The earth has three different layers, which get hotter as you go from the surface to the middle (Picture A). The outside layer where you live is the **crust**. It is made up of hard, solid rock about 100 km thick. In the next layer, the **mantle**, the rock is so hot it has melted into a liquid. It is about 2800 km thick, and much hotter than the crust. The deepest layer, the **core**, is even hotter than the mantle, but the pressure is so great that it is solid.

The Mantle Churns

The mantle bubbles near the crust from the intense heat (Picture B). It moves up and down in huge circles called **convection currents**, which move the molten rock from the core to the crust. The surging currents break the crust into large sections called **plates**. Parts of the crust are sucked down into the mantle, creating ocean trenches. Fresh material from deep in the mantle pushes up forming mountains on the crust. We are usually unaware of this underground activity. But sometimes surging rock causes the plates to move, and then we have an earthquake. Other times the molten lava explodes through the crust as a volcano.

The Earth Shakes

How does the mantle make the ground shake? Although the earth may look solid to you, currents in the mantle have broken it into seven gigantic **plates**.

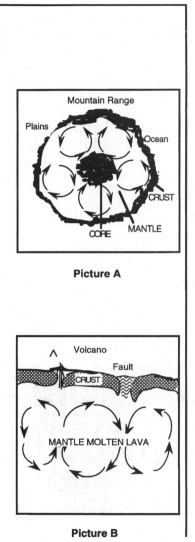

Picture A

Picture B

Figure 3.7 contd.

For example, Picture C shows the American currents cause slow, steady pressure. Picture C shows that America is moving south from the Pacific Ocean, and west from Europe and Africa. The currents slowly press plates in opposite directions, or push one plate over another. You cannot see or feel these movements, because the plates shift only a few inches each year, and most of the action is miles underground. Over time, however, the movement puts enormous strains on the plates. When enough pressure builds up, two plates suddenly unlock and snap in different directions. The earth's crust shakes, and you feel an earthquake.

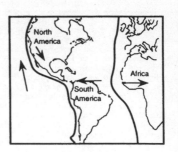

Picture C

You can understand what happens in an earthquake if you and a friend hold hands tightly and pull away from each other. Your arms feel the pressure, and then suddenly your hands slip apart. Keep your balance! Plates on the earth's crust lock together, just as you locked your hands. Your arms stretch in opposite directions, just as convection currents move the earth's plates. The stretchy feeling is like the pressure building between the earth's plates. The sudden jolt when your hands unlock is like the earthquake.

A *Volcano Erupts*

Movement in the mantle also causes volcanoes. Convection currents cause a continual up and down movement of lava in the mantle. As the superhot material from the core rises to the top of the mantle, it expands and causes pressure on the crust above it. Wherever the crust breaks between two plates or at "weak spots" where the crust is thin, the pressure pushes liquid rock through the crust (Picture D). Molten lava explodes to the surface, giving us a glimpse of the mantle.

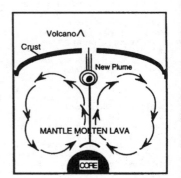

Picture D

Lava spewing from a volcano is like steam spouting from a kettle. When water boils in a kettle, it expands into steam. Steam takes more space than water, so it pushes the steam out of the spout, and you hear the kettle whistle. The pressure in the kettle is like the pressure in the magma. The escaping steam is like the magma exploding between the plates.

The Recycling Earth

Earthquakes and volcanoes may seem different, but both are caused by boiling lava in the mantle. Convection currents in the lava push and pull the earth's crust, breaking it into huge plates, putting the surface crust under constant pressure. Earthquakes happen when two plates, moving in different directions, spring apart. Volcanoes erupt when molten lava breaks through the crust. Deep beneath the oceans, huge blocks of crust are drawn into the molten mantle. On the continents, mountains push up with new material. The earth is continually renewing itself. Earthquakes and volcanoes happen quickly, but most of these amazing events take millions of years.

Will the revised version actually lead to greater student learning than the original? Preliminary research results suggest that young readers find the revised version to be more comprehensible and to lead to greater learning. Two classes of students in upper elementary school read both the original textbook version and a rewrite almost identical to the one in this chapter. They compared the two passages, rating them on understandability, rememberability, and interest. Students consistently rated the rewrite higher on all three dimensions.

Our preliminary results match research using a similar approach with social studies passages. Isabel Beck, Margaret McKeown, and their colleagues propose that designing an explanation so that it leads the reader toward a content goal enhances student learning.[29] For example, they rewrote a textbook passage to guide fourth- and fifth-grade students to understand some of the major events that caused the American Revolution. The passage had a consistent falling domino design, every sentence carefully crafted to advance the causal sequence and render it explicit. After reading, students reported what they could remember and answered several questions. Those students who read the causal explanation remembered more ideas from the passage and answered more questions correctly than another group of students who read a typical textbook version.

Moving from Passages to Complete Textbooks

We have focused in this chapter on the development of a single passage in order to bring attention to the importance of *design* in the development of text materials. Our standards are high. Well-designed textbook passages have the potential to nurture children's minds; to support children as they acquire the lens of the expert. Once it has been crafted, such a design often appears obvious and simple. It clarifies rather than obfuscates.

To be sure, a single passage is a small part of a much larger system – What about the design of chapters, textbooks, and entire series? We address this question further in the next chapter, extending the design concepts developed above. A system is only as solid as its parts; the ideal textbook begins with well-designed passages that mesh with one another to form a coherent and "connected" structure; that collectively present an exemplary curriculum and support student-centered instruction. Design is the key at all levels.

Notes

1   Tyler (1949).
2   Idem.
3   Bloom, Hastings, and Madaus (1971).
4   Whitehead (1929).
5   Tyler (1949).
6   Peters and Waterman (1982).
7   Schwab (1978).
8   Idem.
9   Idem.
10 Idem.
11 Elliott (1990).
12 Tyler (1949), p. 26.
13 Schwab (1978).
14 Idem.
15 Lukins (1990).
16 American Association for the Advancement of Science (1989), National Center for Improving Science Education (1989, 1992), and National Council of Teachers of Mathematics (1991).
17 Cazden (1988).
18 Calfee (1981) and Calfee and Patrick (1995).
19 Cazden (1988).
20 Wilson (1990).
21 Cazden (1988).
22 Piaget (1970).
23 Garner (1987).
24 Brown, Armbruster, and Baker (1986).
25 Calfee and Patrick (1995) and Schon (1987).
26 Brown (1997).
27 Graves (1983) and Proett and Gill (1986).
28 Piaget (1970).
29 Beck, McKeown, and Gromoll (1989), and Beck et al. (1991).

4

DESIGNING THE IDEAL
TEXTBOOK

The previous chapter shows that designing a single passage can be a substantial task for the writer who seeks to connect the young adolescent to the mysteries beneath the earth. This chapter looks at the top-level design of an entire book, or even a complete series. An ideal textbook must sustain themes of comprehensibility, curriculum, and pedagogy over hundreds of individual passages if it is to nurture the minds of children. The passages, chapters, units, divisions, and grade-level books of a series must work together to trace an adequate curriculum path and support student-centered instruction, while exhibiting the three features of comprehensibility (familiarity, interest, and structural coherence). Figure 4.1 shows the relationships among curricular, instructional, and comprehensibility designs on the one hand and textbook design on the other.

It may not be immediately obvious why top-level design is important. Indeed, some teachers have told us that they really do not care how a book is put together. If it covers lots of content and if children can understand the passages, the book meets their needs, these teachers explain. Our goal is to show in this chapter how top-level design can play a crucial role in supporting children as they acquire the lens of the expert. Alfred North Whitehead (and Dewey before him)[1] admonished educators to teach a few things well, implying materials carefully organized around a handful of important ideas and abundant opportunities throughout the year for children to construct their own understanding by trying out the ideas in a community of learners. Textbooks that meet these criteria will not occur by happenstance.

We are not alone in focusing on top-level design. As educators have turned away from behavioral objectives toward broad content understandings and strategies, curriculum frameworks have begun to focus on a larger picture. For example, the *California History–Social Science Framework* outlines the sequence of topics both across grades K–12 and within each grade level.[2] The curriculum framework developed by The Center for History in the Schools, established by the National Endowment for the Humanities, identifies several

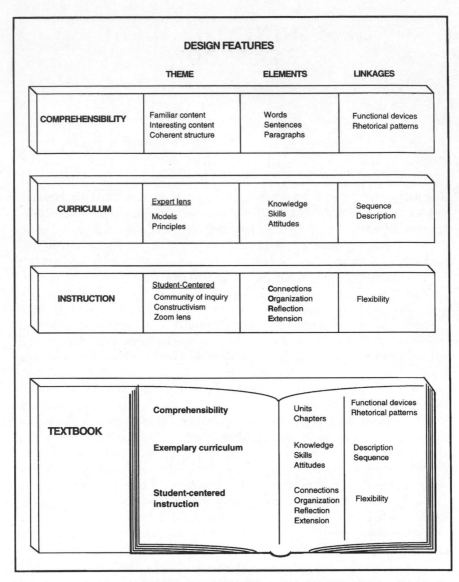

Figure 4.1 The relationships among comprehensibility, curriculum, instruction, and textbook design.

themes to form a top-level design.[3] Analogously, the *California Science Framework* and the curriculum framework developed by the American Association for the Advancement of Science propose themes that are to cut across grade levels as well as to organize the curriculum within each grade.[4] Textbook publishers have shifted focus accordingly. Scope and sequence charts no longer demonstrate how a textbook series meets detailed behavioral objects and factlets but, instead, how it carries out a relatively small number of themes and strategies.

We are unique in proposing a set of analytical lenses that curriculum framers and publishers can use to create a top-level design that adheres to principles of comprehensibility, presents a strong curriculum, and supports student-centered instruction. In the remainder of the chapter, we describe the characteristics of an effective top-level design, highlighting the special features that distinguish well-designed books and series from well-designed passages. To support our discussion, we analyze the design of a curriculum framework in social studies and two current social studies textbooks. We conclude that to create an effective top-level design can be a daunting task, made manageable by considering the elements, linkages, and themes in the design. We demonstrate the possibilities with two redesigns.

But First: A Few Words from the Audience

Before we launch forth on a discussion of "ideal textbook design," what do users have to say? These remarks are typical of what has come our way during the past several years:

- *Students*: "Books ought to interesting and easy to read. They shouldn't be big and heavy. If they're any good, they ought to belong to me, so I can write in them, take them home, and keep them."
- *Teachers*: "Textbooks should be interesting and understandable. They should allow me flexibility in handling different students and situations. But I also need guidance; as a sixth-grade teacher, I can't be an expert in everything."
- *Principals*: "Books need to be cheap, they need to last, and they need to do the job. I'm not a curriculum expert, and I rely on the books to ensure that teachers teach what they should teach and kids learn what they need to learn."
- *State Superintendents*: "Textbooks should be programmatic. My staff doesn't have time to study everything, and so the objectives should be clearly labeled. We ought to be able to see right away how they mesh with our curriculum frameworks. They should incorporate the latest research, and guarantee high scores on state tests."
- *Publishers*: "A textbook series has got to sell; if it's too far off the beaten track, no one will buy it. We try to produce the best materials we can, but we need to be competitive. We want to be responsive to the needs of

different states and districts, but we can't develop different materials for every client."

According to textbook users, books should be comprehensible, present a sound curriculum, and support effective teaching – the same list we described in the previous two chapters. (They also mention size, ownership, and marketability, attributes that we discuss further in later chapters.) But the design task in developing an entire book or series can be complicated. To adhere to sound comprehensibility, curricular, and instructional themes across scores of passages, activities, and ancillary features such as glossaries and indices can be an overwhelming task. Our analysis of current textbooks has led us to conclude that while a few books are well-designed at the top-most level, many more have a list-like quality to them. Most textbooks are revisions of previous editions, and incremental modifications quickly lose the original author's plan and voice in the process. Tradition is an important influence. Social studies books always begin with map skills; the publisher who disregards this practice may lose sales. State frameworks, whether intentionally or incidentally, for better or worse, dictate both content and organization. Professional organizations now add their voice to the cacophony. The result can be a mishmash of content rather than a theme-driven design; countless factlets rather than a small number of well-developed major ideas.

The remedy that we propose starts afresh with the creation of a coherent design that integrates comprehensibility, curriculum, instruction, and text around a few compelling themes. Even if we are willing to take up Whitehead's challenge, what "few things," and how do we do them "well"?

Guidelines for Top-Level Textbook Design

As we have been implying throughout chapters 2 and 3, design implies a designer, someone who fashions the elements and links them to convey a particular theme. In designing a textbook, decisions must be made at several levels: whole-book, unit, chapter, and section.[5] Writing is a recursive enterprise,[6] and so content and organization must be chosen anew at each level according to a theme. For instance, an eighth-grade US history textbook might be organized sequentially according to major historical periods. Historians have found it useful to chunk artificially what otherwise is a long string of small events: exploration of the new world, the colonial period, founding the new nation, growth of the nation, internal conflict, and so on. Each unit, covering one period, could be organized descriptively because historians have also found it useful to study each period according to certain features: the culture of the times, ways of making a living, politics, historical events, and so on. Each chapter, covering one of these topics, could have its own organization. For example, the chapters on culture might be organized descriptively and cover lifestyles, the arts, and religious practices, while the chapters on historical events could be organized sequentially. The decision to organize around major events leaves open the choice of structure within each unit, chapter, or section, although we suspect that both teachers and students would have an easier time if the choices were consistent throughout the book (e.g., chapters on culture always organized descriptively; chapters on historical events always organized sequentially).

The same design principles hold for each of the levels in a book. As with an individual passage, the basic elements or "chunks" must be clearly distinguished, along with the linkages that relate them, and the theme that gives meaning to the enterprise as a whole. In an entire textbook, two of the major elements are the unit and chapter; in a unit, the elements are the chapters and sections; and so on. These elements are linked by the same rhetorical patterns and functional devices that we introduced for passages. And as with shorter texts, the theme casts the "expert's" lens on the entire collection while upholding standards of comprehensibility and student-centered instruction.

Textbooks contain many elements besides prose: an abundance of colorful photographs; graphics and tables displaying maps and population data; skill activities for students to practice concepts such as longitude and latitude; sidebars on incidental topics such as "Merced CA" and "Tomatoes at the creamery"; reviews and tests; and end matter such as glossaries and atlases. In the ideal textbook, these elements would not be ancillary to the substance, but would adhere to the same themes. Graphics, for example, would reflect the structure and content of the prose. A history book the units of which are organized sequentially according to major events would be introduced by a sequential graphic with the same events as the text. A unit with a descriptive design would be introduced with a descriptive graphic that matches the major chapter subtopics. (These suggestions may seem obvious. But we have seen many examples where there is little relationship between the elements and linkages in the prose and those in the graphics.) Sidebars would highlight the major ideas in the prose, rather than trivial, but interesting, details that could "seduce" the attention of a young reader away from the author's important ideas, as we explained in chapter 2.

Student activities in the ideal textbook would give youngsters practice reflecting on what they have read and extending their new understandings. Following through with the history example, students could create a series of large "sequential matrices" on butcher paper, one matrix for each historical period, marching across the wall sequentially. They could use these matrices to keep track of the culture, ways of making a living, politics, and major historical events for each period. As they create the matrices over the course of a year, they could reflect on how the historical periods are alike and different. They also could discuss the effects of culture, ways of making a living, and politics on the major historical events and vice versa for each period. One of their extension projects could be to rewrite history by composing "what if" stories in groups – what if the early settlers on the east coast of the United States had come from Spain instead of Great Britain? What if the revolutionaries had crowned George Washington as king rather than elected him as president?

These suggestions are illustrative rather than prescriptive. We are not history educators. Nonetheless, we have chosen illustrations to demonstrate the relationship that we have in mind between prose and other textbook elements. In the ideal textbook all elements and linkages are guided by the same set of comprehensibility, curricular, and instructional themes, providing students with many opportunities to encounter and experience the same small set of ideas.

Comprehensibility Themes: Familiarity, Interest, and Structure

A comprehensible passage depends on vivid words and sensible sentences to keep students engaged and to foster understanding. Familiarity and interest are critical to motivation and understanding; the writer's challenge is to build coherence into the flow of a few pages of prose. In contrast, an ideal textbook must sustain comprehensibility over hundreds of individual passages. The task is complicated. Familiar and interesting for whom? Today's student demographics encompass a wide array of backgrounds, languages, and expectations. Textbooks can no longer focus on two-parent, two-child middle-class families, the new minority. How can we "clearly organize" the huge array of details identified by myriad special interests? Publishers strive to be all-encompassing out of fear that a selection committee member's favorite fact may be missing. They also tend to sterilize the facts to ensure that no one is offended. Finally, clear and well-organized writing is difficult when done by one author. It becomes almost impossible when completed by committees – and most of today's best-selling series are produced by teams.

Top-level designs must rely on something other than vivid words and familiar examples to be comprehensible. One approach could be to lead off with engaging, familiar topics. Learning to read maps and to tell the difference between latitude and longitude may be important skills, but they are probably not the most interesting or familiar aspects of social studies. Nonetheless, virtually every social studies textbook begins with a section on map skills and the compass rose. History textbooks follow with a unit on the "olden times"; the historical period least familiar to students.

Imagine a book that begins with students studying their own historical period. To follow through with our earlier example, students could start the year by studying the culture, ways of making a living, politics, and major historical events during their life span. The textbook could introduce the project and give students guidance as to where to find information from a wide variety of sources, from newspapers and magazines to trade books at the library. They could start their own matrix to serve as an introduction to the book as a whole. Subsequently, throughout the year, students could refer back to this introductory unit as a "baseline" against which to compare and contrast eras and localities far removed from their own lives.

The third feature of comprehensibility – coherence provided by an appropriate rhetorical pattern – affects comprehension consistently in passages. Those that are coherently organized are easier to comprehend than poorly organized passages. We suggest that the same phenomenon holds true at every level of text design: chapters, units, entire books, and even whole series. In chapter 2, we explained that some patterns have more structure to them than others: matrices and hierarchies, for example, provide a greater number of linkages to the design and should be more comprehensible than topical nets; the additional linkages in branching trees and falling dominoes should enhance comprehension over linear strings; and arguments and explanations should be the most comprehensible of all text structures. Because massive amounts of content are subsumed by the design of an entire book, the particular pattern that links together the units and chapters of a top-level design may be even more important than the pattern used in a short passage.

Picture, for example, a US geography textbook organized around regions of the country. These regions may fit the geographer's inclination, but if the development of each region is a haphazard topical net ("California, the land of excitement"; "Colorado's mountains"; "Farming in Nebraska and Kansas"), readers may fail to comprehend the theme that geographic features affect lifestyles throughout all regions of the country. Imagine, instead, if the same regions were developed according to an orderly matrix (the landforms, waterways, and lifestyles of the northeast, southeast, central plains, and so on). This second design should provide the necessary structure for students to begin to understand the relationship between geographic features and people's lifestyles. Fertile soil and easy access to water encourage people to farm; land rich in minerals that also is sandy and far from fresh water encourages people to mine the minerals; and so on.

Curriculum Themes: Experts and Lenses

Textbooks should present a strong curriculum. It is not enough to entertain students; the aim in textbook design is to guide learning through a course of study that promotes concepts, knowledge, and skills needed to survive (and thrive) after school and in the real world. The question of "What is worth knowing?" remains a major challenge. The times are a'changing. Only a few decades ago, the goal was functional skills – the minimum competency required to get a job and hold it – whatever that meant. Today, high-level thinking and critical literacy – dependent on expert lenses – are indispensable if students are to become productive workers in an information age, to fulfill themselves as informed and involved citizens in a townhall society. These are the authentic curriculum goals that should be explicitly supported in the design of a textbook series. Designing a complex system of 400–1,000 pages of prose and other materials according to an expert's lens is a challenging task. The problems facing publishers multiply as they design several books in a series.

Several years ago, one of us sat in on a meeting of three biology professors, two science educators, a sociologist, and a child psychologist who were designing a middle school biology curriculum that eventually would become a series of materials. Prior to the meeting, this group had identified 26 important topics. While committee members agreed that 26 topics were too many, they could not agree on how to pare the number down. Every topic that they tried to eliminate or merge with other topics had its advocate, who insisted that the topic had to stay. The committee had not begun to address strategies that they would want middle schoolers to learn. We suspect that once they did in subsequent meetings, the number of important ideas increased to far more than 26.

Even when curriculum developers agree on a small number of top-level ideas, the curriculum itself may not adhere to the ideas, as our analysis later in this chapter of a social studies curriculum framework demonstrates. Apparently, designers find it difficult to keep track of even a small number of ideas as they make choices both across and within grade levels. Publishers seem to have a similar problem. The most significant decisions in textbook design center around the selection and organization of the content. What is the best strategy for capturing the essence of a domain? One approach begins with a shopping list; what are the important facts about US history or geography? Such catalogs quickly reach gigantic proportions; in one social studies book written for fifth-graders in the United States, for instance, the six-page index lists almost 1,500 entries, ranging from *abolitionists* and *Emilio Aguinaldo* to the *Yukon River* and *city zoning*, a lot of material for ten- and eleven-year-olds to cover.[7]

A different strategy emphasizes not what to cover but how to look. From the latter perspective, a well-designed curriculum leads students to appreciate the lenses through which various experts view the world. For students in the middle grades, history and geography – the study of how time and place influence social phenomena – comprise the core of the social studies curriculum. Figure 4.2 sketches the lenses employed by geographers and historians to view the United States, showing how elements, linkages, and themes vary with each perspective. These two lenses are quite distinctive, employing different

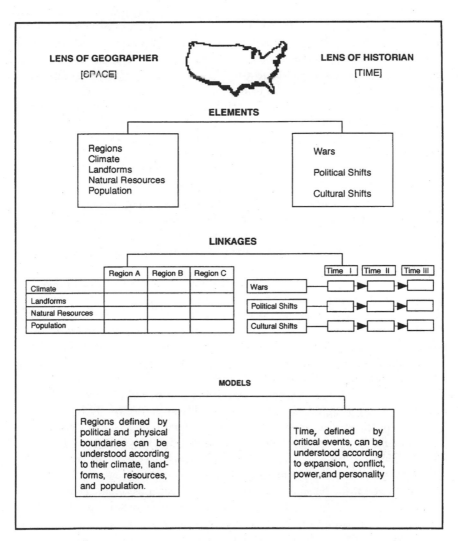

Figure 4.2 Differences in the elements, linkages, and themes that geographers and historians use to study the United States.

concepts and technical language to look at similar social phenomena. To be sure, the geographer is aware that time influences the landscape, and the historian knows that the physical setting affects events in time. For students to understand social studies, they must learn to appreciate the distinctive qualities and contributions of both disciplines.

Decisions about social studies content evoke considerable debate among the experts – and since we all participate in social systems, most of us view ourselves as experts! Whatever the experts believe, certain trends do appear if one looks at existing textbooks. In the United States, the content of social studies begins to take clear shape around fourth grade, when most students study the history and geography of their state (Delaware, Illinois, California). Fifth grade typically looks at US history, sixth grade turns to world geography and history, and so on.

Against the grain of these trends, however, runs a swirling torrent of variations in how to approach these topics – and why. We talked about these trends with two experts in social studies education from the Stanford School of Education. Both Richard Gross and Larry Cuban stressed the diversity of opinions and approaches in this field and the deeply rooted controversies about the appropriate disciplinary perspectives. They both protested when asked to "draw a picture" of the social studies discipline. They both emphasized the roller coaster character of debates about the proper goals of this curriculum domain.

On the other hand, they were in remarkable agreement on several points. For example, both emphasized that the social studies curriculum must encompass three fundamental areas: conceptual knowledge about social and civics topics; skills in dealing with social and civics situations; and the inculcation of democratic responsibilities and values. The first two items on this list are akin to the natural sciences: knowledge and skills. The third item may be the reason why social studies is particularly problematic. The practical application of science in everyday life is certainly a desirable outcome of the science curriculum; the practical application of social studies in everyday life is absolutely essential for the well-being of our democracy. Accordingly, social studies must take students from understanding and appreciating disciplines such as history and geography to applying and extending what they have learned. When Cuban and Gross stressed the complexity of this curriculum domain, they talked repeatedly about the tensions between academic learning versus the practice of citizenship; the purity of the disciplines versus the messiness of practical problems; the steadiness of fixed facts versus the dynamics of real life. These complexities permeate the social studies curriculum, posing special challenges for textbook design. The simple solution, of course, is to select a discipline and create a conceptual framework around it, much as for biology or geology. While this strategy may yield comprehensible texts, the practical dimension – citizenship – may fall between the cracks. This concern was central to the thinking of both Gross and Cuban.

We have already hinted at a possible solution in our choice of vocabulary in the preceding paragraph – "reflecting" and "extending." In chapter 3 we argued that curriculum be domain rather than *socially*, *politically*, or *practically* based; that these other areas, admittedly of crucial importance, be handled instructionally.

Instructional Themes: Connect, Organize, Reflect, Extend

Creating an instructionally sound top-level design presents the third challenge, a design that Connects, Organizes, and supports Reflection and Extension consistently throughout an entire book or series of books. Textbooks need to support instruction that goes beyond rote recitation to promote reflection, problem-solving, and genuine understanding. Learning that is insightful and transferrable comes not from passive reading of factoids, but from engaging in the material at several levels: at the factual level, but also at levels that lead the students to question the facts, to search for broader implications, and to connect the new information with prior knowledge so that the student gains genuine ownership of concepts and skills. To be sure, textbooks do not usually stand alone, but serve as tools for the teacher. However, the teacher's instructional task can be significantly helped or hindered by the textbook. If the teacher's goal is to engage students in a problem-solving approach to social studies, for instance, a textbook portraying social studies as "revealed knowledge" subverts this goal.

As with passage design, comprehensible textbook design sets the stage for student-centered instruction. Familiar and interesting, a comprehensible textbook connects to what students already understand. Its rhetorical pattern organizes the material for students. The more consistently linked the pattern, the more it can be used by students to reflect and extend beyond the content presented in the textbook. The suggestions that we have already put forth for creating a top-level design that is comprehensible would also render a book that supports student-centered instruction.

The CORE model requires that top-level design be more than comprehensible, however. In chapter 3 we noted that CORE allows teachers to "zoom in" to meet student interests and needs, to capitalize on the teachable moment. In order to respond effectively, teachers must have flexible materials at hand. Current textbooks tend to be linear. To understand them, students and teachers must begin on page 1 and progress as far toward the end as the year allows, although the recent development of modules in science textbooks allows for greater flexibility. Unfortunately, what the modules gain in flexibility, they often lose in coherence. Those that we have examined seem to stand alone, sharing no obvious curriculum themes or organizational patterns with other modules in the series. The challenge for top-level design is to create flexibility while retaining coherence.

One solution for creating coherent flexibility is to think of a textbook as a path with variations. Traversing the text from start to finish is one way to understand the subject – to acquire the expert's lens. On the other hand, teachers ought to be able to take alternate routes if they wish, reflecting local priorities and situations. This instructional theme suggests a design in which units and chapters stand on their own as comprehensible "chunks," each chunk a building block for studying one segment of the field. The separate chunks must be linked together, however, by a consistent rhetorical pattern, so that moving from one to another indeed follows a coherent path. The design also must be bounded by functional devices that set the stage at the beginning of the year by introducing the design, and a closing at the end of the year that refers back to the beginning and makes the book complete, even if not all of it has been read in the original order. Ideally, if a curricular theme determines both the chunks and the linkages, the path will lead to student understanding regardless of the exact route that the teacher and students choose.

Some domains are easily handled in this manner. United States geography textbooks typically start in the northeast and move west. But California students are probably more interested in and familiar with Los Angeles than New York. And students in Texas would be more interested in and knowledge-able about the center of the country. Sequential topics such as history pose a greater challenge. The typical course begins somewhere in the past and moves toward the present. One obvious alternative is to reverse this order, starting with the present and moving back in time. The example that we have been developing in this chapter would have the flexibility to present a coherent path whether students began with the past and moved forward or the present and moved backwards. The front "bookend," the initial project, would set up the design. Students could use that design to connect, organize, reflect, and extend whichever direction in time they pursued. And the teacher could choose based on the historical sophistication of his or her students.

Examples of Top-Level Design: Frameworks and Textbooks

In this section we focus on two types of top-level designs: curriculum frame-works and the textbooks that they are intended to influence. Responding to widespread concerns in the 1980s about the quality of public education,[8] states, professional organizations, and national agencies created curriculum frame-works as a way of influencing both curriculum and instruction in educational enterprises, including the design of textbooks. In the late 1980s the California State Department of Education published the California History–Social Sci-ence Framework[9] to present an explicit proposal for textbook design and classroom practice. The California framework is a model study of how a policy body, the California State Department of Education, approaches the "big picture" task. Since states have primary responsibility for schooling, they must go beyond philosophy and generalities to practical specifics for local districts.

It is not surprising that textbook design would reflect the design of curriculum frameworks – for better or for worse. Publishers see themselves as providers rather than educational leaders. They typically look to others for guidance about which content to include, how to organize the content, and what types of instructional guidance to provide. The first textbook that we analyze was designed to match the California framework closely. The second book has a different top-level design. It was produced for a national audience, prior to the development of frameworks and according to the set of criteria prevalent at that time.

A Social Studies Framework: The Historian's Lens

The California framework does develop a top-level design, rather than listing hundreds of factlets for student consumption. Because authors of lengthy texts such as curriculum frameworks (or textbooks for that matter) typically signal their top-level design in the titles and subtitles displayed in the table of contents (TOC), we began our analysis by searching the TOC for the major elements, linkages, and themes in the design. The framework also presents introductory graphics that display the design pictorially. We relied heavily on these graphics as well. As signalled in the TOC, an opening section presents the framework's themes, a large middle section specifies grade-level treatment, and a third section prescribes criteria for evaluating instructional materials. Because the themes reoccur in the second and third sections, this design seems to us to be linked into a topical net.

The opening section starts with 17 statements of principle, the most significant of which are a commitment to history as the curriculum lens ("history as a story well told"), a recommendation to integrate other disciplines (geography, politics, economics, and even literature) within the historical progression, an emphasis on democratic and constitutional principles, an inclusion of the histories of many cultures (particularly those that have traditionally been omitted from textbooks), and a careful examination of selected events and issues rather than "superficial skimming" of everything that has ever happened (following Whitehead's admonition). These principles are organized under three rubrics: Knowledge and Cultural Understanding, Democratic Understanding and Civic Values, and Skills Attainment and Social Participation. The wording is somewhat fanciful, but these three themes are close to those identified by Cuban and Gross.

Figure 4.3 displays in graphic form the design in the large second section of the framework. Note the strong historical lens (represented on the graphic by the time-line at the top), which is integrated with a geography theme

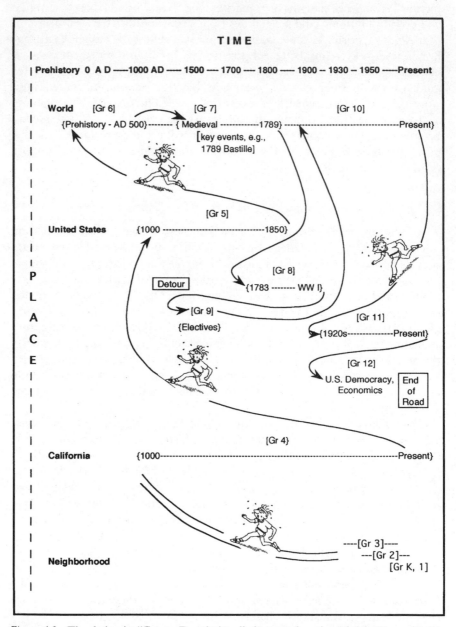

Figure 4.3 The design in "Course Descriptions," the second section of the *History–Social Science Framework for California Public Schools Kindergarten through Grade Twelve* (California State Board of Education, 1988).

(represented by the heading "Place" along the left-hand side). Although our emphasis in this book is grades 4–9, we have displayed the entire K–12 curriculum. The human figures in the graphic trace the path that students are to follow from kindergarten through twelfth grade. Starting close to home in kindergarten, students gradually broaden their focus in time and space. By third grade, students have ventured beyond the local neighborhood to the city, state, and nation, but connected to familiar locales and contemporary events. The scene shifts abruptly in fourth grade to the study of California history. In fifth grade, the framework expands from California to the United States, stretching from the pre-Columbian era through the signing of the Constitution and on to the Westward Expansion. Sixth- and seventh-graders move on to a world perspective, traversing several millennia from prehistory to the 1789 French Revolution. Eighth-graders return to the United States, tracking the nation's accomplishments and travails from Washington's inauguration through the Industrial Revolution and the Civil War up to the First World War (wars are frequently selected as historical mileposts). The path from grade nine onward is partly historical; partly multi-disciplinary.

In this second section the framework gives detailed recommendations for each grade, again in history-book style. For example, fourth-graders, studying the history of California, are to begin with a quick look at the physical geography of the state. Next, students are to move through time from pre-Columbian Indian times to the Spanish colonial period, on through the war for California, independence from Mexico, and the gold rush, and finishing with a look at developments since statehood, including the growth of Hollywood.

The design of the third section on instructional materials is guided by some additional themes. This section lays out the *Criteria for evaluating instructional materials*. The section presents a collection of 15 basic guidelines along with sections on organization of materials, teachers' manuals, assessment and evaluation, and instructional media. The guidelines range broadly, calling for treatment of history and geography in a holistic manner, and one that is integrated with the humanities and social science, writing that is vivid and dramatic but also accurate, and in-depth development of topics and controversial issues. The guidelines recommend formats beyond the single, heavy hardbound book, materials that allow teachers flexibility in emphasis and timing of content and activities. Many of these guidelines we applaud.

The rudiments are here for a design with a strong curricular theme: using the lenses of historians, geographers, and social scientists to focus on the State of California, the United States, and the entire world. At root, however, the historian's lens is the guiding light. If geographers had been in charge, fourth-graders, for example, would follow a different path, traveling through today's California from Death Valley to San Diego, from San Francisco Bay to the Sierra Nevada, looking along the way at historical artifacts. A third type of design might bring an amalgam of lenses to bear on one or more cross-cutting issues, for instance examining the importance of water in California – geographically, historically, economically, and politically. In any event, the framework directs textbook publishers, if they hope to gain acceptance in California schools, to produce a history series.

Unfortunately, themes of comprehensibility do not obviously guide this design. While it is consistently sequential, California students move around almost capriciously as they progress from one grade (and textbook) to the next. We could imagine them scratching their heads, and thinking, "Now, wait a minute. *Where* did this happen? *When* did it happen?"

The early part of the journey is developmental: space and time in the immediate vicinity, gradually spiralling outward. From fourth grade onward, however, the yearly jumps are more discordant. While a general historical trend is apparent, sometimes the locus is California, sometimes the United States, and sometimes the entire world. To be sure, these shifts may not matter to pre-adolescents; Los Angeles, Hong Kong, and London may be equally remote for a ten-year-old living in San Francisco. The 930s and the 1930s may both be "dark ages" for modern youngsters. However, we do not understand the decision to move around in time rather than moving along a consistent path (either forward or backward), the lack of connectedness between US and world histories, and the decision to teach the youngest children the least familiar "oldest times." Historians and geographers view the terrain in a far more orderly manner than the route prescribed by the framework. Their lenses possess a structural coherence that is not reflected in this top-level design. We find it to lack both the familiarity and coherence necessary for many students to gain a basic understanding of the "big picture."

The problems with the top-level design's comprehensibility also affect how well it would support student-centered instruction. The design fails to enhance either connections or organization. The framework does specify flexibility in its guidelines for instructional materials. How, exactly, a publisher would build in flexibility, given the rigid time and place restrictions, is not clear. Because of the basic incoherence in the design, it also is not clear how it would support student reflection and extension.

The real strength of this framework may be more in its themes than in how they are actually fleshed out. Depth rather than breadth, interesting and vivid writing, including the stories of groups of people who traditionally have been left out of history textbooks, are important themes. However, these themes do not clearly show up in the top-level design. And while we certainly applaud them, the framework does not provide much guidance on how to carry out these themes. The responsibility for implementing them seems clearly up to textbook publishers.

In the remaining sections of this chapter, we will look at the annotated teacher editions of two social studies textbooks. *Oh, California*[10], Houghton Mifflin's innovative entry for the fourth-grade California framework, illustrates how a framework description becomes a textbook. Silver Burdett's *The United States and its Neighbors*,[11] which covers US history and geography, is designed for a broad national market. This text, typical of many series, has several design features that foster student understanding and interest; we use this text as a point of departure for redesign based on the principles of exemplary curriculum, comprehensibility, and student-centered instruction. Note that, for both of these books, the teacher edition presents the student edition accompanied by instructional suggestions for the teacher.

A Framework-Based Textbook: Oh, California

To begin our analysis of *Oh, California*, we take a closer look at the fourth-grade design laid out in the California framework on which the book is based. In the second section of the framework, a four-page synopsis, which we have graphed in figure 4.4, sketches a version of California history. Not surprisingly, as for the framework as a whole, the historian's lens predominates, the initial themes are present, but less consistently and explicitly than we would like, and the strength of the design lies in its themes rather than how they are carried out. Because the themes do not really guide the design powerfully, both consistency and coherence suffer, leaving gaps that publishers would be forced to fill in order to produce a well-designed textbook.

The fourth-grade section is divided into seven headings. At the top of the figure, we have listed these headings, assuming that they are meant to signal the major elements in the design. The first major element, you will notice, is actually a brief geography. The remaining major elements are a series of historical events, beginning with prehistory, followed by three centuries of exploring and colonizing up to the gold rush, and finally three half-centuries marking the emergence of modern statehood. These elements are linked by time into a linear string. The "story" follows historical tradition by beginning in the past and ending in the present.

By skimming the entire section, we realize that other elements dealing with culture, economics, politics, and so on are also present, if not signalled by headings. The design is more than a linear string. We decide to diagram it as a sequential-matrix (not unlike the example that we were developing earlier in this chapter) in order to capture these additional elements and highlight ways in which the framework might guide a publisher's design decisions.

We have attempted to portray in the figure how the broad themes of knowledge, skills, and civics presented in the first chapter, "Goals and Curriculum Standards," guide the design. These three themes are presented in the framework as goals, each with a series of subgoals. While the summary for

	The Physical Setting: California and Beyond	Pre-Columbian Settlements and People	Exploration and Colonial History	Missions, Ranchos, and the Mexican War for Independence	Gold Rush, Statehood, and the Westward Movement	The Period of Rapid Population Growth, Large-Scale Agriculture, and Linkage to the Rest of the US	Modern California: Immigration, Technology, and the Cities
Goal	Knowledge Skills Attainment	Knowledge	Knowledge	Knowledge	Knowledge	Knowledge	Knowledge
Subgoal	Develop an understanding of place Develop locational skills and understanding	Understand human and environmental interaction	Understand human movement	Understand the rich complex nature of a given culture	Analyze cause and effect	Analyze cause and effect	Analyze cause and effect
Historical Literacy		Earliest people	Europeans arrive	Europeans settle	California becomes a state	California's population grows	California becomes an industrial power
Ethical Literacy							
Cultural Literacy		Major language groups, legends, beliefs	Variety of cultural groups among explorers	Effect of Christianity	Variety of cultural groups coming to California: effect of women	Tensions among different cultural groups	Development of a strong educational system
Geographic Literacy	Separation from North American continent by deserts. Major regions: mountains, bays, and rivers	Close and natural relationship with environment	Access to California affected by natural barriers	Geographical factors in location of missions, presidios, and settlements	Different routes for traveling to California	Technological links between California and the east	Further development of technological links and environmental projects
Economic Literacy		Economic Activities		European plants, animals and a herding economy	Effects of discovering gold	Effect of transcontinental travel and communication: development of water projects	Commerce, meta-agriculture, communications, aerospace, and trading links with the Pacific Rim
Sociopolitical Literacy		Social organization		Effect of Mexican independence on California	California's statehood and government		

Figure 4.4 The design for fourth-grade in the second section of the *History–Social Science Framework for California Public Schools Kindergarten through Grade Twelve* (California State Board of Education, 1988).

fourth grade does not refer to any of these three goals or their subgoals, we scanned each section, studied the goal discussions in the first chapter, and identified subthemes that the framework designers could have had in mind for the different sections. While, ideally, a designer would choose themes first and use these themes to select content elements, we had to work backwards, synopsizing the content in the framework and inferring possible themes accordingly. For example, the summary for the first subsection, "The Physical Setting: California and Beyond," covers the relation of California to the North American continent, its separation from the rest of the country by deserts, and its major regions defined by mountains, bays, and rivers. We decided that two framework subgoals best capture this content: an awareness of place, a knowledge theme, and locational skills, a skills theme. Following the same procedure for the remaining subsections, we hypothesized themes for each and have placed them across the figure directly under the section titles.

Consistent with the framework as a whole, the fourth-grade summary focuses on the typical lenses of social studies. These lenses are identified explicitly in the framework chapter, "Goals and Curriculum Strands," as historical, ethical, cultural, geographic, economic, and political literacies. The remainder of the figure depicts how the summary treats each of these lenses for each major section. Using the first section again as an example, all of the content falls under geography, while the second section, "Pre-Columbian Settlements and People," has content consistent with the lenses of history, culture, geography, and socio-political science. The last section, "Modern California: Immigration, Technology, and Cities," addresses all of these lenses except for politics.

To understand the framework's design, we begin by focusing on the themes. Note the dominance of the knowledge theme. Having presented the geography of California, the design does not deal with skills and fails completely to include civics. Publishers will be on their own in incorporating these two major themes. Furthermore, the subthemes are general and to some extent could be used for any and all of the historical periods in the design. "Cause and effect" and "human movement" have been themes virtually throughout human history. We suggest that themes this universal lack the power to specify the elements of a framework intended to guide an entire year of study.

Next, we look at the elements, noting patterns in both full and empty cells. Reading horizontally, we see a complete set of elements for the lens of geography and a virtually complete set for the lenses of history, culture, and economics. Switching perspective (and reading vertically), we note that every historical period is viewed according to its history, culture, geography, and economics. In contrast, ethics has skimpy treatment and politics is not mentioned after the founding of the state. Consequently, we have concluded that the theme of civics was not evident in the design. It seems likely, for example, that fourth-graders would have at least some interest in and ability to understand the politics and ethics of modern California. If not, perhaps civics is an inappropriate theme for this age group, a conclusion with which we suspect few would agree.

We also evaluate the quality of the elements. The events in history are coherent, consistent, and explicitly signalled by section headings, with neither overlap between major events nor large gaps. These historical periods are the ones that we would expect historians to use. However, geography, culture, and economics, while consistently treated, lack coherence and are not signalled explicitly (we have arbitrarily assigned content to each of these lenses based on our own content knowledge). Read across the figure, and you will note that "Culture," for example, begins with a focus on the major language groups, legends, and beliefs of a particular type of culture during a particular period (a good start), and subsequently ranges from the influence of a certain religion as well as one gender over the other, the presence of many cultures in California, and the development of one social institution out of many. Even though the development of culture starts well, the good beginning is not maintained, leaving us to wonder what sort of idea – either about culture or how to understand it – a fourth-grader would take away from these elements. Furthermore, we remain unconvinced that anthropologists would pick the influence of women or the development of a strong public education system as the most appropriate content about culture to choose for 1800–1850 or 1940–present. We suspect that these problems with the elements reflect the lack of powerful subthemes guiding the design.

Finally, we attend to the design's linkages. The figure depicts them as a sequential matrix: treating the historical events, ethics, culture, geography, economics, and politics according to the passage of time. Most of the important social studies lenses are linked to one another at least loosely. However, causal connections are missing. We suspect that the problem results, again, from themes that are overly general. "Cause and effect," while specifying causal linkages, is probably not specific enough to guide the design. For instance, why was it that, following Mexico's independence from Spain, significant immigration took place from the eastern United States? What happened to the original Spanish colonizers or to the Native Americans? How was the gold rush linked to statehood? What was the impact of the Civil War on California during this period? How do water rights (a geo-economic–political issue in California) and demographic diversity (a multi-cultural issue whereby east and west, north and south all meet) illuminate the past, present, and future of this complex state? These are just a few of the questions confronting the publisher in transforming the framework into a textbook. Because the themes do not really guide the design powerfully, both consistency and coherence suffer, leaving gaps that publishers would be forced to fill in order to produce a well-designed textbook.

While the section on the fourth grade specifies a curriculum design for fourth grade, we see scanty evidence of comprehensibility and student-centered instruction themes. To be sure, the design laid out for fourth grade is more coherent than the top-level design depicted in figure 4.3; it follows, strictly, a linear string from California prehistory to modern times. Consequently, it should be more comprehensible as well. Otherwise, the fourth-grade section fails to address issues of comprehensibility and instruction. Any guidance given to publishers must come from the document as a whole, with the particular strengths and weaknesses that we have already discussed. Admittedly, our analysis probably fails to do justice to California's framework. Framework designers could only do so much in a short summary.

Figure 4.5 shows in graphic form how Houghton Mifflin used the framework summary to design a textbook. As with the curriculum framework, we began our analysis of *Oh, California* by focusing on the TOC, the device used by authors to signal their top-level design. We have listed the TOC unit headings at the top of the figure as the major elements in the design. Along the side, we have placed the lens headings that we judge are reflected in the TOC. Note that these lenses are identical to those in the framework (see figure 4.4).

To construct the remainder of the figure, we evaluated each chapter and section title, assigning it to a particular cell, chapter titles appearing in block capitals. For example, our best guess is that the chapter SPANISH EXPLOR-ERS chronicles historical events; so we have placed it under the historical lens. On the other hand, we put the chapter MIX OF CULTURES in the cultural lens, and used capital letters to identify both as chapters.

A scan of figure 4.5 reveals the strengths of the textbook design to reflect the strengths of the framework design. To be sure, the framework elements "The Physical Setting: California and Beyond" and "Pre-Columbian Settlements and People" have been collapsed into one textbook unit and given a chapter each. Likewise, "Exploration and Colonial History" and "Missions, Ranchos, and Mexican Independence" have been collapsed into the unit, "Colonial California." Otherwise, the major elements in the framework design form an almost perfect match with the units in the textbook. These textbook elements, like those in the framework, are coherent, consistent, and explicitly signalled by unit headings. Furthermore, as in the framework, they are the historical periods that we would expect historians to use. The result is a coherent top-level curriculum design.

The Houghton Mifflin TOC has an additional strength that is not present in the framework design. Both culture and economics seem to us to possess a coherence in the textbook that is missing in the framework. Use culture as an example. The TOC begins with a lesson on an Indian village, followed by a lesson about life on a mission (cultural changes brought to California by the Spaniards), a chapter on the mix of cultures resulting from massive

	Unit 1 People and Place	Unit 2 Colonial California	Unit 3 Newcomers	Unit 4 Growth and Development	Unit 5 Modern California
Historical Literacy	Ch2 FIRST CALIFORNIANS 2.2 Discovering First Californians	Ch3 SPANISH EXPLORERS 3.2 Early Explorers Ch4 MEXICAN CALIFORNIA 4.2 Missions to Ranchos	Ch5 NEW FROM THE US 5.2 Defeat of Mexico 5.3 Gold Rush Ch6 STATEHOOD 6.1 After the Gold Rush 6.2 Thirty-First State	7.2 Railroad is Born 7.3 Building the Railroad 8.2 Southern California Grows	Ch10 BUILDING CALIFORNIA Ch11 WORLD WAR II AND BEYOND 11.1 Wartime Ch12 NEW STEPS Ch13 FUTURE 13.1 Past and Future
Ethical Literacy					10.3 New Challenges 12.1 Struggle for Rights 13.3 People Take Action
Cultural Literacy	2.3 Indian Village	3.4 Life on a Mission	5.1 Pioneers	Ch9 MIX OF CULTURES 9.1 The New Californians 9.2 Cultural Conflict 9.3 Contributions	11.2 Science and Technology 12.2 New Immigrants
Geographic Literacy	Ch1 GEOGRAPHY OF CALIFORNIA 1.1 Where is California? 1.2 California's Regions			7.1 Link to the East	13.2 Smog
Economic Literacy	2.2 Living with the Land	4.1 Traders	5.4 Gold Mining 6.4 Californios Lose Land	Ch7 RAILROADS Ch8 AGRICULTURE 8.1 Farming Takes Hold 8.3 Agriculture Problems	10.1 Industry Growth 11.1 New Ways of Making a Living
Sociopolitical Literacy		3.3 Presidios, Missions, Pueblos 4.3 Ranchos and Pueblos	6.3 Law & Order		10.2 People's Progress 12.3 Growing State

Figure 4.5 The design for a fourth-grade textbook, *Oh, California* (Houghton Mifflin, 1991b).

immigration during the end of the nineteenth and the beginning of the twentieth centuries, and a final lesson on new immigrants coming to California during the middle and end of the twentieth century. These three lessons and one chapter present the raw material that a teacher could use to help children learn about what can happen when two or more cultures bump up against one another, and how those interactions have influenced and continue to influence the culture of California today. These raw materials are not present in the design laid out in the framework. Unfortunately, even the textbook treatment is embedded for the most part at the lesson level, with large gaps across units where the lens of culture does not seem to make its appearance. Without explicit signaling in the textbook and substantial help from the teacher, we suspect that children would fail to gain an understanding of culture even with these improvements in the design of the book.

Otherwise, the figure suggests problems with the design similar to ones we identified for the framework. First, knowledge is the dominant theme in the TOC. Second, treatment of lenses other than history is inconsistent. Only two other lenses are explicitly signalled by titles, once each (GEOGRAPHY OF CALIFORNIA, and MIX OF CULTURES), and a scan across the figure suggests that the other lenses that are included have gaps. Ethics receives skimpy treatment. And geography occurs with far less consistency in the TOC than it did in the framework. To be sure, we have inferred the placement of all of the unsignalled chapters and lessons. Readers of this volume may not agree with our decisions. However, if the TOC had explicitly signalled the lenses (or "literacies," as the framework labels them), we would not be forced to guess about where they should "fit." More importantly, teachers and students would have been given important cues about the presence of the lenses themselves. Third, linkages are as much a problem in the Houghton Mifflin design as they were for the framework. We see no evidence in the TOC of any causal connections. At least at the top-most level of this book, the publisher did not fix many of the problems that we identified in the curriculum design of California's framework.

Our two experts and the California framework all agree that one of the goals of social studies education is to promote a sense of civic awareness and responsibility. We have already noted how the framework deemphasizes this goal. *Oh, California* likewise fails to promote it adequately. It seems to us that this goal is most likely to be achieved through the development of a few prevailing themes that engage the student's empathetic response to matters that are personally relevant – respect for human diversity, responsibility for the environment, and a willingness to work individually for the well-being of the community. The heavy emphasis on knowledge themes at the expense of all others militates against this important goal. An alternative could be to address it instructionally; to design activities throughout the book that ask students to reflect on the importance of respecting human diversity, of treating the environment responsibly, and of working for the well-being of the community, and then to extend their understanding to designing and carrying out appropriate projects.

Having analyzed the curricular themes of this textbook design, we turn to themes of comprehensibility and instruction. As we have already explained, the framework hopes for textbooks that tell an interesting story (a comprehensibility theme) and support instruction. Story, or narrative, design differs from expository design, as we discussed in chapter 2. We search the TOC for evidence of an overall story. Instructional design is likely to show up in the book as a whole as well as in the TOC, so we look at instructional activities accompanying units, chapters, and lessons to evaluate this aspect of the book's design.

Narratives are sequential, but the sequence links episodes in which characters are confronted in a particular setting with problems that they either do or do not solve; the action in narratives rises as the character works toward solving the problem and falls as the problem is either resolved or not. Narratives have an identifiable set of elements (setting, characters, and episodes) that are linked by a plot according to a theme of universal truth about human nature. To be true to the framework, the TOC should signal these characteristics. Indeed, most of the chapters begin by introducing a set of characters: the "first Californians," Native Americans immigrating from the north and spreading throughout the many ecological niches; Spanish explorers and missionaries making their way north from Mexico, establishing their hegemony over the Pacific coastal regions; "scouts," Forty-Niners, railroad barons, dust bowl refugees, immigrants from the Pacific Rim, and finally the great inpouring during the Depression and World War II. Chapters 2–5 and chapter 9 all begin with one or more lessons about characters. In addition, the first chapter of the book as a whole sets the scene (the geography of California). Missing from the TOC are evidence of a plot structure (we see no headings in the TOC that suggest problems building toward a resolution) or a strong narrative theme. To be fair to Houghton Mifflin, we do not see these elements, linkages, or themes in the framework either, despite the prescription to "tell an interesting story."

We also see no evidence in the TOC of explicit interestingness, an important aspect of comprehensibility. Titles and subtitles tend not either to have vivid vocabulary words or foreshadow topics of absolute interest. However, the vivid vocabulary and interest-enhancing topics used to introduce units, chapters, and lessons should enhance student comprehension. Because they occur consistently, these features are a part of the whole book design even though they are not explicitly signalled in the TOC. Unit 3 introduces the gold rush, for example, with a two-page spread of "Placer mining at Foster's Bar," and a box noting "It was a time of change and a time for decisions. California was free of Spanish rule. Soon, newcomers would arrive in search of gold, in search of dreams."[12] Pretty heady (and heavy) stuff for fourth grade! The next two pages introduce chapter 5 with a pastiche of photographs atop a time line stretching from 1810 to 1860 (only a couple of entries, unfortunately),[13] after which lesson 1 begins with Jedediah Smith struggling through the snow of the mighty Sierra. Captivating material!

In addition, each lesson throughout the book opens with a compelling anecdote:

> Joaquin! The whisper of his name sent chills down the spines of Californians. It was the winter of 1852–1853, and the legend of Joaquin Murieta and his gang was spreading ... Murder, stolen cattle, stagecoach robberies .... No one felt safe.[14]

Vivid and dramatic indeed – very contemporary, something that students can connect with, and in this instance (chapter 6, lesson 3) directly linked to the rest of the lesson.

Finally, we look to see how well the TOC signals instruction consistent with the CORE model of instruction. Even though the framework calls for child-centered instruction, the TOC does not demonstrate the potential for flexibility that such instruction would entail. The simple linear string structure virtually demands a "begin at the beginning and proceed as far as time allows" instructional approach, no matter what. The opening unit on geography and early Californians does not obviously connect with fourth graders. The sequential matrix with its many holes does not provide much organization. To be sure, the book is consistently replete with exercises that potentially could enhance reflection and extension. For example, a two-page spread on the Hetch Hetchy dam, built in the early 1900s over the opposition of conservationists such as John Muir to capture water from the Sierra Nevada wilds for the growing city of San Francisco, provides the foundation for students to develop arguments for and against the project, and to imagine a similar issue in their local community. Another example is a segment on the role of bartering among Californios, Indians, and traders, in which several questions raise the pros and cons of a "moneyless" society upon which fourth-graders could reflect.

Other instructional activities would be far less likely to lead to reflection and extension. For example, the Jedediah Smith lesson concludes with a page describing the misfortunes of the Donner Party, and then a two-page spread on *Measuring distances on a map*, an exercise in trip-planning for visiting California parks (the lake where the Donner Party weathered the winter is now a state park). The point is that the development of skills in this textbook, as in all that we have examined, is not integrated in a coherent and purposeful manner in the overall design, but is a collection of activities pasted into the nooks and crannies of the material. Some examples are powerful. Others are not. They do not adhere consistently to an instructional model, such as CORE.

It is far too easy to criticize and much more difficult to suggest alternatives. If we were to redesign *Oh, California*, what changes would we make? How would we build on the considerable strengths in the current design and remedy the problems that we found? The sequential matrix developed in the framework and carried out in the textbook is a strong basis for a top-level design that reflects and integrates curricular, comprehensibility, and instructional themes. The matrix could be used as a guide to present complete, coherent lenses in the other domains besides history. These lenses could be signalled explicitly in the titles appearing in the TOC.

Separate topics could be linked causally rather than by time passing. Transitions are critical linkages for understanding cause–effect relations in history, particularly if the transitions are guided by powerful themes. What was happening in the 1800s in California? What drove the Eastern pioneers westward? What was the impact of geographic barriers – the Rocky Mountains, the Sierra Nevada, and the deserts? In many respects, economic conditions propelled the pioneers forward and geography both made the trip challenging and determined where they decided to settle. Not only could titles signal these relationships, but the ordering of content in this book could suggest a set of causal linkages. For example, Unit 3 (Newcomers) covers a chapter, "NEW FROM U.S.," with lessons titled "Pioneers," "Defeat of Mexico," "Gold Rush," and "Gold Mining" and a chapter, "STATEHOOD," with the lessons "After Gold Rush," "Thirty-first State," "Law & Order," and "Californios Lose Land." A simple reordering of topics and reframing of content as signalled by titles could communicate the economic impetus and geographic challenges. Lessons for "NEW FROM U.S." could begin with "Defeat of Mexico Makes California a Better Place to Live," "Gold is Found in California," "Pioneers Cross Mountains and Deserts to Get Rich," and "Pioneers Mine for Gold." These lessons would start with economic (and political) causes, highlight barriers, and conclude with effects.

Another set of design changes could improve how well the book at the top level supports student-centered instruction. Wherever possible, topics could be chosen that hold absolute interest for young readers, and titles could communicate the vividness and compellingness of the topics. Instructional activities could be closely integrated with the content, encouraging students to reflect about the history, geography, culture, economics, ethics, and politics of a particular point in time and how they affect one another. Activities could also prompt fourth-graders to extend what they have learned to their own lives as citizens. Our point is not that students should memorize labels – "If it's chapter 8, lesson 3, *Problems facing agriculture*, it must be economics" – but to give them an opportunity to see the discipline themes that illuminate the historical issues, themes implicit in the present design, emerging on occasion like a river in the desert.

In a redesign, *Oh, California* could begin with a unit that presents the curriculum themes using contemporary content to connect with young students and could end with a unit that helps students to reflect back on what they have learned about each theme. The concluding paragraph of *Oh, California* offers a glimpse of possibilities that are currently buried in the writing:

> When you first opened this book many months ago, you saw a big blue ball [actually a rather small one]. That was the earth. When you care for California, you are helping to care for the earth. In 2050, when the space shuttles of the future circle high above the earth, the astronauts may look down on a world that is a little cleaner, a little healthier, and a little nicer because you helped make it that way.[15]

Imagine a book that opens with a discussion about "Spaceship Earth" as one among a handful of themes. These themes would then thread their way through the book, not buried in the details, but highlighted in the TOC, overviews, and summaries. The book would end with a reflection on the themes. For the theme, "Spaceship Earth," the textbook would review the development of California over time and ask students to consider both whether the state is becoming a cleaner, nicer, better world, and, if not, what could be done differently. This thematic design would serve to form connections with the understandings of fourth graders, to organize the content, and to promote both reflection and extension.

Do these recommendations demand too much of fourth-graders, stretching them beyond their capacity to understand abstractions? Given the high level of discourse in other sections of the textbook, we think that the issue is not one of difficulty but design. By fourth grade, for example, students are capable of grasping history and geography as separate disciplines while appreciating their interplay.

Before turning away from *Oh, California* and the California framework, we want to discuss how students are best to understand history. The framework specifies a well-told story. Nonetheless, our redesign would not focus on the narrative quality of history. The prevailing assumption in the framework and TOC is that everyone knows how to read a story – and the research on story comprehension supports this assumption at a certain level. On the other hand, stories and histories are not exactly the same. The narratives of James Michener and Gore Vidal blur this distinction, but in most instances the study of history requires going beneath the surface to the analysis of events, to the examination of cause and effect. One purpose of well-designed exposition is to present content so that it can be easily analyzed. A matrix, for example, lends itself to comparisons; a sequence linked by causality lends itself to an analysis of causal relationships. Narrative designs typically do not easily promote the same kinds of analysis. Moreover, precisely because children find narrative to be easier to comprehend than exposition, they need extensive practice with expository structures. Throughout life they will encounter far more exposition than narrative, both in their homes and at the workplace.

Oh, California offers important lessons about the relation between state frameworks and textbook design. The original intention of guiding textbook development through a framework is a worthwhile goal. The challenge is to create a simple and coherent design that links curriculum, instruction, and comprehensibility with the designers being part of a collaborative enterprise among policy-makers, educators, and (above all) a broad spectrum of classroom teachers. The California framework and the Houghton Mifflin series are a laudable attempt in this direction, offering many lessons along the way.

A Broader View: The United States and Its Neighbors

Silver Burdett's *The United States and its Neighbors* is a broad-based treatment of the history and geography of the Western Hemisphere, designed for fifth-graders. The marketing aim seems to be to cover a range of curriculum outcomes: multiple disciplines, national and international perspectives, content balanced with skill development. The TOC, shown graphically in figure 4.6, opens with sections on "tools for learning," geography first and history second. Four units then cover US history, followed by two geography units, a substantial one on the United States and a tag-end for "neighbors." History receives more attention than geography; the United States enjoys greater coverage than Canada and the countries south of the border.

This textbook has several strengths. As a curriculum, it provides a balance between history and geography and a clear separation between the two disciplines. The history is fairly straightforward; as is often the case, wars mark the episodes of the human chronicle. The geography unit follows a consistent and coherent matrix format. Examining the chapters in unit 6, you can see that each focuses in turn on land and climate, resources, and development. This organization is foreshadowed in chapter 14, although the TOC does not make this structure explicit. The organization of the book as a whole seems likely, however, to leave the student confused about distinctions between history and geography. As the TOC clearly shows, the textbook never contrasts the two subject matters, nor explains how they combine in studying a particular problem (e.g., the expansion of the United States as it gobbled up land originally claimed by the French, Spanish, Russians, and Mexicans). The decision to separate Canada and Latin America from the United States means

CONTENTS

Unit 1 Tools for learning about your country

Ch 1 Reading maps
- What is it?
- How far is it?
- The language of maps
- Mass transit
- Maps are important

Ch 2 Our history
- What is history?
- How do we learn about the past?

Unit 2 An age of adventure

Ch 3 The first Americans
- Native Americans
- Iroquois, Sioux, Pueblo
- Mayas, Aztecs, Incas

Ch 4 Exploration
- Early explorers
- Christopher Columbus
- Explorers of Spain & Portugal
- French, Dutch, English in America

Ch 5 Colonization
- The first colonies
- New England colonies
- The Southern colonies
- The middle colonies

Unit 3 A new and growing nation

Ch 6 Birth of a nation
- Bad feeling between Britain and the colonies
- The move to independence
- War!
- The Constitution
- A summary of the Constitution

Ch 7 Washington through Jackson
- Our first president
- Thomas Jefferson, a remarkable man
- Our national anthem
- Jacksonian democracy

Ch 8 A nation changes
- A changing way of life
- The Lone Star republic

Contents i i

- California
- The Oregon trail

Unit 4 The U.S. comes of age

Ch 9 A nation divides and reunites
- Slavery
- A civil war
- Reconstruction

Ch 10 The nation expands
- Westward movement
- The transcontinental railroads and Indian wars

Ch 11 A modern nation emerges
- The continuing agricultural revolution
- A revolution in industry
- Welcome to our shores
- Growth of cities

Unit 5 U.S. in twentieth century

Ch 12 U.S. becomes a world leader
- Expanding beyond our shores
- The World Wars
- The Cold War

Ch 13 Times of rapid change
- The U.S. since 1900
- The struggle for human rights

Unit 6 [Today] A land of great variety

Ch 14 The geography of the United States
- Tools of geography
- Landforms of the U.S.
- The earth and the sun
- Natural resources

Ch 15 New England
- The land and the climate
- Mining, fishing, and other resources
- Agriculture and forests
- Tourism, people and communities

Contents i i i

Ch 16 Mid-Atlantic
- The land
- Climate and natural resources
- Farming and industry
- Cities

Ch 17 Southeast
- The land
- Climate and natural resources
- Agriculture, industry, and resources
- Population and cities

Ch 18 South Central
- The land and climate
- Agriculture
- Resources and industry
- Population and cities

Ch 19 North Central
- The land and climate
- Farmlands and forests
- Industry and resources
- Population and cities

Ch 20 Mountain West
- The land and climate
- Agriculture, resources, and industry
- Population and cities

Ch 21 Pacific
- The land and climate
- Agriculture, resources, and industry
- Population and cities

Unit 7 Canada and Latin America

Ch 22 Canada
- History and government
- The land and climate
- Physical regions
- Cities

Ch 23 Latin America
- Yesterday and today
- Mexico
- Central America and Caribbean
- South America and Countries of South America

Figure 4.6 The table of contents for a fifth-grade textbook, *The World and its People/The United States and its Neighbors* (Silver Burdett, 1986).

that unit 7 is a pastiche; Canada is organized to parallel the preceding chapters, while the coverage of Latin America is regional, a sprinkling of history followed by a quick trip from Mexico south to Cape Horn.

The design in the TOC appears relatively comprehensible. The organization is certainly coherent, but a fifth-grader reading the two-page TOC will encounter relatively little that is either familiar or interesting, in our judgment. For some reason, publishers often open every social studies book with a section on map-reading, regardless of the topics or the structure. As we have already noted, this topic would not be either compelling or particularly familiar to young readers. Within its pages, however, the textbook is attractively designed and illustrated with numerous photographs and graphics. Page 3 offers an exciting full-page view of Yellowstone Falls, followed by a series of maps ranging from the world through the Northern Hemisphere to the comparison of an aerial photograph of a housing tract with its translation into a map. The writing is largely expository, with occasional embedded anecdotes ("For all of his 12 years Two Rivers had prepared to be a warrior ... , practicing long-distance running on the trails around his house . . . . He had also taken part in the game of lacrosse.").[16] But the thrust of this textbook is the conveyance of information ("Rainfall varies in the Southeast from about 40 inches a year to almost 70 inches . . . . Most rain falls during the summer, when the temperature is at its highest."),[17] with little attention to either familiarity or interest enhancement.

The instructional goals, as laid out for the teacher, reinforce this approach: "[The goal is] to list the nine industries of New England").[18] As for *Oh, California*, the TOC is built around content elements rather than inquiry. The textbook does attempt within some lessons to connect the students to historical and geographic issues, but these are few and far between. "Serious" students may learn a great deal from this textbook, but only if they persist in moving through enormous amounts of factual material. Such is the promise of the TOC, and this promise is fulfilled in the 500 pages that follow the introduction. The intention is clearly to move from the front to the back of the book, despite an aside to be flexible.

As part of the top-level design, Chapter Review and Skills Development sections at the end of each chapter provide additional instruction. The Review includes test questions and a vocabulary quiz, along with activities – "Become a historian and write your family's history."[19] The Skills section is accompanied by a collection of work sheets providing practice on relatively low-level activities (e.g., "The following cities were some of the early settlements in colonial America . . . . [F]ind the latitude and longitude of each city. Then locate and label the cities on the map at the right.").[20] We found few instances of activities that helped students connect, organize, reflect, or extend the information in the textbook.

Designing a Good Text to Be Better

In this section, we lay out two revised TOCs for Silver Burdett's *The United States and its Neighbors*. While the original version has considerable integrity, we have attempted to design our revisions according to the design principles that we have presented throughout this book. We have chosen the elements and linked them together to reflect the lens of either the geographer or the historian, to support student-centered instruction, and to be comprehensible. Our revisions are models, which we offer to exemplify our ideas. We are sensitive to the pressures on textbook publishers and well aware of our freedom, in contrast, to ignore the specifications of frameworks and the heavy influence of tradition. For example, we have chosen to focus on *either* history *or* geography in our revisions. When we attempted to place the two disciplines as equal foci in one design, the result was cumbersome and far too lengthy. Textbook publishers probably would not have the same luxury (although framework designers could give them that freedom). So, here is our redesign of *The United States and its Neighbors*.

The first revision uses geography as the primary lens. Figure 4.7 presents the first TOC. This revision begins not with a skills section but an introduction to the lens of the geographer and a student project in which children apply the lens to their own community. The opening segment, "Where Do You Live?," accomplishes two purposes. First, we assume that students were introduced to geography in previous grades, and so it makes sense to review the earlier material, casting it in a format that is meaningful and interesting to young adolescents. Second, this chapter recapitulates the key elements of a geographic perspective – What does it mean to describe to someone "where you live"? The core of the book presents an imaginary bus tour that moves around North America and views the information that students encounter through the lens of the geographer. This tour can follow a variety of routes. As part of the introduction, a class plans which route they will take. The units and chapters in the TOC are organized around the tour. Note, however, that the tour does not cover Central and South America. The original textbook attempts to cover Central and South America in ten pages. We decided to take seriously the title, *The United States and its [immediate] Neighbors*. The revision ends with a conclusion analogous to the introduction. The introduction and conclusion are examples of the "bookends" that we suggested earlier in this chapter. They present the major themes in the curriculum and help to provide coherence to the book regardless of the particular units that the class has covered in whichever order chosen by the teacher.

The revised TOC has six units and 15 chapters rather than the original single unit and eight geography chapters in the textbook. By focusing on geography

Figure 4.7 A revised table of contents for a fifth-grade textbook on the United States using the lens of the geographer.

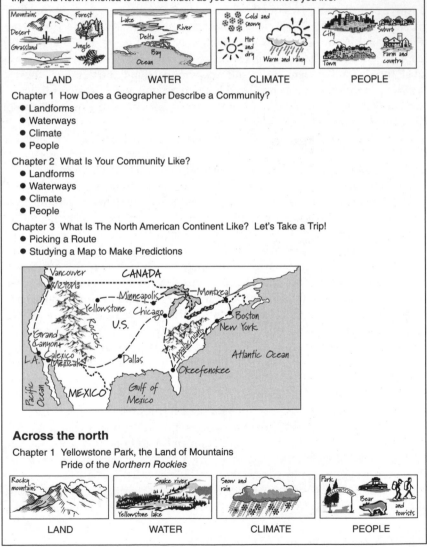

Where Do You Live?

Imagine that you suddenly encountered a Man from Mars who asked, "Where do you live?" Giving your address would not be enough! This book explores life on the North American continent, which is one way of telling about where you live. Unit 1 will give you a new way of thinking about the North American continent. You will learn to think as a geographer, looking at the land, the water, the climate, and how the people who are your neighbors live. In Unit 1 you will describe your own community by making a diorama, writing a story, or acting in a play that would help a Man from Mars understand your community. You will end the Unit by planning a trip around North America to learn as much as you can about where you live.

LAND   WATER   CLIMATE   PEOPLE

Chapter 1 How Does a Geographer Describe a Community?
- Landforms
- Waterways
- Climate
- People

Chapter 2 What Is Your Community Like?
- Landforms
- Waterways
- Climate
- People

Chapter 3 What Is The North American Continent Like? Let's Take a Trip!
- Picking a Route
- Studying a Map to Make Predictions

Across the north

Chapter 1 Yellowstone Park, the Land of Mountains
           Pride of the *Northern Rockies*

LAND   WATER   CLIMATE   PEOPLE

Figure 4.7 contd.

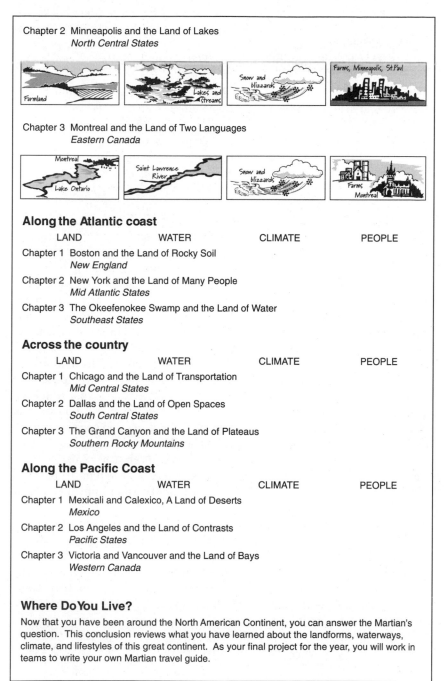

Chapter 2 Minneapolis and the Land of Lakes
   North Central States

Chapter 3 Montreal and the Land of Two Languages
   Eastern Canada

Along the Atlantic coast

LAND	WATER	CLIMATE	PEOPLE

Chapter 1 Boston and the Land of Rocky Soil
   New England

Chapter 2 New York and the Land of Many People
   Mid Atlantic States

Chapter 3 The Okeefenokee Swamp and the Land of Water
   Southeast States

Across the country

LAND	WATER	CLIMATE	PEOPLE

Chapter 1 Chicago and the Land of Transportation
   Mid Central States

Chapter 2 Dallas and the Land of Open Spaces
   South Central States

Chapter 3 The Grand Canyon and the Land of Plateaus
   Southern Rocky Mountains

Along the Pacific Coast

LAND	WATER	CLIMATE	PEOPLE

Chapter 1 Mexicali and Calexico, A Land of Deserts
   Mexico

Chapter 2 Los Angeles and the Land of Contrasts
   Pacific States

Chapter 3 Victoria and Vancouver and the Land of Bays
   Western Canada

Where Do You Live?

Now that you have been around the North American Continent, you can answer the Martian's question. This conclusion reviews what you have learned about the landforms, waterways, climate, and lifestyles of this great continent. As your final project for the year, you will work in teams to write your own Martian travel guide.

exclusively, our book would treat geographic areas with greater depth. The TOC design is more elaborated than the original Silver Burdett book. We actually intend the TOC to be studied as a text at the beginning of the year, a road map to which the class returns throughout the course as a point of reference. The chapter descriptions in the TOC include substance, words, and graphics that highlight the elements and linkages within and between chapters, elaborated to tickle student interest. Words are chosen for vividness and familiarity, and to point up the key topics within each chapter. We envisage the use of artwork and iconic images to support the words and graphics in the revision. We have made a first attempt at graphic elaborations to support the effectiveness of the TOC as a text, and imagine graphics and illustrations for each of the major regions in the TOC analogous to those that we have given for **ACROSS THE NORTH.** The original TOC included photographs, but these were decorative more than substantive.

The alternative revision (figure 4.8) builds on historical elements that are largely the same as in the original textbook. The segments are typical of many treatments of US history: the precolonial and colonial periods, the wars (Revolutionary, Civil, and World), and the intervening segments of economic and industrial development. We have given more attention to events during the past half-century than the original, because we think that students are more likely to connect with the past when they can see it in relation to the present. But rather than simply listing these historical segments in serial order, the revised design attempts to show the cause–effect relations that underlie the shift from one segment to another. Connecting the entire collection are the themes of territory, expansion, and conflict. Expansion and conflict appear as a cause–effect pairing. Human beings, like any other species, expand to fill the available ecological niches. Our opposed thumb (the ability to develop and use tools), language (the capacity to communicate and reflect), and social organiza- tion (perhaps a mixed blessing) give us a potential far greater than that of most other species (one might argue that ants and cockroaches have better track records, to be sure). The task of historical analysis, as indicated in the opening section, "How Did We Get Here?," is to trace the record of human beings in this continent.

In the original TOC, unit 1 introduces the Native American inhabitants in chapter 1, and then the first explorers suddenly appear searching for riches in chapter 2. A student might reasonably ask, "What's happening here? Why were the Europeans exploring? Why did they take so long to find the New World? Why were the Native Americans unable to protect themselves and their land? What was happening in the world as the fifteenth century came to an end? And why should I, a fifth-grader, care?"

The revised TOC attempts to address such questions thematically. Chapters 3 and 4 take shape as a contrast between the Old and New Worlds,

Figure 4.8 A revised table of contents for a fifth-grade textbook on the United States using the lens of the historian.

HOW DID WE GET HERE?

Close your eyes and imagine what life would be like in your neighborhood five hundred years ago. No television, no grocery stores, no hospitals, no schools, no streets. How would you survive? Where would you find food? Water? Clothes? A place to live? The North American continent is very different today than it was in 1492. In this book you will travel through time and space to see how the steady growth of civilization led European explorers to cross the Atlantic Ocean in search of the Orient's riches, suddenly bumping into a new world—the North and South American continents. You will read about how expansion led to conflict and the continuing struggle of human beings to create peaceful and productive lives.

TERRITORY ———→ EXPANSION ———→ CONFLICT ———→ PEACE

Chapter 1 How does it work?

- The search for more good land
- The search for more wealth
- The wish to spread ideas
- The wish for political freedom

Chapter 2 What does it look like in my neighborhood?

- What is expanding in my neighborhood?
- Who is in conflict?
- How could we have peace?

UNIT 1 America and Europe–1492!

TERRITORY ———→ EXPANSION ———→ CONFLICT ———→ PEACE

Chapter 3 The Early Americans: At Peace with the Land

More than 10,000 years ago explorers from Asia crossed the Arctic Ocean and traveled south through Alaska and Canada to all of North and South America. By 1492, Native Americans filled the two continents–farmers, hunters, scientists, artists–living in tribes, villages, big cities, and even large empires. They respected and worshipped nature.

Figure 4.8 contd.

Chapter 4 Europe Entering the Sixteenth Century:
Technology and Industry

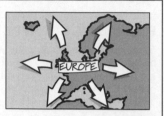

Following the plagues and Black Death of the Middle Ages, the citizens of Europe created the Renaissance, a time of invention and learning, of kings and states, of armies and wars. Europe was crowded with people, merchants looking for new resources, generals and admirals eager for new worlds to conquer, ordinary people hoping to find freedom and start a new life.

Chapter 5 The Explorers:
A Bridge Across the Atlantic

"The earth is round!" Columbus believed that if he sailed westward from Europe, he would reach the Oriental riches of China and Japan. For three months his three ships sailed the "Sea of Darkness," fearful they might drop off the edge of the world. On October 12, 1492, they sighted an island in the Bahamas south of Florida, building a sea bridge between Europe and the Americas, linking two entirely different cultures. Who was more astonished–Columbus' men expecting Chinese silk and pearls, or the Native Americans watching soldiers in armor as they left their enormous sailing ships and marched ashore with banners, swords, and *guns.*

UNIT 2 Creating the Colonies (1500-1700)

TERRITORY ⟶ EXPANSION ⟶ CONFLICT ⟶ PEACE

Chapter 6 European Nations Compete for Land and Wealth
Chapter 7 Development of the Northeast
Chapter 8 Development of the Southeast

UNIT 3 Birth of a Nation–The Colonies Revolt and Unite (1700-1800)

TERRITORY ⟶ EXPANSION ⟶ CONFLICT ⟶ PEACE

Chapter 9 Trouble in the Colonies
Chapter 10 The Revolutionary War
Chapter 11 Building a United States

UNIT 4 Growth of a Nation (1800-1850)

TERRITORY ⟶ EXPANSION ⟶ CONFLICT ⟶ PEACE

Chapter 12 Across the Appalachians to a New Frontier
Chapter 13 The "Purchases:" Free Land to the Mountains
Chapter 14 On to the Pacific Ocean: Gold in California

Figure 4.8 contd.

UNIT 5 The Nation Divided (1850-1875)
TERRITORY ⟶ EXPANSION ⟶ CONFLICT ⟶ PEACE

Chapter 15 Tensions in the New Nation
Chapter 16 Slavery in a Democracy
Chapter 17 The War Between the States
Chapter 18 Reconstructing the Country

UNIT 6 The Nation Grows (1875-1900)
TERRITORY ⟶ EXPANSION ⟶ CONFLICT ⟶ PEACE

Chapter 19 Factories and Cities
Chapter 20 Industry and Invention
Chapter 21 The Raw Goods
Chapter 22 Democracy for All

UNIT 7 The Nation Becomes a World Power (1900-1950)
TERRITORY ⟶ EXPANSION ⟶ CONFLICT ⟶ PEACE

Chapter 23 Isolation and Adventurism
Chapter 24 Fighting in Europe– World War I
Chapter 25 A World Economy
Chapter 26 Fighting Throughout the World

UNIT 8 The End of the Frontier; A Time of Challenges (1950-Present)
TERRITORY ⟶ EXPANSION ⟶ CONFLICT ⟶ PEACE

Chapter 27 Struggles on Many Fronts
Chapter 28 The Limits of Power
Chapter 29 The Way Ahead

HOW FAR HAVE WE COME?
Close your eyes and imagine how far we have come in five hundred years. What would an American living five hundred years ago exactly where you live now think about your life? In this book you have traveled through time and space to see how the steady growth of civilization has brought us to this time and place. You have read about how expansion led to conflict and the continuing struggle of human beings to create peaceful and productive lives.

Chapter 30 Territory ⟶ Expansion ⟶ Conflict ⟶ Peace. How did it work?

- Moving ever Westward: The search for more good land
- Exploring the New World: The search for more wealth
- The Nation Divided: The wish to spread ideas
- A Nation is Born: The wish for political freedom

Chapter 31 Challenges for the Future. Peace without Conflict?

between fifteenth-century America with its rich resources, primitive technologies, and generally peaceful civilizations, and Europe with its depleted assets, thriving technologies, and bitter internecine warfare. Separated by an ocean barrier that was then impassable, the two continents had undergone several millennia of development along very different courses. Europe was worn out, while America was ripe for the taking. This contrast provides a basis for explaining the impact of the early explorers, who found a land open for exploitation, a new frontier with virtually no barriers. It also sets the stage for the turmoil that followed as the Europeans fought one another as well as the Native Americans. Europe was not a unified entity; rather, the national divisions of previous centuries were immediately recapitulated in the New World.

The transferral of national strife is further developed in unit 2. In the original textbook, territorial divisions appear incidentally: a chapter each on the Spanish, the Portuguese, the French, the Dutch, and the English. In the revised TOC, these divisions are related to geography: Who came ashore where? They are also related to distinctions within nations. In the English colonies, for example, different groups occupied different regions: the merchants and traders looking for a profit, the poor and persecuted seeking relief, and government representatives fighting for a profit on the enterprise. Again, the linkages are designed to support a cause–effect analysis of the tensions that eventually led the British settlers into the War for Independence, tensions that led less than a century later to the War Between the States. The Spanish explorers, on the other hand, loyal to their monarchs' mandates to exploit and settle, sustained a hegemony for more than a century; the internal strife that did occur was about money and territory more than independence. Geography played a large role in separating the combatants. The English occupied the Atlantic seaboard, the Appalachians forming a barrier that pushed development north to the St. Lawrence River and south to Georgia. The Spanish moved from the Caribbean north through Texas and California, while the French used the Great Lakes and the Mississippi to occupy Canada and the northern part of the Great Plains. The French and Spanish gave priority to exploration over settlement, so that while the English were building farms, factories, homes, and families, the French and Spanish were spreading themselves sparsely over large regions, with little staying power.

The graphics in the TOC highlight the cause–effect and thematic features in the revised version. We have designed these graphics to reveal the structural features of the textbook. Specifically, they highlight the interplay among the thematic elements: expansion, territorial competition, conflict, and resolution among nation–states. As with the previous example in figure 4.7, we also intend them to aid teachers and students in comprehending the TOC as a text in its own right.

The remaining units are briefly sketched in this revision to give an idea of how we think a TOC that is familiar, interesting, and organized, that lays out a comprehensive curriculum, and that has instructional value could take shape. As with the first redesign, the concluding section serves as a "bookend," reviewing the major features of the year's study, and projecting students into their roles as future citizens.

The revised TOC has 31 chapters rather than the original 13 history chapters in the textbook. By focusing on history exclusively, our book would treat events with greater depth analogously to the treatment of geographic regions in the first revision. This TOC, too, is meant to be studied as a text in its own right: chapter descriptions include substance, to highlight the elements and linkages within and between chapters and to peak student interest; artwork and iconic images support the words and graphics in the revision; and titles use vivid, familiar words that point up key unit and chapter topics.

In summary, we have used curriculum, instructional, and comprehension themes to create two whole-book designs in which the separate elements work together to trace an adequate curriculum path and support student-centered instruction, while exhibiting the three features of comprehensibility (familiarity, interest, and structural coherence). The designs differ primarily in the particular curricular lens used to frame the book. The differences in the lenses have strong implications for the content covered and the structural backbone used to organize the content: the geographic design links features of the United States into a descriptive matrix structure; the historical design links causes and effects into a sequence. Otherwise, the two designs adhere to similar comprehension and instructional themes. Both books should support comprehension and student-centered instruction. The structure of both is consistent and coherent, and the bookends accompanied by the TOC word choice and graphics of both should enhance student interest and topic familiarity. We expect that these designs would be comprehensible to young readers. The thematic treatment of the two designs should support student reflection and extension and allow for flexibility in instruction. However, the geographic treatment would allow for greater student and teacher choice in how to order the year than the historical treatment, a difference that is discipline based, we suspect. Finally, the TOCs in both cases can stand as texts in their own rights, providing a "road map" for students to follow as they construct their own understanding of an entire year of work.

We have focused on TOC revisions in this section. We imagine similar designs for each unit introduction, two-page spreads that provide a road map to students and teachers, enlarging on the image provided in the TOC, providing coherence and connecting to student background and interest. Textbooks similar to those that we have analyzed in this chapter are likely to provide the foundation for subject-matter instruction for some years to come. We think that it is possible to enhance these materials so that they meet the criteria of comprehensibility, curriculum adequacy, and instructional support, so that they are effective when employed in a traditional manner, but also provide a springboard for teachers to explore alternatives to "beginning at the start" and "finishing at the end."

Notes

1   Whitehead (1929, 1974) and Dewey (1902).
2   California State Board of Education (1988).
3   Crabtree et al. (1992).
4   American Association for the Advancement of Science (1989) and California State Board of Education (1990).
5   Calfee and Chambliss (1987) and Chambliss & Calfee (1989).
6   Calfee & Curley (1984).
7   Silver Burdett (1986).
8   See, e.g., US Department of Education (1983).
9   California State Board of Education (1988).
10   Houghton Mifflin (1991b).
11   Silver Burdett (1986).
12   Houghton Mifflin (1991b), p. 104.
13   Ibid., pp. 106–107
14   Ibid., p. 146.
15   Ibid., p. 305.
16   Silver Burdett (1986), p. 51.
17   Ibid., p. 333.
18   Ibid., p. 289.
19   Ibid., p. 42.
20   Ibid., p. 16.

5

FINDING THE DESIGN IN TEXTBOOK MATERIALS

In early chapters, we imagined textbooks designed around a handful of important ideas, while meeting standards of comprehensibility and providing students with many opportunities to participate actively and think reflectively. We presented rewrites to demonstrate our ideas. We proposed that such materials would nurture the minds of all students. In this chapter, we demonstrate how a small set of rubrics can be used to evaluate the design of texts of various lengths, from an entire book to a section of several paragraphs.

As we have already demonstrated, not all text designs are equal. Content can build on reader knowledge and interest or be unfamiliar and boring. The content may be linked coherently or may take the form of a long list or loosely related network. The design may or may not reflect the knowledge, themes, and ways of knowing in a domain. It may support good instruction or fly in the face of everything known about how children learn. Figure 5.1 represents what we see as the difference between well and poorly designed textbook selections at various levels, from whole book to section. The challenge is to acquire the expert's lens for analyzing textbook materials; for recognizing well-designed textbook offerings.

Evaluating Textbook Design

Evaluating the design of textbooks has proven to be a knotty problem. It has been by no means obvious how to recognize curricular, comprehensibility, and instructional themes in a passage of several hundred words; few have tried to analyze books of several hundred pages. State, district, and classroom textbook selectors have used readability formulas and checklists to evaluate, compare, and choose textbook series. Publishers have often designed their books to meet readability and checklist criteria. Readability formulas and checklists each have strengths and drawbacks.

COMPREHENSIBILITY

Key Question: How comprehensible is the text design?

GOOD DESIGN	POOR DESIGN
Themes: The text is interesting, familiar, and coherently structured.	The text is uninteresting, unfamiliar, and poorly structured.
Elements: Words, sentences, paragraphs, and text are familiar and interesting.	The words, sentences, paragraphs, and text are unfamiliar and uninteresting.
There are only a handful of separate elements in the design.	There are many separate elements in the design.
Linkages: The rhetorical pattern is consistent and complete.	The rhetorical pattern is inconsistent or incomplete.
The rhetorical pattern is tightly linked (e.g., matrix, hierarchy, branching tree, argument, explanation).	The rhetorical pattern is loosely linked (e.g., list).
The text uses functional devices (i.e., introductions, transitions, conclusions, paragraph topic sentences).	The text has no functional devices.

CURRICULUM

Key Question: How well does the text design communicate the lens of a domain expert?

GOOD DESIGN	POOR DESIGN
Themes: Text design reflects expert models or principles.	Text design fails to reflect expert models or principles.
Elements: Text topics or events are important to experts.	Text topics or events are trivial to experts.
Linkages: Text structure matches a relationship important to experts.	Text structure fails to match a relationship important to experts.

INSTRUCTION

Key Question: How well does the text support student-centered instruction?

GOOD DESIGN	POOR DESIGN
Themes: The text Connects to student knowledge and interest, Organizes topic and events, and sets the stage for students to Reflect and Extend in a community of inquiry.	The text fails to Connect to student knowledge and interest, to Organize topics and events, and to set the stage for students to Reflect and Extend in a community of inquiry.
Elements: At least some text topics and events are familiar and interesting.	Virtually no text topics and events are familiar and interesting.
Linkages: Text structure is flexible (e.g., a matrix, hierarchy, branching tree, or falling dominos; an argument or explanation).	Text structure is inflexible (e.g., a list, topical net, or linear string).

Figure 5.1   Characteristics that differentiate between well and poorly designed textbook materials.

Readability Formulas

As we explained in chapter 2, all textbooks, regardless of content, may be evaluated by examining the complexity of words and sentences. Readability formulas use both features to produce a grade-level score.[1] The formulas have been designed on the reasonable assumption that students with immature reading skills will find textbooks with familiar words of one or two syllables and short sentences to be easier to comprehend than books with unfamiliar, multi-syllabic vocabulary and convoluted sentences.

Unfortunately, while word familiarity and word and sentence length can correlate with comprehension scores, readability formulas have serious draw-backs. Different readability formulas applied to the same reading passage can produce scores differing by as much as 6.2 grade levels.[2] Furthermore, scores fail to represent important writing features, such as text organization or interestingness.[3] As we demonstrated with our example in chapter 2, publishers who use readability scores to guide textbook writing often produce passages that are actually more rather than less difficult to comprehend. Their passages are replete with vocabulary that is familiar, but vague and ambiguous, and sentences that are short, but unrelated to one another. To comprehend these passages, readers must resolve ambiguity and infer relationships, two sophisti-cated comprehension tasks.[4]

Textbook Selection Checklists

Customarily based on the objectives, goals, or themes of a curriculum, check-lists provide a different lens through which to evaluate textbooks. These instruments vary from a large number of scales used to rate individual textbook characteristics[5] to global analyses guided by a set of scoring rubrics.[6] In both cases, the outcome of the evaluation is a numerical score that can be compared across the textbook series under consideration. Textbook evaluators can tailor checklists to text features that they value. Hence, checklists have several advantages over readability formulas. They can focus heavily on content.[7] They also can address important writing features not computed into readability formulas (e.g., interestingness).

Unfortunately, checklists have their own problems. They tend to be long, superficial, and to emphasize content to the exclusion of important writing features.[8] The final score no longer represents the particular strengths and weaknesses in the book. Two books with ratings of "50," for example, might actually have quite different features.

A Text Design Taxonomy

We have found that graphic depictions represent textbook design more validly than either readability formulas or checklists. Because graphics display words and statements in meaningful patterns, graphic organizers are an efficient means of clearly communicating large amounts of interrelated content.[9] When content is presented graphically, important information is distinguished from less important details, and relationships are displayed visually rather than explained verbally. The well-designed graphic can communicate complex relationships – such as comparison, contrast, cause, effect, superordination, and subordination – in an eye span, preserving limited human processing resources. It depicts the separable elements in a design and the pattern that links them. We have found common organizational patterns in college fresh-man composition books, and many of these patterns map well on to the semantic networks and hierarchies that cognitive psychologists have used to represent how humans link their knowledge.[10] The graphic organizers that we pose for evaluating textbooks combine these two traditions.

In chapter 2 we proposed that all designs, including textbook designs, have three ingredients: identifiable *elements*, *linked* according to a *theme*. In designing a textbook, we assumed, an author indeed chose particular content to include and a structural pattern to organize the content. We also assumed that the author made these design decisions anew at each level of text: whole book, unit, chapter, section, paragraph, and sentence. We further suggested that all well-designed textbooks adhere to curricular, comprehensibility, and instructional themes. To analyze a textbook, our task is to find the elements, their linkages, and any overarching themes implied by the resulting pattern, diagram the designs, and evaluate their comprehensibility, curriculum, and instructional support

We have presented examples of materials that either reflect or neglect effective design principles. We also introduced a handful of patterns (see figure 2.4) that can describe the design of virtually any textbook. Using a passage, a curriculum framework, and a TOC as examples, we modeled how to use the taxonomy. First, we identified the elements, linkages, and themes that the author built into the text. Having found these design ingredients, we repre-sented them in a graphic organizer that matched one or more of the patterns in the taxonomy and evaluated the graphic for its comprehensibility, curricular, and instructional features. Throughout the sections of this chapter, we describe the patterns more fully. We present examples of tables of contents and passages to illustrate the approach and provide practice in using it for interested readers.

Finding the Design in a Text

Our examples to follow are from social studies and science textbooks for grades 4–8. These grade levels represent the greatest challenges for young readers and also offer the most opportunity for improving the system dramatically. Up until fourth grade, children are acquiring the reading skills that they will need throughout life. At fourth grade they are suddenly expected to be reading to learn rather than learning to read. Science and social studies textbooks begin to assume a major role in their instruction, a role that continues to increase through eighth grade and beyond. Unfortunately, as we explained in chapter 2, children's early reading experiences have prepared them poorly for comprehending and learning from the exposition so common to content area textbooks. This problem is compounded by the quality of the writing in textbooks for young readers, which tends to be poorly structured. Readers frequently must mentally reconstruct the text to represent it coherently before they can comprehend it, a process that causes significant challenges to novice learners. By considering the design in social studies and science texts for the middle grades, publishers can improve the comprehensibility, curriculum, and instruction in instructional materials for these crucial grades, and educators can make better choices. Instructional materials will improve.

Even though our examples come from particular domains and particular grade levels, the approach transfers readily to most other content and grade levels. Language textbooks, such as basal readers, do present a special case. Basal readers are typically anthologies with accompanying explanation and practice exercises. The separate readings, explanations, and exercises in the anthologies (the elements) can be linked into descriptive patterns such as topical nets according to literary themes ("Friendship," "Danger," "Fantasy," and so on) or genre (poetry, short stories, and essays). The approach can be used well to analyze the top-level designs of entire basal reading series and grade level anthologies. It is less effective with designs of poems, plays, and stories within the readers, because these designs do not match the expository patterns in figure 2.4. While the patterns cannot adequately picture these designs, the same principles of comprehensibility, curriculum, and instruction apply.

We have designed this chapter to follow a common pattern. First, we will model how to recognize, diagram, and evaluate the design in a TOC or passage, sharing our examination in some detail. Next, we will present a similar TOC or passage and briefly summarize our analysis. We repeat this pattern several times. The set of second examples gives you the opportunity to practice finding and evaluating the design of TOCs and passages on your own before you read our summary. We suspect that you will best appreciate the power of the approach if you try it yourself.

Before tackling the examples, you may be reassured by the experiences of others who have found the text analysis approach worth learning. As we write this book, we have taught over 200 classroom teachers and district administrators to find the design in social studies, science, language, and mathematics materials. We have trained at least as many more to teach their students how to apply the same lenses to planning and executing their own writing tasks. Colleagues have taught fifth-, sixth-, and eighth-graders, including groups of ESL youngsters, to search out the design in social studies and science texts.[11] Research studies have demonstrated that students' comprehension of new materials improves after this instruction. Finally, we have held successful training sessions with groups of editors from major textbook publishers. Trainees have typically responded positively. Teachers and administrators have told us the sessions were "outstanding." Some of the comments are as follows: "I feel that I learned so much on how to analyze a textbook and practical ways of going about it;" and "You provided a specific 'procedure' which makes the evaluation of textbooks a workable, objective task. Invaluable!" A group of mathematics editors approached us at the end of a training session: "We are impressed with your approach and can already see ways we could use it to improve the math series we are developing," they told us. We trust that whether you are a textbook publisher, a practitioner charged with selecting instructional materials, an educational researcher, or an interested "uncategorizable" reader, you will find the lenses useful as well.

Informational Patterns: The Building Blocks of Textbook Design

Textbook designs are multi-faceted, not unlike the Lego or Tinker Toy designs of a creative eight-year-old. Building-block patterns can be combined in virtually endless combinations to form the paragraphs, sections, chapters, units, and books that comprise a series of instructional materials. In chapter 2 we explained that the patterns in the taxonomy initially depend on whether the author's purpose seems to be to inform, argue, or explain – and informational patterns are the most basic. Some of these informational patterns are descriptive, a design that presents the static characteristics of an object analogous to a snapshot (lists, topical nets, hierarchies, and matrices); other patterns are sequential, a design that presents events progressing over time somewhat like a movie (linear strings, falling dominoes, and branching trees). Authors use these building blocks to describe cultures, geographic areas, and the characteristics of physical phenomena, or to present the sequence of events in historical eras, of the stages in various processes, and so on. These building-block designs differ in how many linkages join the separate parts, and the differences in the linkages seem to affect comprehension, as we reported in chapter 2. Our first examples focus on these informational patterns.

Examples 1 and 2: Descriptive Tables of Contents

To model the approach, we begin with the table of contents for *Our United States* (see figure 5.2). One approach to evaluating a textbook is to read it from cover to cover. A far more efficient approach focuses on a book's table of contents, in which authors can clearly signal the design of the book, a TOC feature that we demonstrated in chapter 4.

We begin by scanning the table of contents for clues to the author's design. Our scan reveals that the book is divided into seven units and two or three chapters within each unit. The first unit, "OUR COUNTRY, THE UNITED STATES," gives characteristics of the country as a whole, while the remaining units divide the country into six geographic regions. These units characterize the country rather than presenting events. We decide that the book is designed as a description.

A set of defining text characteristics, presented in figure 5.3, helps us determine the precise design. We focus on **Description**. The first set of characteristics states, "If each subtopic deals with the same attributes then the design is a matrix." We scan chapter and other bold-faced headings for each unit and note that all units have one chapter on the geography of the region, at least one on the people of the region, and a unit review. In addition, all units with the exception of the first unit include a historical narrative (e.g., "Long Ago in the Northeast Region: The Pilgrims.") We also note that there is a hierarchical relationship between the first unit, "OUR COUNTRY, THE UNITED STATES," and the remaining units (see the second set of characteristics under **Description** in figure 5.3). As we look at chapter titles within the unit, it appears to us that this unit is functioning as an introduction to the design of the book as a whole. We decide that a matrix best represents the book's design and diagram it as in figure 5.4. We also leave the short section on Puerto Rico, the Glossary, and other ancillary features out of the diagram as peripheral to the book's top-level design.

Having pictured the design, we are in a position to evaluate it. To what extent has it been guided by the comprehension, curricular, and instructional themes that we value?

Design comprehensibility   The graphic representation suggests that it has at least one of the characteristics of comprehensible text: coherent linkages that are signalled in an introductory unit (an important functional device). The matrix pattern is consistent throughout and complete. The design has no empty cells. However, it lacks the two other features of comprehensible text. We see

Figure 5.2 The table of contents for *Our United States* (Klein, 1983).

Table of Contents

Figure 5.2 contd.

Figure 5.2 contd.

no evidence that it builds on reader knowledge. Nor does it look particularly interesting. The topic itself is probably not intrinsically captivating to fifth-graders. We see no use of vivid vocabulary or personalization, at least at this whole-book level.

Curriculum The design does reflect a particular domain theme in part: the lens of the geographer. The book is divided according to geographic regions and considers regional attributes of importance to geographers. Otherwise, the book's design does not reflect any significant geographic models, although it could quite easily do so. For example, geographers propose a causal link between the physical characteristics of a region and lifestyles that people who

Text Characteristics		Building Block Design
If the text presents . . .		
. . . attributes	then the design is	Description
. . . events	then the design is	Sequence
Description		
If each subtopic deals with the same attributes	then the design is a	Matrix
If subtopics present categories that are hierarchically related	then the design is a	Hierarchy
If there are 3-5 main subtopics	then the design is a	Topical Net
If subtopics are none of above	then the design is a	List
Sequence		
If there is more than one sequence covering the same period of time	then the design is a	Branching Tree
If there is a cause and effect relationship among events in a sequence	then the design is	Falling Dominoes
If the events are linked by time only	then the design is a	Linear String

Figure 5.3   Text characteristics that differentiate among the rhetorical patterns that serve as building-block designs.

live in the region develop. People who live on flat plains with easy access to water are far more likely to become farmers and to build their houses out of brick, for example, than to mine for minerals and construct wood houses. To be sure, causal principles may pervade the units and chapters of the book, but titles in the TOC do not signal them.

Text Structure

We have omitted Unit One from the matrix because, as is typical of social studies texts, this unit is a broad introduction and overview to the subject of the textbook, the United States.

REGION	GEOGRAPHY	PEOPLE	HISTORICAL NARRATIVE	UNIT REVIEW
UNIT 2 NORTHEAST	Ch 4 Geography of the Northeast Region	Ch 5 People of the Northeast Region	Long Ago in the Northeast: The Pilgrims	Unit Review
UNIT 3 SOUTHEAST	Ch 6 Geography of the Southeast Region	Ch 7 People of the Southeast Region	Long Ago in the Southeast: Two Famous Americans	Unit Review
UNIT 4 NORTH CENTRAL	Ch 8 Geography of the North Central	Ch 9 People of the North Central	Long Ago in the North Central: The Treeless Plains	Unit Review
UNIT 5 ROCKY MOUNTAINS	Ch 10 Geography of the Rocky Mountains	Ch 11 People of the Rocky Mountains	Long Ago in the Rocky Mountains: Mountain Men	Unit Review
UNIT 6 SOUTHWEST	Ch 12 Geography of the Southwest Region	Ch 13 People of the Southwest Region	Long Ago in the Southwest: The Comanche	Unit Review
UNIT 7 PACIFIC	Ch 14 Geography of the Pacific Region	Ch 15 People of the Pacific Region	Long Ago in the Pacific: Gateway to America	Unit Review

Figure 5.4   The rhetorical pattern for *Our United States* (Klein, 1983).

Instruction   Recall the CORE instructional model that we have used throughout chapters 3 and 4: Connect, Organize, Reflect, Extend. To what extent does this book, as signalled in the TOC, fit the model? We have already noted that the design does not explicitly connect with the knowledge and understandings of the typical fifth-grader (as a contrast, see our textbook redesign in chapter 4). It does *organize* information about the country. The matrix organization supports some strong instructional possibilities. First, it lends itself well to group work, enhancing the social construction of children's learning. Different members of a group can each become "an expert" on one of the three columns of the matrix and share their knowledge with other members of their group to construct complete pictures of the five geographic regions. Second, because it organizes information so coherently, a matrix organization can support student reflection and extension. Each region is viewed through the same set of lenses: geography, sociology and economics, and history. Children could reflect on what we need to find out about a region to be able to understand it. They also could reflect on how the different characteristics affect one another, using the geographer's causal model even though the textbook apparently does not. Through their reflections, students may identify other categories (such as recreation) that the book fails to address and extend their reading to additional resources to fill in this gap.

A second example TOC, *Our World*, written for sixth-graders, is pictured in figure 5.5. Our brief analysis follows in figure 5.6. As we have already suggested, if you want to try your hand at identifying and evaluating the design of a textbook linked descriptively, we suggest that you do not look at our analysis until after you have sketched out the design on your own piece of paper and answered the following questions:

- How comprehensible is the design? Does it use a pattern with strong linkages? Does it connect with reader knowledge? Does it appear interesting?
- How well does the design reflect the lens of an established knowledge domain?
- How well would the design support the CORE instructional model?

Examples 3 and 4: Sequential Tables of Contents

Consider *A Message of Ancient Days* (see figure 5.7), also written for sixth-graders but with a very different design. As before, we begin by scanning the table of contents for design clues. The table of contents is divided into six units and two or three chapters within each unit. The first unit, "The World Past and Present," gives an overview for the entire book. Its title suggests a series of events. The remaining titles appear to be descriptions of characteristics (e.g., "Early Middle Eastern Civilizations," "Early Asian Civilizations"). However, we note a passage of thousands of years between the second unit ("The Earliest People") and the final unit ("Rome: A World Power"). We tentatively decide that the book is designed as a sequence of events. To confirm our choice, we skim through the contents of the units (a luxury that you may not have) and note that each unit indeed spans at least several hundred years. Incidentally, if unit titles better signalled events (e.g., "Early Civilizations Develop in the

Figure 5.5 The table of contents for *Our World* (Canjemi, 1987).

Table of Contents

Figure 5.5 contd.

Figure 5.5 contd.

Figure 5.5 contd.

Figure 5.5 contd.

Middle East") and if the time frames covered by units appeared in the table of contents (e.g., 5300 BC to AD 350), the sequential design would be far more obvious both to us and, we suspect, to young readers.

As before, figure 5.3 helps us to determine the precise design. We focus on Sequence. The first set of characteristics states, "If there is more than one sequence covering the same period of time then the design is a Branching Tree." As we scan individual units, we notice quite a bit of sequential overlap. For example, unit 3 covers 5300 BC-AD 350 while unit 4 spans 2500 BC-AD 467. We also note that many of the chapters are related sequentially within units, and that many of the sections are related sequentially within chapters. For example, within unit 6, chapter 13, "The Rise of Rome," and chapter 14, "The Roman Empire," are sequential, as are some of the sections within each of the chapters ("The Early Empire," "Social Rank in the Empire," "Daily Life in Ancient Rome," and "The Fall of Rome.") We decide that the book is designed as a branching tree, as diagrammed in figure 5.8.

Now we ask how well the design of *A Message of Ancient Days* seems to have been guided by important comprehensibility, curricular, and instructional themes.

Design comprehensibility   The graphic representation suggests that, similar to the two descriptive books, this book has an introduction (units 1 and 2) that functions to foreshadow the design as a whole. It also has coherent linkages. Rather than one sequence stretching from beginning to end, the design divides the time period into somewhat parallel subsequences. Note that, while the subsequences overlap, they are not strictly parallel, with "beginning" and "ending" dates that can differ by one or two thousand years. Likewise, as we

Text Structure

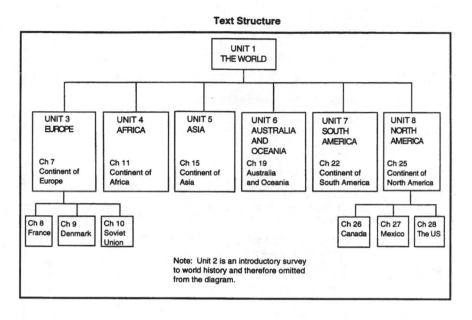

Text Analysis

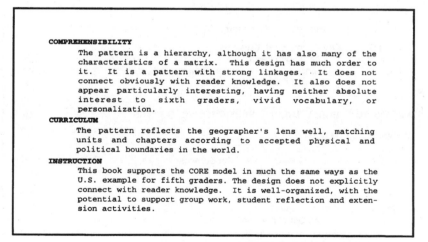

COMPREHENSIBILITY

The pattern is a hierarchy, although it has also many of the characteristics of a matrix. This design has much order to it. It is a pattern with strong linkages. It does not connect obviously with reader knowledge. It also does not appear particularly interesting, having neither absolute interest to sixth graders, vivid vocabulary, or personalization.

CURRICULUM

The pattern reflects the geographer's lens well, matching units and chapters according to accepted physical and political boundaries in the world.

INSTRUCTION

This book supports the CORE model in much the same ways as the U.S. example for fifth graders. The design does not explicitly connect with reader knowledge. It is well-organized, with the potential to support group work, student reflection and extension activities.

Figure 5.6 The rhetorical pattern and brief analysis for the table of contents for *Our World* (Canjemi, 1987).

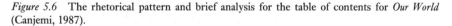

saw in the two examples of description, the design does not appear to build on reader knowledge, nor does it look particularly interesting. The topic itself is

Figure 5.7 The table of contents for *Houghton Mifflin Social Studies/A Message of Ancient Days* (Houghton Mifflin, 1991a).

Table of Contents

Figure 5.7 contd.

Figure 5.7 contd.

probably not intrinsically captivating to sixth-graders. And we see little use of vivid vocabulary (with the possible exception of the action words "Rise" and "Fall") or personalization (except for an introduction titled "Your Book" and a chapter called "Peoples of Our World").

Curriculum   The design does reflect a nice focusing on the world of two domain lenses: the lens of the geographer and the lens of the historian. One way to understand the world is to look at the different historical sequences occurring in different regions of the world at approximately the same time. The book is divided according to major geographic regions and offers an historical account of each. As we have already noted, geographers propose an important causal link between the physical characteristics of a region and the social system that people who live in the region develop over time. At the whole-book level, we see little evidence of this causal model. Historians propose repetitive patterns as civilizations rise, become established, and fall. The design does reflect this pattern in the unit on Rome. It is not obvious in the other five units.

Instruction   How well would this book support the CORE model? We have already noted that the design does not explicitly connect with the knowledge and understandings of the typical sixth-grader. It does organize information about a vast time period by dividing the historical sequence according to geographic areas. A branching tree organization can support students' group work almost as well as a matrix. Different members of a group could each become "an expert" on one of the four branches in the tree and share their

Text Structure

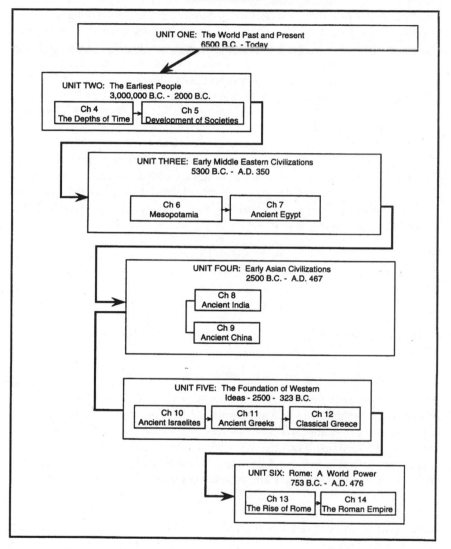

Figure 5.8 The rhetorical pattern for *Houghton Mifflin Social Studies/A Message of Ancient Days* (Houghton Mifflin, 1991a).

knowledge with other members of their group. However, the subsequences may very well be too extensive (spanning at least several hundred years) to be handled in this way. Unlike a matrix, the branching tree design does not in and of itself support either reflection or extension. The design exhibits no recurring patterns cutting across subsequences at the unit or chapter level that students could use either to reflect or to extend beyond what the textbook has to offer. Suppose, instead, that the sequence for each civilization started with its rise, chronicled its heyday, and ended with its fall, and that the titles of chapters and lessons clearly marked this pattern. Youngsters could reflect on and identify the pattern. They could extend their new understanding to a variety of cycles, including life cycles. While the savvy teacher could superimpose this design on the text (the raw material is already there), the text design itself does not support either reflection or extension.

A second sequential TOC, *Legacy of Freedom Volume I: United States History Through Reconstruction*, written for eighth-graders, is pictured in figure 5.9. It is accompanied by our analysis in figure 5.10. If you want to practice finding and evaluating the design of a textbook linked sequentially, draw the design and answer the questions that we introduced for the descriptive TOC before you look at our analysis:

- How comprehensible is the design? Does it use a pattern with strong linkages? Does it connect with reader knowledge? Does it appear interesting?
- How well does the design reflect the lens of an established knowledge domain?
- How well would the design support the CORE instructional model?

Extending the Approach to Units and Chapters

The same approach to describing and evaluating TOCs can also be used to describe and evaluate the design of units and chapters by relying on titles, headings, and subheadings. Textbooks typically divide units into chapters and chapters into sections. The chapters within a unit and the sections within a chapter are linked somehow. Likewise, the approach can be employed with entire series of books by combining tables of contents. Entire series are divided into textbook materials for each grade level, linked according to a pattern. The same analytic lenses can be focused as easily at large blocks of text within a book, or upon the entire series of books, as they can be directed toward an individual textbook.

Examples 5 and 6: Descriptive Sections

As important as the comprehensibility, curriculum, and instruction of larger amounts of text are, youngsters typically encounter a textbook as a succession of paragraphs, sentences, and words. Well-designed books, units, and chapters

Figure 5.9   The table of contents for *Legacy of Freedom Volume I: United States History Through Reconstruction* (Linden, Brink, and Huntington, 1986).

Table of Contents

Figure 5.9 contd.

Chapter 8   The American Revolution
The Early Battles
Political and Financial Problems
Winning Independence
Fruits of Victory

Chapter 9   Creating a New Government
Problems Facing the New Nation
Drafting the Constitution
The Ratification of the Constitution

Chapter 10   Constitutional Analysis
Federalism
Separation of Powers
Elasticity and Flexibility
Ensuring Individual Rights

Chapter 11   The Federalist Era
Making the Constitution Work
Maintaining Neutrality
Federalists vs. Republicans

Chapter 12   The Republicans Assume Control
The Election of Jefferson
The Nation Grows Under the Republicans
Foreign-Policy Challenges
The War of 1812

UNIT THREE   THE AMERICAN NATION EXPANDS: 1815-1850

Chapter 13   The Growing Nation
A Spirit of Nationalism
Economic and Social Developments
Westward Expansion and the Growth of Sectionalism
Politics in the Growing Nation

Chapter 14   The Jackson Period
A Period of Change
Jacksonian Politics
New Political Alliances after Jackson

Chapter 15   Expansion to the Pacific
Moving West
Annexing New Territories
More Land from Mexico

Chapter 16   Different Societies in the North and in the South
The Land and People of the North
The Land and People of the South

Figure 5.9 contd.

will lose much of their power if textbook sections are poorly designed. Finding the design in a succession of paragraphs can be somewhat harder than finding the design suggested by titles, headings, and subheadings in a larger chunk of text. The design in a passage is often opaque without the help of headings. Fortunately, the analytic lenses that we used to describe and evaluate tables of contents can be used to highlight the design of a passage.

We begin with "Reptiles," presented in figure 5.11. Incidentally, you will note ellipses in this and subsequent figures. We have used them to replace references to pictures or maps in the original textbook materials that we have not included in our versions.

As with larger amounts of text, we scan any titles and subtitles to identify the author's design. We also focus on introductions, conclusions, and topic sentences, functional devices that authors use to help the reader identify and remember the design of a text. The passage title, "Reptiles," with accompanying question suggests a descriptive, informational text. Sure enough, the

Text Structure

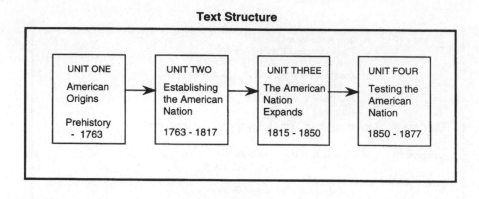

Text Analysis

COMPREHENSIBILITY
The pattern is a linear string with events linked by time only. Such a design does not have particularly strong linkages. Fortunately, the book has only four units, a number that eighth-graders should be able to keep easily in mind. It does not connect obviously with reader knowledge. It also does not appear particularly interesting, lacking absolute interest to eighth-graders, vivid vocabulary, and personalization.

CURRICULUM
The pattern reflects the historian's lens, matching units to accepted historical time periods in United States history. We see no evidence of important historical causal principals or models, however.

INSTRUCTION
This book offers little support for the CORE model. The design does not connect explicitly with reader knowledge. It is organized according to the passage of time. We see no obviously repeating patterns crossing the design. It would not support group work, student reflection, or student extension.

Figure 5.10   The rhetorical pattern and brief analysis for *Legacy of Freedom Volume I: United States History Through Reconstruction* (Linden, Brink, & Huntington, 1986).

opening introductory paragraph provides information about the defining characteristics of reptiles and foreshadows the design of the section. The closing paragraph ends with the characteristics of turtles. To verify our original hunch, we read the rest of the passage. Our reading shows paragraphs to present

REPTILES

What Are the Main Characteristics of Reptiles?

A **reptile** is a cold-blooded vertebrate that has lungs and dry skin. Almost all reptiles have scales. Most reptiles live on land and lay eggs. Some give birth to live young. The eggs of reptiles are laid on land. These eggs have a tough covering that prevents the eggs from drying out on land.

There are four main groups of reptiles. These are the alligators and crocodiles, the snakes, the lizards, and the turtles.

Alligators and crocodiles make up one group of reptiles. They are large four-legged reptiles. They look alike, but their color and the shape of their snouts help to tell them apart. Crocodiles are green and gray, while alligators are gray and black. Crocodiles have a more slender and pointed snout than do alligators. . . .

Snakes make up the largest group of reptiles. They do not have legs, and their bodies are covered with thin scales. Snakes can be large or they can be small. The anaconda, from South America, can be more than 9 m long. The thread snake is only about 12 cm long.

Snakes have an interesting way of eating. They swallow their food whole. . . . Most of the things snakes eat are larger than their mouths. When a snake eats an animal larger than its mouth, the snake's lower jaw separates from the upper jaw. This allows the snake's mouth to open very wide. Also, the snake's teeth are curved backward. This makes it hard for an animal to escape from the snake's jaws.

Another group of reptiles is the lizards. There are many different kinds of lizards. Many live in deserts and other hot, dry areas. Lizards have claws on their toes. . . . The body of a lizard is covered with scales.

The chameleon is one of the most interesting lizards. Chameleons live in trees and catch insects for food. They can change color. These lizards can change from brown to green to gray. . . . These changes help these animals to blend in with their surroundings. How can this be helpful?

Turtles make up the last group of reptiles. The body of a turtle is protected by a shell. When in danger, a turtle pulls its legs and head into its shell. How does this help it to survive? . . . Box turtles can close their shells very tightly. Some turtles live on land. Others spend most of their time in water.

Figure 5.11 "Reptiles: What are the main characteristics of reptiles?" (Mallinson et al., 1985b).

attributes that signal a description rather than a sequence. We decide that the passage is a description.

We use figure 5.3 to fine-tune our decision. Paragraphs 1–4 suggest to us that the text does not consider the same set of characteristics for each subtopic. The same paragraphs do suggest hierarchical linkages. The superordinate category, reptiles, subsumes four subordinate groups. Each of these subgroups subsumes individual types. As we begin to sketch the design, we notice a problem. We cannot directly map paragraph divisions on to the hierarchy. The third

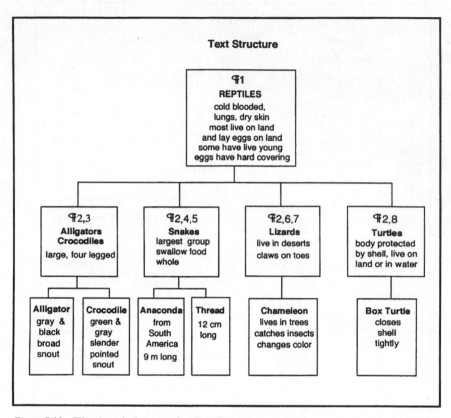

Figure 5.12   The rhetorical pattern for "Reptiles: What are the main characteristics of reptiles?" (Mallinson, et al., 1985b).

paragraph describes alligators and crocodiles as a group (surely this group must have one label...) and then distinguishes between them. The fourth paragraph also combines characteristics shared by all snakes and distinguishes individual types. Paragraph 5 returns to snakes as a group. The last paragraph begins by characterizing all turtles, inserts the example of box turtles, and returns to more general characteristics. Only paragraphs 6 and 7 match the hierarchical pattern. We have indicated this problem by identifying the paragraph numbers for major elements of the hierarchy (figure 5.12). We ask: To what extent has the design for "Reptiles" been guided by effective comprehension, curricular, and instructional themes?

Design comprehensibility   You may recall from our account in chapter 2 that comprehensible exposition has well-designed introductions and conclusions that connect to reader background knowledge and summarize the entire passage. Paragraphs are organized around explicit topic sentences. Hence a comprehensible passage will not only be well organized, connected to reader knowledge, and interesting, but it also will have well-functioning introductions, conclusions, transitions, and paragraph topic sentences.

The picture suggests coherent linkages, but a problem with design elements. The design links the description according to relationships of super- and subordination. The author gives the reader some help in parsing the design. The second paragraph introduces it. Paragraph topic sentences signal its parts. However, the paragraphs (the elements) do not consistently divide the text according to the hierarchy. And the pattern is incomplete, since the passage only offers one example each for lizards and turtles. Note that the passage has an introduction, but lacks a conclusion that recapitulates the design. We do not see any content in the design that connects explicitly with reader knowledge and experience, although we suspect that children already know more about reptiles than they do about some other animal groups, such as crustaceans. The topic itself, as well as most of the vocabulary, should be at least somewhat familiar. Nonetheless, we would be happier if the opening paragraph properly served its function and connected with knowledge that youngsters typically have about reptiles. The design does demonstrate interest-enhancing features. The topic itself probably is intrinsically interesting to many fourth-graders. Two of the examples – how snakes eat and how chameleons change color – may further heighten reader interest.

Curriculum   The design reflects the biologist's lens in part, since biologists typically categorize living organisms hierarchically. It does not, however, highlight the principles that underlie this categorization. How does a biologist decide that a type of animal belongs in this category and not another? What do crocodiles and alligators, snakes, lizards, and turtles have in common that they end up in the same superordinate category rather than another? What characteristics distinguish them one from another? Alligators and crocodiles are described according to color, snout size, and number of legs; snakes according to absence of legs, scale size, eating behavior, and jaw and teeth configuration; lizards by the presence of toe claws, scales, and camouflage ability; and turtles by body shells and protective behavior. While these features distinguish them one from another, the distinctions appear somewhat capricious rather than principled. If each of the categories had been described according to features that are important to biologists, such as physical configuration, habitat, and behavioral manifestations, the design would have better matched the lens of the biologist.

Instruction   Consider how well the passage would support the CORE model. While the design does not explicitly connect with reader knowledge, youngsters should already have some background knowledge about the topic. Instruction could quite easily make the connections that are missing in the actual passage. The design does organize descriptive information about reptiles (albeit with the problems that we have already mentioned). Because the design reflects an important organizational pattern in the larger domain, youngsters could reflect about this pattern. If the same categorization principles had cut across the categories, however, students' reflection on how a biologist views the world could have been enhanced. This design could also support groups of children extending the lesson. The passage sets up the hierarchy but actually offers very few examples. Groups of children, one per reptile group, could turn to trade books and encyclopedias to learn more about each category and add to the number of examples. Of course, every extension costs time. Alternatively, the textbook passage that offers many examples efficiently provides children with the content that they need – all in one place – to construct their own understandings about the taxonomic relationships among animals, a savings in time. However, the children's involvement with the material would be less. Teachers who are aware of differences in passage design are in a good position to align their instruction with the characteristics of the particular passage they choose.

A second descriptive passage, "Major Land Regions," written for sixth-graders, is pictured in figure 5.13, accompanied by our brief analysis in figure 5.14. As with the TOC designs, if you want to practice finding and evaluating the design of a passage linked descriptively, draw the design and determine its comprehensibility, curricular, and instructional characteristics before you look at our analysis.

Examples 7 and 8: Sequential Sections

"The Wonders of a Feather" in figure 5.15 comes from a trade book written for elementary school youngsters rather than a textbook. Even though the title has a descriptive flavor, the opening paragraph, particularly the sentence chronicling the development of bird feathers, suggests a sequence, as does the concluding paragraph. Reading the rest of the passage, we note that paragraphs present events in the life cycle of the feather rather than feather attributes – an informational, sequential design.

As we work through the sequential characteristics in figure 5.3, we find no parallel sequences. We do note several cause–effect linkages. True feathers push and shove the down out. Veins and arteries develop to bring food to feathers and cause them to grow. Veins and arteries dry up to cause feathers to

MAJOR   LAND   REGIONS

Despite its small size, Europe has a wide variety of land forms ranging from low plains to high, rugged mountains. The continent of Europe is divided into four main land regions... .

In the north is a rocky, hilly region known as the Northwest Highlands. It covers most of Iceland, the British Isles, Norway, and Sweden.

In this rolling country, there is little good soil for growing crops. Instead, the fields are used as pasture for the hardy sheep and cattle that graze there.

The people of this region get much of their food from the sea. Many of these people make their living catching or processing fish. Since early times, people from the Northwest Highlands have been known as great sailors.

South of the Northwest Highlands is the largest single region of Europe, the Central Lowlands. It stretches from the Atlantic Coast all the way to the Soviet Union. This region consists of a series of plains fitting between the upland areas. In some places in the western part, the plains are about 80 kilometers (50 miles) wide. In the eastern part, the plains widen to over 1,930 kilometers (1,200 miles).

In this region, farming is good because much of the land is flat and the soil fertile. The plains of the Central Lowlands are a checkerboard of cultivated fields. People here grow many different kinds of crops, such as rye, potatoes, and sugar beets.

No other region in Europe has more rivers and canals than the Central Lowlands. Ships and barges carry goods on these waterways from the interior areas to the seacoast... . The Rhine [River] is the busiest waterway in western Europe.

A third land region, the Central Uplands, includes Portugal and most of Spain and central Europe. This is the heart of Europe. It is a region of forests, valleys, hills, plateaus, and low mountains. There are some lowland areas. The hillsides are formed of ancient rock and are rich in minerals. Europe's important coal fields are found here.

The land formations in the Central Uplands have an effect on the way of life in this region. Where the land is not too steep or rocky, people have small farms. In the hills, they raise cattle and sheep.

The steepest of Europe's mountains belong to the Alpine Mountain System. This region stretches across southern Europe. The name comes from the mountain chain called the Alps. The Alps first curve northward and then eastward along the borders of Italy, France, Switzerland, West Germany, Austria, and into Yugoslavia. Other mountain ranges are also part of the Alpine Mountain System. The Pyrenees, for instance, lie on the border of France and Spain.

Streams flow swiftly down the slopes of these mountains. Many of these streams are used for hydroelectric power. In the mountain valleys, grapevines and olive trees are grown. In the coastal areas between the mountains and the Mediterranean Sea, many people earn their living from fishing.

Figure 5.13 "Major Land Regions" (Canjemi, 1987, pp. 132–3).

Figure 5.14   The rhetorical pattern and brief analysis for "Major Land Regions" (Canjemi, 1987, pp. 132–3).

Text Structure

	Location	Landforms	Relation of Landforms to How People Make a Living	Relation of Waterways to How People Make a Living
Northwest Highlands	¶2 Iceland, British Isles Norway Sweden	¶3 Rocky Hilly	¶3 Little good soil for crops. Raise sheep and cattle	¶4 Catch and process fish
Central Lowlands	¶5 Atlantic Coast to Soviet Union	¶5 Series of Plains	¶6 Flat fertile soil good for farming Grow rye, potatoes, and sugar beets	¶7 Ship goods on many canals and rivers
Central Uplands	¶8 Portugal, Spain, Central Europe	¶8 Forests, valleys, hills, plateaus, low mountains, rich in minerals and coal	¶9 Farm where land is not steep and rocky. Cattle and sheep in hills.	
Alpine Mountain System	¶10 Across Southern Europe, borders of Italy, France, Switzerland, West Germany,Austria, Yugoslavia, Spain	¶10 Mountains	¶11 Grapevines and olive trees grown in mountain valleys	¶11 Produce hydro-electric power on swiftly moving streams. Fish in the sea at base of mountains.

Text Analysis

COMPREHENSIBILITY

The pattern is a matrix. Each of four regions of Europe is described according to four categories.   Unfortunately, these elements do not always match paragraph divisions. For example, "Location" and "Landforms" are combined into one paragraph throughout.   This pattern has strong linkages.   It is almost complete--all but one cell is filled. The passage begins with an introduction that foreshadows the design, but does not connect with reader knowledge. Paragraphs typically start with topic sentences that also serve as transitions. The design has no conclusion. Throughout, the design does not connect with reader knowledge. Also it does not appear particularly inter-esting, lacking absolute interest to sixth-graders, vivid vocabulary, and personalization.

Figure 5.14 contd.

CURRICULUM
The pattern reflects the geographer's lens, matching paragraphs to geographically defined regions in Europe and categories of characteristics used by geographers to describe an area: location, landforms and their effects on how people make a living, and waterways and their effects on how people make a living. An important geography model -- the social institutions (how people make a living) are affected by conditions in the environment--cuts across the design, even though it is only hinted at in the beginning of the ninth paragraph.

INSTRUCTION
This design does not connect with reader knowledge and experience. However, it supports the CORE model in almost every other respect. It organizes the description well. It also could support reflection and extension. Students could reflect both on categories to use to describe an area in the world, as well as the relationship in a region between the environment and how people live. They could extend the text by adding other categories (recreation for example) and researching them or by describing another region, such as their own community, by the same categories.

stop growing. Because of these causal linkages, we decide that the design is a falling domino and diagram it as in figure 5.16. We then evaluate the design's comprehensibility, and its curricular and instructional support.

Design comprehensibility   The design seems to us to have several features of comprehensible text. Many of the linkages are strong, adding causal relationships to the passage of time. Note that it is not unusual for a domino pattern to have some linkages that are not causal. This design is no exception. The paragraph divisions consistently match the design. Down develops in the first paragraph. True feathers develop, pushing the down out, in paragraph 2; true feathers grow thanks to nutrients brought to them by arteries in paragraph 3; and so on. The text also has an introduction that foreshadows the design and at least refers to the knowledge of most people. About half of the paragraphs begin with a topic sentence that subsumes the sequence in the paragraph (e.g., "But every feather still has a lot of growing to do.") In the remaining paragraphs, the first sentence serves as a transition while the topic sentence follows as the second sentence (e.g., "Meantime important changes are going on in those pits, as different sets of cells start making the true or contour feathers.") While we do not see content in the design that explicitly connects with youngsters' knowledge, surely all elementary school children have experience with birds and feathers. The basic topic is familiar, as, we judge, is most of the vocabulary.

THE WONDERS OF A FEATHER

The whole principle of bird camouflage depends upon the feathers. In fact, there is nothing more truly wonderful than the way a bird's feathers grow from tiny, tiny specks into some of the lightest, strongest and most beautiful objects in the world. Few people have the least idea how feathers do this, or how perfectly they serve the purposes for which they are intended.

Each feather starts in a very small pit or hollow in the inner layer of skin, fitted with a tiny artery and vein. Even before the young bird breaks out of its eggshell, a group of cells begins to grow toward the outside of the skin. When they reach it, they break through, separate, and harden into those shreds of fuzz that you see on most young birds as soon as they dry off after hatching.

This soft down is not like real feathers, but for a little while it works very well as a covering. Meantime important changes are going on in those pits, as different sets of cells start making the true "contour" feathers. Each of these will have a central quill of its own. Pretty soon the tips of these new baby feathers push out into the open air, shoving the shreds of down ahead of them. Each baby feather is rolled tight inside a sort of skin. This keeps the feather so thin and pointed that we call it a pinfeather.

When a young bird has been out of its shell for a week or so, nearly all its true feathers have appeared. Perhaps there are as many as three or four thousand of them in dozens of different sizes, shapes, and colors.

But every feather still has a lot of growing to do, and that requires a supply of food. This food is in the bird's blood, which is brought into the pit by that tiny vein and artery. As the feather gets longer and broader, the special artery and vein carrying the blood stay right with it. Gradually they reach out farther and farther within the protection of the strong center quill. In this way the food that the feather needs is always ready for use. Because food from the blood is at work every minute, the feather grows bigger and prettier.

Finally it is fully grown. But it can't keep on growing or it will become too big to fit the bird. So deep down in that little pit where the whole thing started, the artery and vein are sealed up. Then no more blood can get through. The feather stops growing and dies. But its quill stays stiff, springy, and tightly anchored in its socket down in the skin.

Months later, when the feather has become so worn that it loses some of its usefulness, it simply drops out. And immediately those same little cells in the underskin start making another one. The new feather may be a bit different from the one it replaces. This is because some changes in the feather's colors or markings usually take place when a bird grows up. Or changes may occur when the bird shifts from summer to winter plumage and back again the following spring.

Figure 5.15 "The Wonders of a Feather" (Lemon, 1955).

Text Structure

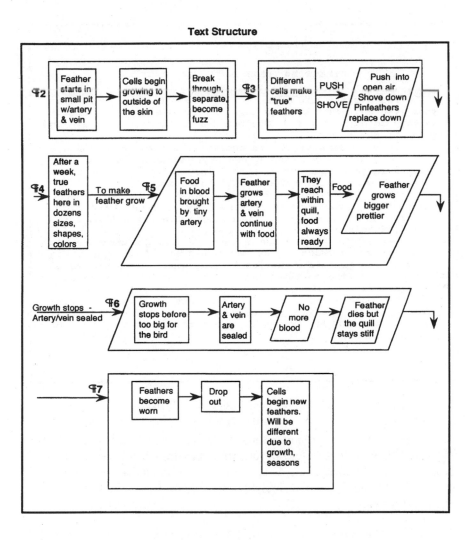

Figure 5.16   The rhetorical pattern for "The Wonders of a Feather" (Lemon, 1955).

We also note interest-enhancing features. The topic of bird feathers may have intrinsic interest to some children. The tone of the author is personalized as well, sprinkled with references to "you" and "we" and informal phrases such as "Pretty soon" and "where the whole thing started.' The author also conveys enthusiasm for the topic, choosing superlatives (e.g., "lightest," "strongest," "most beautiful objects in the world") and vivid vocabulary (e.g., "specks," "breaks," "shreds of fuzz," "tiny").

DIRECTING YOUR BODY TO MOVE

The alarm clock wakes you up in the morning. You open your eyes and reach over to turn off the alarm. This action is easy to do, isn't it? But how did you direct your arm to turn off the alarm?

In your ears are nerve endings. These nerve endings join together to make up a sensory neuron. The sensory neurons in your ears sense sound. They carry messages about the ringing sound from the ears to the brain.

When you open your eyes, your brain gets more information. The sensory neurons in your eyes sense light and also carry messages to the brain. The brain then forms a kind of "picture" of what you see.

The brain then sends a message along other nerves called motor neurons. The motor neurons from the brain carry a message to the muscles in your arm. The arm muscles contract, pulling on the bones in your arm. You reach over and turn off the alarm.

The muscle and skeletal systems are involved in moving the body. The nervous system coordinates these movements. In fact, the nervous system keeps all the parts of your body working together.

Figure 5.17 "Directing Your Body to Move" (Cooper et al., 1985a).

Curriculum   This falling domino design reflects an important biologist model. Individual living things follow a cycle: they start from a few cells, grow and develop, reach maturity, and drop out or die. But individuals are being continually replaced by new individuals, who or which may be at least somewhat different.

Instruction   Not surprisingly, because this design is comprehensible and reflects the lens of the biologist, we find that it would support the CORE model quite well. Even though the passage fails to *connect*, instruction could easily build on reader knowledge about and experience with feathers, making the connections that the passage misses. The design *organizes* the sequence well. Youngsters could *reflect* about the model in the passage and *extend* their thinking to other, analogous life cycles, such as their own hair or fingernails.

To give you practice in diagraming a sequential passage, "Directing Your Body to Move," written for fifth-graders, is pictured in figure 5.17. Our analysis is in figure 5.18.

This section has presented examples of TOCs and passages with basic building-block designs. We have used these examples to demonstrate tools for analyzing the comprehensibility, curricular, and instructional features of text-book materials. The examples as a whole are quite well-designed textbook materials. You will have noticed that we did not sort the examples into categories of "better" and "poorer"; nor did we reach a final judgment about the design of each. Instead, we characterized each example individually and pointed out its strengths and weaknesses. Typically, it is very difficult to compare the designs of passages that cover different content. As we will demonstrate in chapter 7, comparisons have the most validity when two or more examples are compared that cover essentially the same content.

Finding the Design of Arguments and Explanations

Most textbook passages are designed to be informational. However, authors may want to do more than present characteristics of an object or chronicle a sequence of events. They may wish to *argue* a claim or *explain* the underlying principles of a phenomenon. These two purposes add additional layers of structure.

Example 9: Argument

Before presenting example 9, we discuss the special features of written argument. Consider an argument from a second-grade text that claims, in the opening sentence, "Some animals change many times as they grow." The following sections present the evidence for the argument, which consists of two sequences: frogs changing from eggs to tadpoles to adult frogs, and insects changing from eggs to caterpillars to cocoons to adult moths or butterflies. The argument's claim and evidence are linked by a third argument part, which we are going to call the *warrant*, borrowing from a term used by the philosopher Stephen Toulmin.[12] Warrants are analogous to major premises in syllogisms and represent the underlying reasoning in the argument. For this argument the warrant is "Animals that change dramatically three or four times in their lives are indeed changing many times as they grow."

The warrant is probably the argument part that is least familiar to you. Toulmin first proposed the three argument parts and suggested the warrant as the logical glue that holds the claim and evidence together; the warrant is the *reason* why a reader should accept the claim given the particular evidence that has been offered.[13] Typically, readers must infer the warrant in an argument,

Text Structure

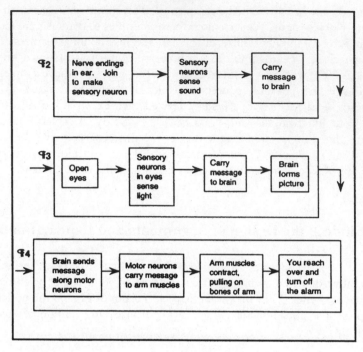

Text Analysis

```
COMPREHENSIBILITY
     The pattern is a linear string.  A linear string does not have
     particularly strong linkages, but at least there are only three
     major events, a number that fifth-graders should be able to keep
     in mind.  The passage begins with an introduction that connects
     with reader experience, but does not summarize the sequence to
     follow.  It ends with a conclusion that draws implications, but
     does not summrize the general sequence.  Paragraphs three and four
     have topic sentences, which also serve as transitions.  The design
     connects explicitly with reader knowledge while presenting a
     scientific model.  This sequence may have intrinsic interest for
     some fifth-graders.   Furthermore, the passage sprinkles
     personalization throughout.
CURRICULUM
     The design reflects the biologist's lens, chronicling an important
     model for one of the sequences that occurs when humans react to a
     stimulus.
INSTRUCTION
     This design connects with reader experience. It organizes the
     information according to an important domain model. Consequently,
     fifth-graders could reflect on how humans respond to various
     stimuli.   They could extend the example to other scenarios,
     tracing the path from sensory organs to the brain and back to the
     musculo/skeletal system.
```

Figure 5.18 The rhetorical pattern and brief analysis for "Directing Your Body to Move" (Cooper et al., 1985a).

ELECTRICITY: ENERGY FROM ENERGY

You have seen a number of ways to produce an electric current. In fact, by now it may very well seem as if we can make electricity out of thin air. Don't be fooled. You cannot get something from nothing. To produce electric energy, we must first have some other form of energy.

Think about when you scuffed your feet on the rug and made a spark of current electricity. Although you probably didn't realize it at the time, by rubbing your feet on the floor you were providing a form of energy--mechanical energy. If you didn't first rub your feet, there would be no spark. A similar thing happened when you moved a magnet through a coil of wire. You provided the mechanical energy by moving the magnet with your muscles. Without this mechanical energy, the magnet would not move and there would be no current.

The dry cell you used in your activities also produced an electric current. Again, the current did not simply appear. The energy from chemicals in the dry cell was converted into electric energy.

The same is true for the generators that produce most of our electric energy. At Hoover Dam, for example, the energy provided by moving water turned the turbine. The mechanical energy from the spinning turbine turned the electromagnets. Only then did an electric current flow. In each and every case, the only way you could obtain electric energy was to start with another form of energy.

Figure 5.19 "Electricity: Energy from Energy" (Cooper et al., 1985b).

because it is missing from the text entirely. Often, the warrant is so obvious that its presence in a passage seems needlessly redundant. Nonetheless, we urge you to consider the warrant when evaluating any argument design. While, of course, the calibre of the evidence can always be questioned (fact or opinion?), problems in arguments show up most clearly when the warrant is made explicit.

"Electricity: Energy from Energy," written for sixth-graders, is presented in figure 5.19. We initially scan the passage, focusing on the introductory and concluding paragraphs and the title. The introductory paragraph seems to link back to earlier passages in the chapter, to raise an issue that might occur to young readers, and to present a contradictory assertion, which sixth-graders may find counterintuitive: "To produce electric energy, we must first have some other form of energy." The concluding paragraph ends by linking the examples with the assertion.

Since the assertion is a generalization, we suspect that the passage may have an argument structure that offers support for it. Alerted to this possibility, we skim the rest of the passage, looking for any support. The design has three remaining paragraphs, each presenting one or two sequences that begin with one form of energy and end with electrical energy. These paragraphs seem to be presenting evidence for the assertion. We decide that the design is an argument and diagram it as in figure 5.20.

The electricity text actually concludes with a warrant-like statement. In our diagram of the design, we have turned the statement from the text into an if–then construction that highlights the logical linkages between the claim and evidence. While we would not necessarily recommend that warrants be added to the text, they are useful to the analysis, for they enable us to ask "Is the logical relationship valid?" What do you think? Is the claim justified? We think so.

As with informational texts, once we have chosen and diagrammed the overall design, we can evaluate its comprehensibility, curriculum, and instruction. Because arguments superimpose a claim/evidence/warrant relationship on the basic building-block designs, the linkages in the design should be strong and enhance student comprehension and learning. We conclude that the tight, consistent organization, well-formed introduction and conclusion, connections to reader background knowledge, and interest-enhancing personalization suggest a comprehensible text. The design reflects the physicist's model of conservation ("You can't get something from nothing") and has coherent patterns, which could support both student reflection and extension. We have chosen this passage because it demonstrates the power of text design principles. The passage makes a typically abstract notion understandable and usable for the sixth-grade reader.

Example 10: Explanation

Explanations have a different set of linkages.[14] Imagine an author who wants to explain to fifth-graders what causes differences in seasons. The author might begin "Many people think that it is hot in the summer because the earth is close to the sun and cold in the winter because the earth is farther away. Actually, in North America, the earth is closer to the sun in the winter than in the summer. Astronomers can show that the real difference is how directly the light waves from the sun hit different parts of the earth during different times of the year." This author is using the first of three structural features in an explanation. He or she is moving the reader from the understanding of a novice toward the understandings of the expert. An explanation fills gaps through the use of familiar examples, analogies, definitions, and statements juxtaposing novice and expert understandings. Next, the author might present the scientific

Text Structure

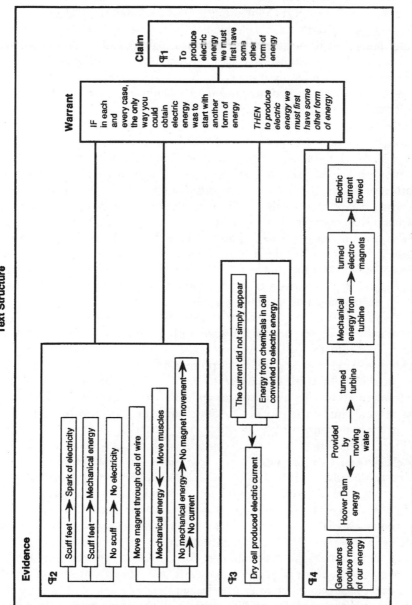

Figure 5.20 The rhetorical pattern for "Electricity: Energy from Energy" (Cooper et al., 1985b).

model, chronicling how the earth orbits the sun at an angle and how the light waves strike the earth at different parts of the orbit. He or she might follow the model by giving steps that children in the class could follow to act out the sun and the orbiting earth using a flashlight. By presenting three "subexplanations," the author demonstrates the second structural feature of explanations. Well-designed explanations have *tiers*.[15] Each tier is a subexplanation. The "seasons are not caused by distance from the sun" example is one tier, the scientific model is a second tier, and the flashlight demonstration is a third. Notice that the tiers in this explanation progress from general principles to specific examples. Logical order is the third structural feature of an explanation. Other possible logical orders are specific to general or question/answer chains, in which the author raises a question about a phenomenon (How does a thermos work?) and provides an answer (thermodynamics), that leads to another question (What is thermodynamics?) and answer (The scientific model involving groups of molecules).[16] The plate tectonics rewrite that we shared in chapter 3 is an example of an explanation.

The example that we have chosen, "How Heat Moves Through Solid Matter," is presented in figure 5.21. This passage is from a general science textbook written for fourth-graders. We skim the title and both opening and closing paragraphs, where we find indications of an explanation. The word "how," accompanied by questions that the text supposedly is answering, can signal an explanatory purpose. Furthermore, the section begins by referring to a common everyday experience and ends with a "scientific" depiction of heat energy. We read the passage to discover if it follows a logical progression, building on reader understanding to present underlying relationships. Since the passage begins with a concrete phenomenon that is familiar to young readers and ends with the details of an underlying scientific model that is abstract and unfamiliar, we decide that the section is an explanation and diagram it as in figure 5.22.

This design exhibits many strong comprehensibility, curricular, and instructional features. In many ways, it is a good example of explanatory text. It connects directly with student experience. The tiers of subexplanations, progressing from the concrete to the abstract and back to the concrete, add additional linkages to the design. Both personalization (lots of "you's") and a few vivid vocabulary words ('hit," "vibrate") add to its interest value. The text reflects an important sequential scientific model, a feature of strong curriculum design. And the design shows support for the CORE instructional model, connecting to student background knowledge, and partially organizing knowledge about heat transfer according to the sequential model.

However, the design also exhibits problems. Tiers of subexplanations follow a mishmash of patterns, from argument to informational; from description to sequence. The last explanatory tier, tier 4, raises the most concern. First, tier 4

HOW HEAT MOVES THROUGH SOLID MATTER
How does heat move through a solid?

Have your ever touched a metal spoon that has been in hot soup for a time? The handle of the spoon was probably hot. Heat moved from the soup to the spoon. How did this happen?

Suppose you could see the particles of matter in the spoon and in the soup. A spoon is a solid. Particles of matter in a solid vibrate or move back and forth. But the particles do not move around. Soup is a liquid. Particles of matter in a liquid are free both to vibrate and move around....

The particles of matter in the hot soup have a lot of energy. They are moving quickly. The particles in the spoon have less energy. They are vibrating slowly. Some particles of matter in the soup hit some particles of matter in the spoon. The particles in the spoon that were hit begin to vibrate faster. These particles hit other particles in the spoon, causing the other particles to vibrate faster. This keeps happening all along the handle of the spoon. The heat energy is being passed from particle to particle along the handle. The way heat energy moves through a solid is called **conduction.**

Heat energy does not move at the same speed through all kinds of matter. Heat energy cannot move easily through some materials. These materials are called good **insulators**. The particles that make up a good insulator are spaced far apart. . . .[P]izza box[es], pot holders, and home insulation. . .are made of good insulating materials. So is [a] thermos--it uses a layer of air to keep hot liquids hot and cold liquids cold. Particles of air are spaced far apart.

Heat energy can easily move through other materials. These materials are called good **conductors**. The particles that make up good conductors are close together. ...[P]ans and irons...are made of good conducting materials.

Figure 5.21   "How Heat Moves Through Solid Matter" (Mallinson et al., 1985a).

presents examples as descriptions rather than sequences. Second, the tier requires the reader to engage in reverse reasoning. The examples are described according to how far apart their "particles" are rather than by whether they change temperature quickly. The author offers the *model* as evidence, rather than the phenomenon. The design could be improved by presenting the *fact* that some materials change temperature faster than others to suggest the scientific model.

Text Structure

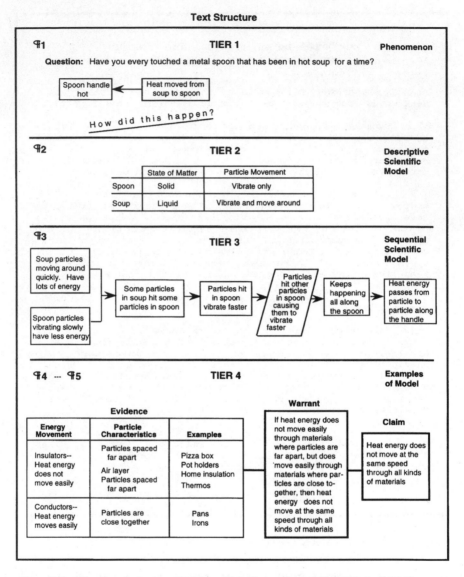

Figure 5.22   The rhetorical pattern for "How Heat Moves Through Solid Matter" (Mallinson et al., 1985a).

Suppose that the author chose, instead, a branching tree structure to chronicle the sequence of heat transfer through the four insulators and two conductors. The content would have a more consistent sequential organization that would match the scientific model and highlight patterns. Because the text structure would emphasize patterns, children would be able to reflect about the various causal relationships (e.g., "Why aren't all materials affected by heat the same way?"). They would be able to use the patterns to *extend* the model to other instances of heat transfer (e.g., "What would happen if you put a wooden spoon into the hot soup? How could you design a pot handle so that you wouldn't get burned?"). As they reflected and extended, youngsters would be using the lenses of the scientist. Rhetorical, curricular, and instructional themes would have consistently guided the elements and their linkages in the text.

Most textbook materials have informational designs. In some respects, this section on analyzing arguments and explanations is superfluous. However, we believe that designs structured as arguments and explanations have a greater potential than informational designs to be comprehensible, offer a strong curriculum, and support student-centered instruction.

The Versatility of the Lenses

In this chapter, we have presented a set of lenses for describing and then evaluating textbook materials of all lengths and sizes, from entire series to passages of several paragraphs. While the lenses lend themselves to analyses at many levels, the choice of how detailed an analysis to conduct is made by the analyst. Our examples have ranged from global considerations of tables of contents to detailed analyses of sentences within paragraphs within passages; from comprehensibility to instructional support. We suspect that some of our readers will be more comfortable with the global examples and others with the more detailed versions. Reading specialists have the expertise to analyze text comprehensibility; curriculum specialists have the knowledge to analyze curricular themes; and so on. While we have demonstrated complete analyses, the tools are meant to be applied to meet the needs of a particular analysis and the expertise of a particular analyst.

In the next part of this volume, we turn away from written text design to focus on the designers themselves – people who publish, adopt, and select textbooks. In chapter 6, we describe current practices of textbook publishers, state textbook adopters, and district textbook selectors. Chapter 7 reports our recommendations for redirecting each of these tasks. In both chapters, we rely heavily on the same principles of design that we have been developing thus far.

Notes

 1   Chall and Dale (1995) and Fry (1968).
 2   Lovitt, Horton and Bergerud (1987).
 3   Armbruster, Osborn and Davison (1985) and Davison and Kantor (1982).
 4   Armbruster, Osborn, and Davison (1985).
 5   Dole, Rogers, and Osborn (1989) and Farr and Tulley (1985).
 6   See, e.g., California Department of Education (1991).
 7   Farr and Tulley (1985).
 8   Idem.
 9   Tufte (1990).
10   Calfee and Chambliss (1987) and Chambliss and Calfee (1989).
11   Avelar La Salle (1991), Curley (1990) and Whittaker (1992).
12   Toulmin (1958).
13   Idem.
14   Chambliss (1993).
15   Wong (1991).
16   Idem.

Part II

WELL-DESIGNED TEXTBOOK PUBLISHING, STATE ADOPTION, AND DISTRICT SELECTION

6

CURRENT PRACTICES: PUBLISHERS, STATES, AND DISTRICTS

Who determines the textbooks that our children pack into their book bags and our teachers place on their laps or lecterns? The system is seemingly straight-forward. Adoption states and large urban districts set policy by deciding which series they will approve for purchase. Publishers design textbooks accordingly. Districts select the books and spend the money. Teachers integrate the books into their instruction. All important tasks are covered, from the establishment of goals by the policy-makers to eventual instruction of children.

Improving textbooks should be a straightforward matter as well. Policy-makers could insist that future textbooks be written with an explicit structure that links the separate parts to be comprehensible and reflects both a powerful curriculum and current wisdom about instructionally effective texts. Publishers would then design the books. Districts would purchase them. They would become pervasive in classrooms.

Why is the system not as successful as it could be? What happens at each level, from the design of a textbook to its selection for use in the classroom? In this chapter, we switch our perspective from the characteristics of textbooks to the system that produces instructional materials. To understand the dynamics of this complex system, we conducted interviews, attended meetings, read public documents, and scoured the research of others. We interviewed editors at major and small "niche" publishing houses, state employees responsible for state textbook adoption, and district curriculum specialists responsible for district selection. We attended meetings at several of the major textbook publishers, in meeting rooms as an adoption state opened up its adoption procedures to the public, and at district offices while district selection commit-tees completed their tasks. We read public documents describing state adoption in the two largest adoption states; we read curriculum frameworks and the many forms used by districts. We studied research conducted on textbook publishing,[1] state adoption,[2] and district selection.[3] In this chapter, we present our understanding of the current system for producing textbooks, in order to lay the groundwork for a contrasting scenario that we propose in chapter 7.

Understanding the Present by Looking at the Past

The current textbook system in the United States has evolved from decisions made by thoughtful people responding to significant problems. The history of textbook development is not haphazard, capricious, or corrupt. Some of the most talented educators and policy-makers of the past helped to shape the current system, influenced by a noble goal: to educate a large, diverse, and mobile school population. Both the goal and the problems are still with us. We begin our characterization of the present system by first summarizing the history of textbook development, adoption, and selection.

Developing Textbooks to Educate Everyone

Until the 1800s, the development of textbooks was not particularly systematic. School children were an elite group with educated parents, and textbooks – moralistic, alphabetic, and phonetic – were designed to teach them how to read. Because parents provided the books, there was no guarantee that all children in a classroom would have the same book. In fact, diversity of books and age levels typically marked the early American classroom. Despite this diversity, parents, children, and teachers shared a common background. Children used the books their parents had used, and most people valued both the moralistic content and the instructional approach.[4]

Textbook design began to evolve into a serious enterprise with the introduction of universal elementary education in the mid-1800s. Large numbers of children came to school whose parents did not know how to read and did not necessarily share or appreciate the traditional content. Teachers could no longer manage large classrooms of students whose backgrounds as well as ages diverged greatly. Schools responded by dividing the students into grade levels. Textbooks evolved into graded textbook systems to be used uniformly in the large classrooms.[5] The content became far more inclusive, based on various disciplines rather than shared morals.[6] Workbooks and teacher editions evolved to give teachers help in educating the diverse school population.[7] Educators developed readability formulas to determine the difficulty level of textbook materials, so that teachers could match the reading abilities of their students with the difficulty levels of textbook materials.[8]

Throughout most of its early history, textbook development was the province of educators from major universities. The first of the national publishing companies located close to large university centers such as Boston and Cambridge, New York, and Chicago. During these early days, university scholars dominated the development of textbook materials. Gradually, however, this academic monopoly diminished. University scholars were replaced by practicing teachers, and publishing companies moved throughout the country. During the latter half of the twentieth century, textbook design has continued to be the province of textbook publishers, although large, powerful states and organized citizen groups have increasingly exerted planned pressure on publishers.[9]

Adopting Textbooks for Everyone

While publishers were developing textbook series to be used nationally, many state governments began to legislate free textbooks for all students and adoption procedures for controlling what those textbooks would be. In the late nineteenth century, family mobility was high. With every move, parents were forced to buy new textbooks, because different districts used different books. To save parents money and to provide books for children whose parents could not afford to buy them, states responded by providing free textbooks and adopting books to be used uniformly across a state. In 1882, Massachusetts became the first state to require all districts to provide free textbooks for all students. Other states quickly responded. In addition, by 1915, almost half of the states controlled textbook selection to at least some extent.[10]

States began to adopt textbooks to address administrative concerns; besides uniformity, they wanted to keep textbook costs down. A state is in a much better bargaining position than a district to demand lower prices of publishers. More recently, some of the largest adoption states have also used textbook adoption to attempt to improve the quality of textbooks.[11]

Selecting Textbooks for Everyone

Even before states formally entered the picture, the need for uniform selection within districts was apparent. As early as 1847, the State of New York Superintendent wrote in *The Statutes of New York Relating to Common Schools* that one of the "greatest evils to afflict [the] schools was the great variety of textbooks in use." He explained that teachers were required to divide students into as many classes as there were kinds of books.[12]

To match textbooks with student characteristics, educators developed systematic selection procedures. According to Lee Cronbach, a prominent educational psychologist, measurement was king: "The textbook was judged by a score card not unlike the card used in selecting a prize cow. Certain characteristics of the text were singled out for inspection, scoring weights were assigned on each characteristic, and the summary score was used to decide whether the text should be adopted," he explained.[13] Today, the most conscientious districts take pains to develop systematic measurement procedures.

Nonetheless, The Problems Remain

Whether the focus is on changes in textbook publishing, adoption, or selection, the situation looks the same. Over the decades, changes have been made, but they have not solved the problems, and have sometimes even caused new, unanticipated problems. Critics decry the gargantuan, hefty, all-inclusive textbooks, incoherent because of their adherence to readability formulas;[14] the mindless workbook exercises that fail to promote "higher order thinking skills";[15] and the overloaded teacher manuals that replace the teacher's professional judgment.[16] They fault adoption states for sending publishers detailed and conflicting directives that make it impossible to design a worthy product.[17] They cite districts for selecting textbooks by using invalid, unreliable measures and for failing to report their selection criteria back to textbook publishers in a useable form.[18]

While keenly aware of the problems, we are less pessimistic than many other critics. The size of the entire enterprise is one facet of the problem. Multiple voices all singing a different tune is a second facet. The lack of a coherent strategy leading to complexity of mind-boggling proportions is a third facet. Nonetheless, when we studied people at work, we saw many tasks that were well-designed, along with those that were less well-conceived. In the next section, we analyze current publishing, adoption, and selection practices, in order to identify those practices on which a more effective system could be built.

Present-Day Publishing, Adoption, and Selection

In the United States, school textbooks today are produced by textbook publishers, adopted by 22 adoption states, and selected by individual school districts around the country. Publishers strive to turn out quality products while satisfying as many states, districts, and classroom teachers as possible to remain a profitable enterprise. States, districts, and classroom teachers purchase materials that they believe will best match their needs. The stakes are high. Millions of dollars are spent. Thousands of people work at the various tasks. Children across the country know what they know, think what they think, and value what they value in some measure because of the textbooks they use. As these children become adults, the materials from which they learned will affect what they know, think, and value well into the twenty-first century.

To understand the complex system that brings textbooks onto the market, we applied a task model to characterize how publishers produce, states adopt, and districts select textbooks. According to the model, all participants establish

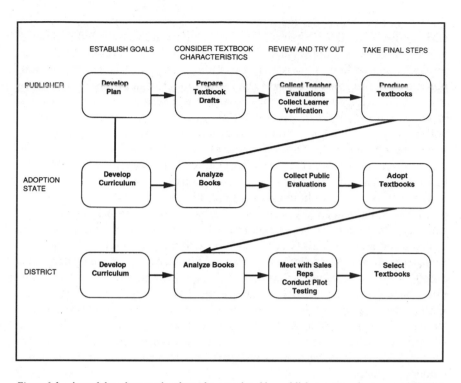

ESTABLISH GOALS   CONSIDER TEXTBOOK   REVIEW AND TRY OUT   TAKE FINAL STEPS
                      CHARACTERISTICS

PUBLISHER

| Develop Plan | Prepare Textbook Drafts | Collect Teacher Evaluations Collect Learner Verification | Produce Textbooks |

ADOPTION STATE

| Develop Curriculum | Analyze Books | Collect Public Evaluations | Adopt Textbooks |

DISTRICT

| Develop Curriculum | Analyze Books | Meet with Sales Reps Conduct Pilot Testing | Select Textbooks |

Figure 6.1   A model to characterize the tasks completed by publishers, state adopters, and district selectors.

goals, consider textbook characteristics, review and try out textbook materials, and take final steps (see figure 6.1). To establish goals, states and districts prepare statements that specify curricular objectives, instructional tasks, and comprehensibility features that will characterize whatever materials they buy. (We have already described one example: the Calfornia History–Social Science Framework published in the late 1980s.) Publishers survey these state and district documents, review educational research, and interview both classroom teachers and administrators to formulate their own goals. Publishers gather together editors, authors (who plan the overall characteristics of a textbook series), writers (who prepare first drafts), consultants (who advise on curricular, instructional, and comprehensibility issues), and graphic artists to produce textbook series with particular characteristics. States and districts analyze these characteristics. All three collectives bring in outside experts to review textbooks, and some of them try out textbook materials in classrooms. As a final step, publishers produce textbooks, state committees decide which ones to adopt for potential district selection, and districts buy them.

Applying the model has led us to important general conclusions about the entire process. First, participants currently demonstrate a sincere willingness to improve textbooks. Publishers seek out opportunities to develop new, better products. One editor told us that her publishing house looked upon new literature requirements from California as a wonderful opportunity to experiment. Adoption states turn to subject matter and pedagogical experts for their input. The three largest adoption states have revamped their adoption process within the past few years to become more systematic, more curriculum based, and more representative of diverse student backgrounds and interests.[19] School districts send representatives to seminars on textbook selection and work with university researchers to improve their procedures.

Within this general willingness to change, strong constraints bind each of the participants. Publishing is a business and must please its primary customers – teachers – to remain viable. One publishing executive described the challenge as first designing materials to get them "through the gate" erected by the state or district and then slanting the materials to the teacher. "If teachers don't like a new design, we can't afford to make it," explained another executive. "We must be able to excite teachers before we have a crack at the students. Unfortunately, what excites the teachers may not be the best text for the students," he added. States and districts have other constraints. The choices of adopters and selectors can only be as good as the available products, no matter how skilled they may become in recognizing a textbook that would support student learning.

In addition, voices for change are diverse and divisive. The market shouts loudly, but the message that it speaks is typically muddled. States issue directives that frequently are at odds with one another. Some states toss out readability formulas; others require them. Some states insist on a strong treatment of evolution; others want it downplayed. Academic voices are also discordant. "Teach [or "Don't teach . . ."] reading skills." "Tell the reader the theme" – or "Leave it up to the reader to figure it out." "Use narrative to carry the message as often as possible" – or "Use well-written exposition so that young readers will learn to comprehend it." "The well-designed textbook has yet to be fully exploited" – or "Toss out textbooks altogether and substitute with hands-on activities, trade books, and original sources." Voices from the public are no clearer: "Include information on the dangers of unprotected sex" – or "Leave children's sex education up to their parents."

The entire process is so large as to be unmanageable. States and districts often produce scores of goal statements, too many for adopters, selectors, and publishers to keep in mind. This number expands rapidly as each adoption state or influential district adds to the national list. Publishers struggle to hold on to this unmanageable collection of goals across the one hundred or so people working on a series and the thousands of pages comprising series that span several grade levels. Individual states and districts wrestle with the task of finding textbooks that match all of the goals. Often, they are comparing several textbook series, each of which, stacked on the floor, could reach a height of at least three feet. How can they tell whether all of these books meet their curricular, instructional, and comprehensibility goals? How can they analyze them, how can reviewers critique them, and how can classrooms try them out? Lacking a systematic approach, adopters and selectors settle either for a cursory skim or for a detailed examination that can take as much as two years and produce enormous amounts of information that are impossible to synthesize. Whether the look is cursory or detailed, districts find themselves setting aside their formal analysis and deciding "intuitively." And so, because the system lacks a careful design, textbooks indeed change, but do not necessarily improve.

It is not immediately obvious who can best lead the system out of this quagmire. In many important ways, major publishers are the only participants who are in a position to understand and influence the national market. Their nationwide view is implemented by a trained professional staff with the knowledge and wherewithal to implement and "sell" new ideas. Because publishers are running a business, however, their impact is blunted. Rather than leading, they typically follow marketplace trends.

Currently, some state governments have taken on the challenge to improve textbooks. We have already described California's efforts in social studies and the impact of the California framework on subsequent textbook design. However, the concerns of states are local rather than national, and each has its own notion of the changes to be made.

Clearly, publishers, adopters, and selectors must work together to bring about improvement. And, in some cases, we see the beginnings of such influence and cooperation. Typically, however, the hard work of each of these collectives falls short, failing to bring about the changes called for by the many critics.

Within these general trends, we identified two opposing stances as we watched publishers, states, and districts complete their tasks. In the *Responder* stance, those responsible for textbook materials primarily respond to outside influences. This stance is the one most often criticized and least likely to lead to improvement. *Designers*, on the other hand, act customarily according to their own design decisions. They, too, are likely to be criticized by those who disagree with their design. Furthermore, the overall effects of their work are blunted because the system as a whole lacks a design. Nonetheless, we propose that only Designers, whether they be publishers, adopters, or selectors, will be able to bring improvements to school textbooks. We contrast the two stances as a basis for recommendations in the remaining chapters of this book.

Admittedly, this dichotomy is simplistic. At times, any of the groups that we studied assumed one stance or the other. However, we found that we could distinguish among particular tasks by whether publishers, states, and districts were responding or designing.

Responding to Outside Pressures

Publishers, adopters, and selectors who took the stance of a Responder based their own work on someone else's decisions, needs, or effort. Publishers developed their products to match the requirements of curriculum frameworks and the results from market research; states and districts depended on publishers to produce good books. If Responders did play an active role, it was based on practical goals: what would sell; what would save money; what would last; what looked inviting. And they either produced or looked for textbooks that met these goals.

Producing textbooks   Textbook publishers were in the business of producing textbooks that would sell. For Responders, each major task was strongly influenced by the results of market research. Outside voices from focus groups, teachers who have tried out the materials, and sales representatives influenced the final product substantially. Unfortunately, because these voices often spoke mixed messages, the various publishing tasks were frequently disconnected from one another, and the final product suffered. Editors had no effective response if focus groups wanted to scuttle something that the editors knew was good instruction or writing. When talking with us, editors who were Responders tended to be apologetic about their product rather than proud. They explained the shortcomings by describing negative teacher reactions to textbook features that were subsequently scrapped even though the editorial staff had suggested them for sound curricular, instructional, or comprehensibility reasons.

Through input from sales representatives and consultants, teacher focus groups, teacher surveys, and classroom observations, Responders began to get a feel for the market and to establish goals for a new series. One science editor described how she and her staff, planning to revise a middle-school science series, sent a survey to teachers who had used the program. The survey asked the teachers to evaluate whether they liked the order of the chapters and the content covered in the chapters, whether the computer aids accompanying the program were helpful, and whether the program included a sufficient number of laboratory exercises. The editor was not able to describe the direct influence of this survey on the new series, but she did tell us confidently that the goal for the new series had been to produce a textbook that teachers would like. She argued forcefully that the role of a textbook publisher is to meet the needs of teachers, not to take any leadership in establishing other goals.

Goals in hand, publishers began to produce the textbook series. First, all publishers hired authors who were experts in the curriculum. At times, authors were responsible for initial drafts of each book. Responders had little initial influence over these authors, who often worked virtually independently on the first draft of the first edition. Two authors with whom we talked drafted their own outlines and crafted their own texts without *any* prior specifications from the publishers. One of these authors explained that he dealt with the text only, and that all chapter beginnings, headings, and so on were provided by the publisher after he submitted his drafts. However, once an author had submitted the first draft, the influence of editors (and the results of sales projections) could be substantial, without any input from the author. "I had to keep fighting to have my book on the western hemisphere remain according to my vision," complained one author. "With the first edition, there were 54 changes even when the text was already in galley form, because the publisher had heard from several sales representatives that content in the draft was too politically sensitive. With the second edition, the editor completely rearranged the units. I had designed the opening unit on how a geographer views the world to set the stage for the entire book. Instead this unit was boxed off as a thinking skill, 'Thinking Like a Geographer.' The integrity of the entire book was compromised. The book lost its overview and consequently the glue that I had designed to hold the separate pieces together." The publisher was a Responder, trying to reconcile the voice of the author with the voice of several sales representatives. And because publishing is a business, the representatives had the greater influence.

Responders also tended to turn over major parts of the production to outside firms that employed freelance writers. Often, authors would outline what each book was to cover, but writers from outside firms would prepare some of the text, or produce teacher manuals and other ancillary materials. And, as with authors, Responders provided very little initial guidance to the outside firm, becoming dissatisfied only if subsequent market feedback suggested a problem. The staffs from the publishers and the outside firms lacked a common set of curricular, instructional, and comprehensibility goals and had little contact one with another. Not surprisingly, critics have noted that textbook materials can have a piecemeal flavor that is reflective of having been developed by diverse groups, working independently. In these books, some chapters were better written than others; some activities in workbooks matched the text, while others had no obvious connection.

Once Responders had drafts to share, they began to solicit *reviews* on their developing product. They sent out national surveys, asking teachers to give their opinions on various features of the package. Teachers were asked to evaluate page formats, to order a listing of possible topics, or to decide whether the package should be in a notebook or in file boxes. The same kinds of questions were asked in focus group meetings of 15–20 teachers.

Teacher opinions had a potent effect on the product developed by Responders. One editor provided a particularly telling example. Her staff was considering beginning a life science textbook with a unit on human biology. The unit would use humans to exemplify topics covered later in the book. The publishing staff reasoned that such a unit should capture the students' interest and enhance their understanding, because it covers topics close to home and of concern to middle schoolers. However, life science textbooks have historically ended with a unit on human biology. In focus groups, teachers reacted negatively. Their courses were organized to end the year with human biology, they explained. They would not buy a book that *began* the year the way they customarily *ended* it. The staff decided to drop their idea after teachers reacted so negatively to the new ordering. "Placing human biology first would have been a disaster," the editor explained. And so the human biology unit was placed at the end of the book; the editorial staff made no effort to change the teachers' minds, even though beginning the year with a unit that connects with student knowledge and interests makes good instructional sense.

Publishers produced basal reading series somewhat differently from books in science and social studies but, for Responders, the decisions were as likely to be based on market research. Much of the content came from preexisting children's literature. It was not written anew for the series. A major task was to choose which pieces of literature to include in the series and at what grade level. Executive editors told us that the in-house staff, which included editors and children's librarians who were highly familiar with children's literature, compiled a corpus of titles to which the company owned the rights. One editor described gathering thousands of selections, both narrative and expository. Next, the staff submitted the selections to extensive review with children's librarians, teachers, and samples of students. The staff placed those selections with the most votes into their textbooks.

Editors told us that feedback from sales representatives influenced product development throughout the process. One editor described a scenario in which district sales managers had pushed for eight last-minute changes in the design of a reading series. The editor in charge did agree to five of the eight, although she worried about making changes with so little forethought.

James Squire, an eloquent and knowledgeable spokesperson for the publishing industry, summed up the role of review and try out in publishing. He explained that publishers who continue to publish successfully make extensive use of impartially chosen teacher focus groups to check their ideas against teacher perceptions: "If too many of today's textbooks seem overly traditional or overly similar in content, quite possibly this is what teachers in America say they want," he concluded.[20]

The *final task* for Responders was to use input from review and try out to redesign and produce a product. Because Responders had been collecting input from the market as they completed their tasks, this final step actually occurred along the way rather than as the final task. Where it had the most obvious impact, however, was on the production of new editions. By the time authors were preparing a second edition, publishers had large amounts of feedback from teachers on the first edition, either through formal surveys or comments passed on by sales representatives. Two authors of social studies books told the same story. With the first edition, they had been given a free hand in writing an original draft. Before they began to rewrite the second edition, they were sent large binders filled with detailed changes that they were to make. Both of them were so discouraged at the number of unconnected details with which they had to contend that they refused to write a third edition.

When publishers responded to the many forces from without, their products suffered as a result. If various constituents – state adopters, district selectors, classroom teachers, university researchers, and so on – had designed their requirements with greater care, publishers could have directed their considerable resources toward producing well-designed textbook materials that nonetheless would sell.

Textbook adoption   Only a handful of the 50 states have a major impact on textbook publishing – and this impact is substantial. The majority of the states actually have very little impact on the characteristics of textbooks. Twenty-eight states choose not to adopt textbooks. Many of the 22 adoption states have created only a minimal system for textbook selection. We have classified all of these states as Responders. Critics have often pointed a strong finger at the negative effect of textbook adoption, arguing that if states would only bow out and leave textbook choice up to districts or classroom teachers, many of the strongest constraints on publishers would be lifted. They argue that publishers would have been able to develop much more effective products if they had not had to please so many different audiences.[21] This argument champions Responder states. However, we are not completely convinced that states should bow out of the work to improve textbooks, and we will rejoin the argument when we consider states as Designers.

Responders who adopted textbooks articulated with a broad brush curriculum, social, and practical *goals*, with the intent of screening out only books that failed to fit the broad standards. They deliberately chose requirements that were inclusive, to leave districts as many options as possible in making their own choices.

When they considered textbook characteristics or reviewed and tried them out, Responders aimed to screen the many textbooks that met the goals from the few that did not. For example, in one of these states, the committee in charge set up sites at which textbook publishers could display their series.

Announcements in local newspapers and professional association newsletters encouraged school administrators, teachers, university researchers, and lay citizens to come to the sites. These field evaluators completed a standard evaluation form, the only analysis or review conducted in the state. The books that passed the evaluation were placed on the adoption list as books that the state would contribute money toward buying. Public review could have a strong influence on which books Responders chose. *Education Week* reported that, "The state textbook advisory committees in Georgia and North Carolina have recommended against the adoption of a widely used reading-textbook series that has been the target of attacks by parents and conservative groups across the country."[22] Public review had a strong impact in these two Responder states.

Other Responder states requested *try outs*, called "learner verification," to show that children indeed benefit from the publisher's materials. However, the publishers themselves, not the states, designed the try out, from establishing goals, describing measurable learning objectives, and developing assessment items for the objectives, to conducting recursive rounds of data collection and revision. Most adoption states did not consider the results in their final decision. Those that did used learner verification to screen books. They excluded those from publishers who failed to complete learner verification according to state requirements but made no use of the actual outcomes.

The textbooks for Responder states resulted from the work and influence of others: the three or so influential adoption states, large districts, and textbook publishers themselves. A good example was the effect of the adoption in the late 1980s of the California History–Social Science Framework, which we described in an earlier chapter. The California framework carved up history/social science from fifth grade on differently than it had been parsed in the past. *Education Week* predicted shortly after the adoption that because California had been able to influence publishers to produce books with particular characteristics, children all over the country would be using textbooks dictated by California's standards.[23] And, we propose, this effect would be particularly true in Responder states.

District selection   Districts buy textbooks. Their buying patterns can influence publishers substantially. Indeed, editors-in-chief from major textbook companies have told us that if no more than 10 per cent of districts nation-wide were to request a particular feature, publishers would produce textbooks with that feature. While we suspect that some of the districts within that 10 per cent would need to be large districts, the point remains that district decisions are potentially very powerful. Responder districts relinquished their power. Similar to Responder states, they relied heavily on the work of others to determine the characteristics of the textbooks among which to choose.

Responder districts did not officially *establish goals* for selecting textbooks. If they were in adoption states, Responders often accepted state goals wholecloth. Other Responders relied on the expertise of different textbook publishers, concluding that the "experts" hired by the publishers knew more than they did about curriculum, instruction, and comprehensible writing. In neither case did Responders consider whether the state or publisher goals matched student characteristics, curricular standards, or instructional practices in their district. And some Responders left as many of the selection tasks as possible in the hands of their curriculum coordinator, including establishing goals. We talked with the science curriculum coordinator for a district, appointed to direct the selection of an elementary school science series. The coordinator explained that he had formulated the selection goals. The coordinator communicated the goals, he thought, to the members of his district selection committee, but he admitted to us that they were never written down and never approved by either the superintendent or the school board. Consequently, the members of his committee proceeded as if the goals had never been formulated. If this coordinator were ever to conduct a district selection again, he said he would be sure to have philosophies and goals put in writing and approved by the district board of education.

To *analyze* the characteristics of the candidate textbooks, Responders relied heavily on their initial impressions. Publishers signaled the content and organization of their books in the table of contents. They included letters to teachers at the beginning of teacher manuals to describe special features of their materials. They included eye-catching multi-colored graphs and pictures. Those who have studied district selectors at work even have a term to describe the most superficial of the intuitive analyses – "the thumbing test." Researchers have reported watching district selectors flipping rapidly through books as they "analyzed" a stack of textbook series. When asked what she was looking for, one answered "I just know I take this book . . . and I do this [flips pages] . . . if those pages are too busy, I set that down for a while." Another explained, "I guess just to see if it appeals to me, or you know, if I would be interested in it."[24]

Even when Responders used a checklist to rate textbook materials, the analysis was impressionistic. Farr and Tulley reviewed 70 criteria checklists, and found that most checklists encouraged a cursory examination of text materials, emphasizing the presence rather than the quality of a characteristic.[25]

We watched a group of classroom teachers rate basal readers according to a checklist developed by the reading coordinator in the district. The coordinator had chosen these teachers because they all had tried out one of the basal readers in their classrooms. They were to complete the checklist on the basal reader they had piloted. The teachers had never seen the checklist before they arrived, and the coordinator gave them no training in how to use it. The checklist asked the teachers to determine whether a particular feature (e.g., unabridged literature) was present and then to assess the book's "correlation with the [California] framework." Teachers were concerned. Almost all of them were unfamiliar with the framework, other than what they had heard about it "here and there." The coordinator reassured them that because the features listed on the checklist were based on the framework, if they found many examples in the book of a particular feature, the correlation would be high. Subsequently, teachers completed the checklist according to how the publisher had labeled text selections and activities rather than what a careful analysis would reveal. Teachers, working in pairs, would say to one another comments such as "Here is a summarizing activity," or "This book has journal writing," because the textbook labels identified the activities as such. One pair became bogged down on the first checklist item, which listed different types of genre that were presented in the framework as important for children to read (e.g., fairy tales, ethnic folk tales, biographies, and so on). These teachers spent 20 minutes trying to define each type of genre and then find an exemplar of it. They never got to the other items, but put the checklist aside and discussed problems at their respective schools.

Responders who did *try out* textbook materials in classrooms did so very informally. They were reluctant to constrain teachers who were using the materials, explaining that they did not want to influence teachers' reactions unduly. Indeed, teachers may have felt free to do whatever they wished with the textbooks, but the result was often too chaotic to affect the selection decision. One district coordinator admitted to us that she did not know exactly who had tried out the materials or whether all of the series had been piloted. When it came time to gather information from teachers, she did not know who to invite to the feedback session, inadvertently failing to contact eight of the teachers. We attended a working session of the coordinator and six teachers who each had piloted a textbook. Not all of the series were represented, and of those that were, several grade levels were missing. The group did not discuss the books systematically, and by the end of the four-hour session had reached no conclusions. Subsequently, their work had no influence on the final selection.

To *review* textbook series, Responders turned to publishers' sales representatives, asking them to attend meetings at which they highlighted distinctive features of their books. Sales representatives came to these sessions carefully prepared, pointing out features in their series, reading testimonials from satisfied teachers, showing pictures of teachers and students working together, and so on. Responders were reluctant to place any constraints on either teachers or sales representatives. Consequently, they made sure that teachers and district administrators who attended the meetings were free to ask the representatives whatever they wished. The questions that they asked sales representatives from different publishers differed markedly, making direct comparisons across series difficult if not impossible. Furthermore, because sales representatives were biased reviewers, the answers to the questions did not provide objective, informative data. While it was difficult for us to determine which of the tasks that they completed influenced the final decision for Responder districts, textbook sales representatives assumed that their presentations had an impact. They certainly participated willingly.

The final step for Responders was to *select* the books to buy. This final step was often completed by the district school board, although superintendents, principals at each school, or individual teachers also made the decision at times. Even if checklists had been completed, even if the series had been reviewed and tried out, Responders made this final selection intuitively. They described getting a "sense" of which would be the best textbooks for their district and making a recommendation to the school board. At times, the superintendent, teacher groups, or citizen groups disagreed with the recommendation. At such times, the school board responded to the recommendations coming from these different sources, and made a final decision. Because districts that were Responders were so heavily influenced by the work of others – their state, publishers, and individuals – they were far more likely to support the status quo than to push toward change. And they were far more likely to be dissatisfied with their choice. "Most of the books have never been removed from their shrinkwrap. Despite all our hard work, the final choice did not match either the curriculum or the instruction in our schools," explained the science coordinator who we described earlier. "And, now we have spent so much money on these books that the next time science adoption comes around, we won't be able to afford to replace them."

Publishers responded to states, districts, and teachers. States responded to what the publishers provided. Districts and teachers responded to states and publishers. And while Responders might have brought changes to textbooks – while textbooks might not always look exactly the same – Responders did not improve them substantially either.

Building from a Vision

Designers completed their tasks quite differently. Whether designers were publishers, adoption states, or district selection committees, they established explicit goals, based on the latest scholarship in curriculum and instruction. Designers articulated the goals clearly. They communicated the goals to everyone involved in the production, adoption, or selection of textbooks. They attempted to conduct analyses and make decisions based on the goals. Publishers established and articulated goals, subsequently producing textbook materials according to the goals. States established goals that they communicated to textbook publishers early on, so that publishers could produce books that matched the goals. Subsequently, they analyzed how well textbook materials met the goals and adopted only those that indeed matched. Districts likewise established goals and analyzed whether textbook materials met them.

Despite establishing goals early on and using them to produce, adopt, or select textbook materials, no publisher, adoption state, or district that we studied completed all of the tasks according to the initial goals. As we describe what we have found, we explain why publishers, states, and districts seemed to have so much trouble assuming a designer stance throughout. The enormity of the enterprise, from conceiving a textbook series to placing it in the hands of children and teachers, almost guarantees that the initial design will be lost along the way.

Producing textbooks   No less than for Responders, Designers who produce textbooks must design a product that will sell. The goals for Designers, however, came from their knowledge of scholarship in both curriculum and instruction, and in comprehensibility to a lesser extent. The goals for Responders came primarily from market research.

To articulate *goals*, Designers educated themselves in current theory. "We take care to know the latest research. For example, we know the curriculum guidelines in Math developed by the National Council of Teachers of Mathematics and the National Science Teachers Association," explained one executive editor. A reading editor listed goals for a recently marketed basal reading series that reflected current theory on how best to develop youngsters' literacy: "First, children are to learn to read by reading. Second, activities, wherever possible, are to be enjoyable to children. We also had three additional subgoals: lots of variety in literature selections, more student interaction and responsibility than in the past, and a heavier reliance on having students write." Another executive editor explained that he had insisted that his firm set as a goal in all subject areas the design of *comprehensible* text. He described being heavily influenced by research in the characteristics of comprehensible writing and by criticisms that textbook writing often is not comprehensible.

Based on what they had learned, an editor–author team articulated goals early on. The editor in charge of the series gathered together all participants, from the executives to the sales force, and educated them in the goals. One executive editor explained that this approach requires a *dream* (articulated goals) and a *team* (an educated staff dedicated to the dream).

After the goals had been articulated, editors, authors, writers, selected sales representatives, and consultants came together to *establish the design* for a textbook series. "We start with everything we want to see in the series and place it within a scope and sequence," explained an executive editor describing the design of a science series:

At this point we decide what should be taught at each grade level based on a combination of what is specified by state frameworks and our knowledge of what children at a particular age can comprehend. As we assign content to a level, we create the table of contents for each book. This process is carried out at the in-house level since we are the ones who have studied the total situation. Publishers try to build through the strands in a scope and sequence some spiralling, so topics are returned to at each grade level, each topic building on what was presented earlier. Spiralling is one way to handle all the topics required by the various state frameworks. Finally, we draft an outline or a concept map for each chapter.

Incidentally, this executive editor, with his explicit goal to design comprehensible text, was the only editor who described using concept maps not unlike our graphical patterns to plan the content and structure of textbook prose. Otherwise, his comments typify content areas such as science and social studies. We attended the meetings of a comparable group who were also working on the initial planning of a science series – and our experience matched his account.

For Designer publishers, the editorial staff closely supervised the authors and writers who were responsible for turning the outlines into prose. Authors and writers were given a template to follow, which provided a common format across the series. The same people responsible for writing the student print also produced the student activities at the end of textbook units and chapters, and any accompanying student workbooks, teacher manuals, assessment packages, and other ancillary materials. Not all Designers, to be sure, use in-house staff to prepare drafts. We met with two executive editors, one from the textbook publisher and one from an outside firm responsible for drafting the series. They and their staffs had worked closely throughout, jointly developing goals and overseeing the materials that were produced. The story that they told us differed dramatically from how Responders relate to outside firms.

Finally, editors sent draft materials out to subject-matter and reading specialists for *review* to ensure that authors and writers had remained true to the original goals. For example, the executive editor with the strong interest in comprehensible text sent all of the drafts in his K–6 science series to Bonnie Armbruster, a leading researcher in textbook comprehensibility. She described to us creating her own concept maps of every chapter to test whether the chapter had structural coherence and fulfilled the original comprehensibility goals. On the basis of her maps, she suggested changes, most of which the editor made.

Designers are in an excellent position to bring about substantial improvement in textbook materials. We analyzed this science series before we knew anything about the steps involved in its design. Our analysis revealed fourth-through fifth-grade textbooks that were coherent at the level of the table of contents but, even more strikingly, had well-structured units and chapters within units. Concept mapping, similar to the design graphics that we have introduced in earlier chapters, seems to hold great promise for improving textbook design.

However, because textbook publishing is a business, any leadership assumed by publishers must at least overlap the goals of states, districts, and teachers. Executive editors ruefully admitted to us that they each have one magnificent failure in their past – a textbook series guided by important curricular, instructional, and comprehensibility goals that failed because not enough school districts bought it. The editors explained that magnificent failures deviate too markedly from the goals of the marketplace.

Textbook adoption   Responder states accepted whatever textbooks publishers offered. If they did adopt textbooks, they screened the few that did not meet their broad, practical, goals from the many that did. In contrast, Designer states played an active role, attempting to improve education in their states by requiring publishers to change textbook materials. Designers specified a detailed curriculum, developed a system closely matched to the curriculum to analyze the books, trained evaluators to recognize the curriculum in textbook series, and accepted only materials that met the curricular goals. These states were in an excellent position to improve textbook materials when the state goals had been carefully designed and communicated clearly: the analysis was both true to the goals and manageable, and the final adoption procedures were closely based on the analysis.

We do not believe that state adoption is *ipso facto* an obstacle to well-designed textbooks. States have access to excellent expertise and resources and are not under market constraints. The state that carefully considered how to integrate curricular, instructional, and comprehensibility themes, and how such an integration would look in textbook materials, could bring market support to publishers developing such a design. Consequently, we propose that adoption states could have an important role to play in any major improvements to textbooks.

The Designer states that we studied established curricular, instructional, and comprehensibility *goals*, which were publicly approved and distributed to all interested publishers. These goals were developed by experts in curriculum and instruction to reflect the latest curricular and instructional scholarship. In contrast to the goals established by Responders, Designer goals were intended to influence textbook development rather than screen out a few textbooks that failed to meet broadly defined standards.

For example, social studies textbooks until relatively recently focused on Western civilizations and their impact on the United States. Current approaches to curriculum have greatly broadened the focus to the impact on the USA of civilizations around the world. This change in curriculum is related to the move toward child-centered instruction. To be child-centered, textbook content must connect with the histories of the children in American class-rooms, who come from every major cultural group on earth, and many of the smaller ones as well. Accordingly, one Designer state required that students reading sixth-grade textbooks learn about people and events "that ushered in the dawn of major Western and non-Western civiliations." Textbooks were to include " . . . the early societies of the Near East and Africa, the ancient Hebrew civilization, Greece, Rome, and the classical civilizations of India and of China."[26] Each of these civilizations was to be considered according to "the major contributions, achievements, and belief systems that have endured across the centuries to the present day." Another Designer state stipulated that textbooks for seventh-graders include " . . . the role of and contributions of notable individuals and groups representative of the racial, ethnic, religious, and cultural backgrounds in the exploration, colonization, and development of [the state]."[27]

These states were unwilling to leave important curricular and instructional goals up to what they considered to be the whims of the textbook market. Furthermore, note that each of these goal statements hinted at a design that could organize an entire book: perhaps a matrix for the first set of goals that would consider each of seven civilizations according to three types of influences and a parallel branching tree for the second set of goals to treat the history of several groups that differed racially, ethnically, religiously, or culturally as they explored, colonized, and contributed to the development of the state. To be sure, we have superimposed our design rubrics on these goal statements, but nonetheless, it occurs to us that a publisher could have exploited the relationships implied by these states and designed a textbook with curricular integrity.

Besides curriculum goals, Designer states also established instructional and comprehensibility goals. One of these states included subsections in its curriculum frameworks to specify writing guidelines, organizational goals, and standards for teachers' manuals and reference materials. For example, one of these subsections explained that, among other features, instructional materials should provide "A format for printed materials that incorporates research relative to the features that best promote reading comprehension, learning, and retention."[28] Another Designer state has included a subsection in its proclamations that specifies goals for instructional strategies. One of these subsections lists eight goals. For example, textbooks shall " . . . include lessons and activities that are designed to have students work individually and cooperatively in small and large groups."[29]

Unfortunately, these instructional and comprehensibility goals failed even to hint at what design a publisher might develop, an evaluator might reward, or the state might adopt. Which "research" did the first state have in mind? What, exactly, did the second state understand the relationships to be between particular kinds of lessons and activities and individual versus cooperative work in small or large groups? This second set of goal statements appears to us to have been too broad, too vague, to influence more than superficially the instruction provided in textbooks or the characteristics of the prose.

To *analyze* textbook characteristics, Designer states appointed committees that turned the goal statements into analysis instruments, applied the instruments, and summarized the results. Classroom teachers, librarians, curriculum specialists, and scholars in the content area – all representative of the state's ethnic make-up – served on the committees. In one of these states, staff members from the state's Department of Education trained committee members to complete detailed evaluation forms. During the training, the evaluators studied the state's goal statements and practiced completing the form. This form directed the evaluators to compare textbook characteristics with a set of criterion descriptors that specified the features of a close, moderate, or poor match with the state's goal statement. The evaluation form was closely tied to the goal statements and, for some items, repeated them verbatim. During training, committee members learned to rate each item, to quote examples that supported the rating, to weight each item for importance, and to sum individual scores for a grand total.

Following the training, committee members spent three months completing the analysis for a subset of the textbooks submitted by publishers for state adoption. They began by reviewing the tables of contents, to gain a general sense of the parts of the instructional program for different grades. Next, they were asked to read carefully both the students' materials and the teachers' materials (a gargantuan task) and complete the evaluation form. After three months, the committee reconvened into grade-level panels to arrive at a recommendation. They compared scores, reached consensus, and drafted a written description of each of their analyses. The state's board of education, who would make the ultimate decisions, had established a minimum score below which a book would be automatically eliminated from contention. The different panels of evaluators used this cut-off to recommend to the board whether to adopt each textbook that they had analyzed.

Unfortunately, as closely as this Designer state linked its goals to the analysis, the state's *review* of potential textbooks was no different than the review completed by Responder states. Perhaps because review was so poorly designed, it had only minimal impact on the final decisions (although in this state, public review has overridden committee analyses in the past).

We attended the public review sessions held before two official state committees that made the final adoption decisions. Public interest was high. The meetings were packed, with every seat taken and overflow crowds lining the aisles. Each speaker had only two minutes to comment, there were over 100 speakers, and speakers appeared according to the order of the original sign-up sheet. Furthermore, each speaker was supposed to add something new. The chair interrupted and reprimanded any speaker who repeated a comment made earlier. Several times, the proceedings became unruly, with speakers refusing to leave the microphone when their two minutes had passed, or audience members calling out loudly to attempt to be heard over the comments of the current speaker. Indeed, twice the chair of the board of education had to threaten to call in marshals to clear the room, because participants at the public review were becoming too belligerent.

This environment virtually guaranteed that comments would be random one from another and that speakers would address narrow, specific issues. And, indeed, most speakers mentioned specifics: the wording on page 69 in the fifth-grade textbook, the pictures on page 350 in the seventh-grade textbook, and so on. Speakers' comments tended to center around particular wording and graphics that they believed unfavorably distorted the history of the ethnic or religious group to which they belonged. The committees responded by directing the textbook publishers to replace the wording or redo the graphics accordingly.

States that otherwise are Designers virtually ignored *try out* tasks. In fact, they seemed far more wary of pilot data than of public review. Most states did not consider data from classroom try outs, and those few that did ignored the results when making a decision. For example, one of the major Designers considered any try outs conducted by publishers as field testing and allowed the data to be reported early on to the state's Department of Education as "additional information." Committee members could ask to see the results, but pilot data were not to be considered when recommending particular materials to the state's board of education and, consequently, were to have no effect on the ultimate adoption decision. An official with the Department of Education admitted to us that he distrusted piloting and would not recommend that it become a part of the state adoption process.

The problems that all states had with review and try out concern us. Review by the loudest and most persistent, rather than the most knowledgeable, insightful citizens may have held undue sway. By failing to look systematically at whether teachers indeed could use particular textbooks to help students learn, know, understand, and be able to do what the state originally had in mind, Designers had no check on their analysis. We do not understand why Designer states, with their abundant resources, have steered clear of conducting impartial try out of materials.

In Designer states, the results of textbook analysis did affect the *final adoption*. The people in charge of the analysis gathered together their data and recommended to the state's board of education that the state adopt some of the many books submitted by publishers. If districts chose from this list of books, the state would provide money to buy the books. When the sequence worked as it should, the board accepted the recommendations and adopted books accordingly. And when the written recommendations described how each book either did or did not meet the state's goals, both districts selecting books to buy and publishers planning future editions had useful information. Designers consequently affected the quality of both current as well as future textbooks.

Even when textbooks adopted in Designer states clearly reflected the state's goals, these textbooks could still have serious design shortcomings, as we demonstrated in chapter 4. Unfortunately, while Designer states indeed created a design that guided most of the adoption tasks, the design usually was not well-conceived. It may have had too many elements – we counted 83 separate goal statements for one major Designer and 72 separate goals for another. Most of these elements were not strongly or tidily linked – the curricular, instructional, and comprehensibility goals that we described earlier in this section either had no obvious linkages or only the hint of some possiblilities. And no strong curricular, instructional, and comprehensibility themes guided the design. (If there had been obvious themes, the designs would have had neither too many elements nor nonexistent linkages.) These poorly conceived designs failed to provide publishers with the road map that would have led to better textbooks. Furthermore, problems that the states had with review and try out – two tasks that might have demonstrated whether the textbooks indeed met the goals – may well have sprung at least in part from problems with the original designs. We turn to these issues in greater detail in the following chapter, suggesting specific design lenses that states (and districts) can use both to create a well-crafted design, and to make use of it as they analyze, review, try out, and adopt textbooks to support student learning.

Textbook selection Designer districts have the power to change textbooks substantially, if they are large enough or if a number of districts begin to look for similar textbook characteristics. Across the country, districts are the collectives that spend the money. And some of those districts follow a thoughtful, thorough approach to textbook selection, looking for materials that can carry their curriculum, support their instruction, and be comprehensible to their students.

The Designer districts that we studied tended to perceive the ideal textbook series as one that would carry their curriculum, and appointed a curriculum coordinator to oversee the selection tasks. They established *goals* by articulating a new district curriculum statement. The statement grew out of months of prior study and discussion, led by the curriculum coordinator. One district committee in a nonadoption state met for *two years* of in-service training in the latest curricular and instructional theories and held discussions with members of the community, publisher representatives, educators, and university researchers. After the two years, the committee prepared a philosophy of reading, defined statements of purposes for reading instruction, and constructed the reading outcomes for a pre-K to 12 reading program. Two other districts in a major Designer state completed comparable tasks in half the time. Because they could rely on work completed by the state, they were able to establish their goals more quickly.

To *analyze* whether textbooks "match" the district's goals, someone in the district prepared a textbook checklist that was closely linked to the district's goal statements. One of the Designer districts that we studied had developed as goal statements a list of standards for each grade level. The kindergarten oral language standards, for example, included "Children will be able to (1) identify and use suitable words based on context cues; (2) gather information from oral reports; and (3) listen and make judgments." The checklist instructed evaluators to indicate on a scale of 1 (poor) to 4 (outstanding) how they felt the publisher addressed each of the standards for this grade level. The checklist for this district also included sections on textbook design features. Part II of the checklist directed evaluators to rate the format and design of the teacher's edition and the student text: "Size of print [in the teacher's manual] same as students' [text] or at least readable without magnification . . . . [Teacher's manual] clear and to the point regarding procedures for lessons and pacing . . . . [Student text] durable . . . . [Student text has] high quality selections . . . ," and so on.

Designers trained evaluators to apply the checklist. Two of the district coordinators whom we interviewed described the training that they provided. The reading specialist in one of the districts assembled a committee chosen to represent each school site, personnel working for categorical programs, parents throughout the district, and community members. Then she trained them in the evaluation process, using a training program developed the preceding spring for the state adoption panels. This training included both instruction in how to recognize reading materials that matched the state framework as well as training in group dynamics that would help group members come to consensus. Members also practiced on one section of the checklist until they produced reliable ratings across reviewers.

Designers converted checklist ratings into numerical summaries and included them with more qualitative "impressions." Once committee members completed the checklists, the district coordinator added the ratings and averaged across raters for each publisher at every grade level. The coordinator then ranked the books from different publishers according to the average ratings. Coordinators at this point reconvened the trained selection committees to make a nonnumerical evaluation called "coming to consensus." Typically, the committee divided into subcommittees according to grade level. Subcommittee members studied the numerical scores, expressed their own impressions, and "reached consensus" on a small number of series for pilot testing.

We share a concern with others who have looked at district selection about how even Designer districts conducted a textbook analysis, although we may frame our concern differently.[30] The initial goals did not clearly guide the development or use of their checklists. First, the checklist items used by the Designers that we studied were either trivially specific (e.g., "Size of print [in teacher's manual] same as students [text] or at least readable without magnification.") or globally vague (e.g., "Develops a variety of comprehension strategies for different reading materials and purposes," or "Has high quality selections.") Second, these districts had no workable system for grappling with the task of evaluating the design of an enormous mound of materials: student textbooks, teacher manuals, and ancillary materials for series from several publishers, and sometimes for several grade levels, a problem for state adoption as well. Finally, all Designer districts tended to convert the separate analyses to numbers, compute an average, and arrive at a final score. Unless a total score is close to either perfect or zero, it is essentially worthless for distinguishing textbook designs in a meaningful manner. One has no idea which combination of individual scores has produced totals in the mid-range without going back to look at the original ratings. Perhaps, given these problems, it is not surprising that committee members tended to rely on their impressions rather than the scores from checklists, despite the time that they had put into the rating task.

No Designer district conducted *review and try out* designed to discover whether textbooks differed in how well children using them learned what the district hoped they would learn, even though one coordinator told us "The feedback from piloting teachers was the most valuable data we collected." Designer districts *did* try to control for teacher bias, which they described to us as the tendency of teachers to fall in love with whatever they pilot. For example, each piloting teacher in one district tried out books from three publishers, one chapter from each book. And Designers also developed systems to be sure that all books would be piloted at every grade level in schools with student characteristics representative of the entire district. Eighty-one teachers in a large, urban district pilot tested nine basal reading series, for example.

However, the actual try out stage for all districts was free-form. Once teachers received the materials, they used them however they wished, and typically figured out for themselves how to evaluate the success of the try out. Any instructions for teachers tended either to be minimal or inadequate. One district coordinator advised teachers to look for "useability in the classroom." Another district had publisher consultants provide their standard training for teachers. No district designed instructions for teachers that related specifically to the original goals or developed teacher and student assessment to determine whether the goals had been reached.

After the pilot period was over, teachers gave feedback to the selection committee. They completed written questionnaires, were interviewed by committee members, or came together in a group to reach consensus on the outcome.

The success of review and try out is dependent on how well districts follow standards of effective evaluation: representative sampling, well-conceived measures, and steps to ensure validity and reliability. The districts that we studied, both Designers and Responders, had trouble with all three. Those who tried to be representative often had overwhelmingly enormous sample sizes. Those who abandoned the attempt had biased results. Measures focused solely on teacher reactions rather than student outcomes. Finally, training teachers would help to ensure validity and reliability, but no district trained teachers specifically to conduct try outs.

To *select* a textbook, the selection committee members of Designer districts gathered the information they had collected, came to consensus, and made a final choice. The committee presented its recommendation to an official group, either the board of education or the district management team. This official group made the final decision on the basis of the committee's recommendation.

The process of coming to consensus ranged from taking a democratic vote to getting together to discuss the various series informally. The curriculum coordinator from one district described her experiences in detail. Most of the other districts that we studied selected basal textbooks comparably. On what she described as a "final day," members of the selection committee gathered at her house to choose one series from among the five that had been piloted. First, some of the pilot teachers met with the selection committee to share teacher reactions to each series. Following these presentations, the coordinator gave committee members a matrix that summarized the average checklist scores assigned to each item for each publisher. She also gave them 57 pages of comments that she had compiled from both members of the selection committee and piloting teachers. According to the coordinator, committee members discussed the matrix and comments (although to us the task sounds overwhelming). They studied the reviews published by the state. Wherever discrepancies between raters appeared, committee members looked through the books in question. Members also shared their own perceptions of the materials and any reactions that they had heard at their school sites.

By early afternoon, the coordinator called for a secret ballot vote among the five series. The final decision was based on how committee members voted, not on how particular series fared on either the rating task or the pilot. The coordinator explained that, while committee members used these sources of information in their discussion, they were free to vote however they wished. Two series "won," one for kindergarten through sixth grade and a second for seventh and eighth grade.

Following the final day, the coordinator prepared a summary to present to the board of education for final approval of the selection. The board quickly gave their approval, neglecting to request justification for the two winning textbook series. Textbook selection was complete.

The success of textbook selection depends on how closely all prior tasks affect the final decision. All but one of the Designer districts that we studied held a session analogous to the final day in which committee members studied summaries of all information collected and made a final choice. However, each district shared the same problem: how to summarize the information to make it understandable without distorting it. Some districts computed means of ratings wherever they could and compared the means across publishers. But averages can be difficult to interpret. What does an average score of 53 *mean*, for example? To stay "true" to the data, other districts prepared many pages of comments collected on each book. However, so many randomly ordered comments undoubtedly created information overload.

Selection committee members had spent years, in some cases, collecting information on basal textbook series. Repeatedly, however, curriculum coordinators explained to us that the committee members had not been able to use what they had collected directly. The data had influenced the *impressions* of committee members, but no curriculum coordinator could show us a documented, direct relationship between the work of the committee and the final decision.

In Conclusion

Our account depicts an armada of talented, educated, motivated people devoting large quantities of time to the production, adoption, and selection of textbooks. As we have already proposed, this armada followed no overall design, leading to competing influences, materials that were less well-conceived than they could be, and little improvement.

To be sure, individual collectives within the armada differed in their dedication or effectiveness, ranging from true Responders to authentic Designers. However, even the efforts of the Designers were less powerful than they could be. First, few people involved in the process, including Designers, had a clear understanding of what makes a textbook a good learning tool and how to recognize a well-designed textbook. In earlier chapters of this volume, we proposed a set of curricular, instructional, and comprehensibility rubrics to address this problem. Second, all participants were overwhelmed by the massive scope of their tasks. In the following chapter, we apply design rubrics to textbook publishing, adoption, and selection. We demonstrate that publishers, states, and districts could *design* their tasks by identifying the elements, linkages, and themes and then representing the design graphically. Having pictured the design, they could decompose, or break down, an overwhelming task into more manageable subtasks that nonetheless maintained the integrity of the original design.

In the final chapter of this book, we propose appropriate leadership roles for publishers, states, and districts, as well as ways in which they could collaborate that would bring true design to the system that places textbooks into America's classrooms. All participants tend to underestimate their power to change the situation. Publishers have both a national vision and strong expertise, but they explain that they cannot go against the market. States have both a large market and powerful expertise of their own, but they claim that they cannot get publishers to make the books they would like. Districts spend the money and have the clearest notion of the needs of their teachers and students, but they have the same complaint about publishers, and add that the major adoption states also have too much power. In addition, participants often fail to communicate with one another clearly enough to bring about positive changes. States prepare poorly conceived goal statements that fail to give publishers clear guidance. Districts cannot give publishers guidance either, because their intuitive decisions render them unable to explain clearly to publishers why they bought a particular series. Publishers fail to describe the underlying curricular, instructional, or comprehensiblity designs in their series well enough for states and districts to be able to match, competently and confidently, their own goals with a particular series.

Notes

1   See, e.g., Chall and Squire (1991).
2   See, e.g., Tyson (1990).
3   See, e.g., Farr and Tulley (1985).
4   Squire and Morgan (1990) and Westbury (1990).
5   Moore, Readence, and Rickelman (1983) and Tulley and Farr (1990).
6   Moore, Readence, and Rickelman (1983).
7   Squire and Morgan (1990) and Westbury (1990).
8   Chall (1988).
9   Squire and Morgan (1990).
10   Tulley and Farr (1990) and Westbury (1990).
11   Squire and Morgan (1990).
12   State of New York (1847), p. 181.
13   McMurray and Cronbach (1955), p. 14.
14   Armbruster, Osborn, and Davison (1985), Center for Education Studies/ American Textbook Council (1994), and Tyson-Bernstein (1988a, b; Yager (1983).
15   Anderson (1993), Osborn (1984), and Osborn and Decker (1993).
16   Woodward and Elliott (1990).

17   Carus (1987) and Holden (1987).
18   Farr and Tulley (1985).
19   Tyson (1990).
20   Squire (1985), p. 20.
21   Tyson-Bernstein (1988a, b).
22   Viadero (1990b), p. 13.
23   Viadero (1990a), p. 33.
24   Dole, Rogers, and Osborn (1989), p. 3.
25   Farr and Tulley (1985).
26   California State Board of Education (1988), p. 57.
27   Texas Education Agency (1991), p. 134.
28   California State Board of Education (1988), p. 118.
29   Texas Education Agency (1991), p. 137.
30   Farr and Tulley (1985).

7

CREATING A DESIGN FOR PUBLISHING, ADOPTING, AND SELECTING

In this chapter, we refocus the design lenses on the development, adoption, and selection of textbooks. As we have already suggested, successful human enterprises hew to a design. The well-educated human mind is no exception; nor is the well-crafted textbook. The successful system for publishing, adopting, or selecting textbooks would be no exception either. A design always implies a designer who chooses and organizes *planfully*. The problem for publishers is how to design an effective textbook series. The problem for adopters and selectors is how to design an effective approach for recognizing an effective series when they see it. Throughout this chapter, we promote the same analytic lenses that we used toward textbooks: consider the elements, linkages, and themes in a design, represent the design in a diagram, and evaluate it against explicit standards. We demonstrate how the basic design for a textbook series can be explicated early on and maintained as the series is being developed by publishers or evaluated by practitioners, tried out, and finally published or chosen.

In the last chapter, we painted a picture of well-meaning, capable, intelligent people designing, adopting, and selecting textbooks. Many of these people committed to their tasks hundreds of hours of time, large amounts of creative resources, and millions of dollars. For some, reform was in the wind. Several publishers and state adoption bureaucracies were changing, and instructional materials were changing as a result. All too frequently, however, the publishers, adopters, and selectors in chapter 6 were less effective than they had intended. Their tasks were typically overwhelming – far too many content objectives to juggle; no effective system for keeping track of what was happening to the objectives in the design of the student textbook, teacher's edition, ancillary materials; no valid approach for assessing whether youngsters using the materials indeed reached the objectives; reams of analyses that defied easy summarization; decisions reached impressionistically or as the result of political pressure. Many of these problems would have been solved if all participants had a clearer understanding of what makes instructional materials a good learning tool and analytic rubrics useful for applying this understanding.

Well-Designed Publishing, Adopting, and Selecting

In chapter 6, we introduced a model to organize and analyze the tasks that publishers, state adopters, and district selectors complete as they ply their separate trades. This model highlights several separable elements – the four tasks:

- establishing goals
- considering textbook characteristics
- reviewing and trying out
- taking final steps

and the three participants:

- publishers
- states
- districts

These elements are linked into a design by a sequential linear string composed of the separate stages completed by each group of participants – somewhat like a sequential matrix. The model lacks either a theme or evidence of a designer. As we have already suggested, the process by which textbooks eventually are placed in the hands of teachers and children is not well-designed. It is not surprising that publishers, adopters, and selectors frequently appear buffeted by outside forces.

How would the tasks look if the process adhered to a theme? In figure 7.1 are shown improved, "thematic" models for considering curriculum (see the top panel), instruction (see the middle panel), and comprehensibility (see the bottom panel). The figure depicts how curricular, instructional, and comprehensibility themes would guide the goals that publishers, states, and districts set, the kinds of textbook design that they consider, what they look for in reviews and try outs, and what they finally produce, adopt, and select. For example, in the curriculum model (top panel), a publisher (first row in the figure) designs a hierarchical curriculum plan, prepares drafts with a hierarchical structure, submits for review and try out this draft with its hierarchical design and the topical net design of the current textbook, but finally produces a textbook with a hierarchical design that matches the original plan. A district (third row in the figure) designs a plan with a matrix design instead, but analyzes books with both hierarchical and matrix designs, reviews and tries out

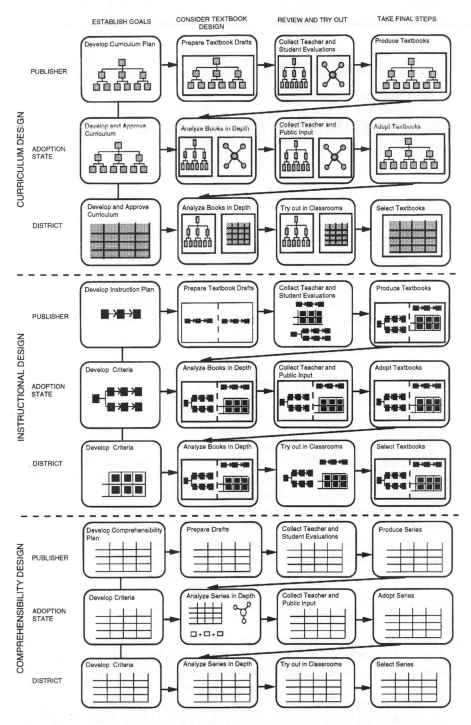

Figure 7.1 Improved "thematic" models whereby curricular, instructional, and comprehensibility themes guide the tasks completed by publishers, state adopters, and district selectors.

both designs, and decides to select a book with the matrix structure. To explain this model further, we rely on a scenario of a publisher developing and an adopter and a selector choosing a science series for youngsters in grades 4–6. This scenario is illustrative only, and is not meant to range the depth and breadth of the tasks for each of these groups. The scenario and figure complement one another.

A Textbook Publisher

We focus first on the staff of a publishing house, whose tasks are depicted in the first row of each panel in the figure. As is typically the case, the editors and authors begin by identifying the goals for the series. Rather than listing them or arranging them into a standard scope and sequence chart, however, this staff creates a design for their goals that links the parts into meaningful patterns. They specify curricular, instructional, and comprehensibility goals: "The curriculum shall reflect the lenses of science, encompassing the major domains of life, physical, and earth science each of which shall cover the disciplines (zoology, botany; physics, chemistry; geology, meteorology)." "Activities shall be student-centered and shall encourage students to think like scientists." "All materials shall enhance comprehension by connecting with reader knowledge, being well-organized, and increasing interest."

Guided by the curriculum goal, the staff designs a *hierarchy* according to the major divisions of life, physical, and earth science, each of which is in turn divided into the domains of zoology and biology, physics and chemistry, and so on (see the first cell in row 1 of the top panel). To encourage students to think like scientists, they construct a linear string design: observe, analyze, report (the first cell in row 1 of the middle panel). The staff represents the comprehensibility goal as a matrix that crosses the different components of the series (i.e., student textbook, teacher's manual, and so on) with the three features of comprehensible text (the first cell in row 1 of the bottom panel).

These curricular, instructional, and comprehensibility designs guide the staff as they plan and bring into being their textbook series – the second task. To match the original goal plan, the staff develops design diagrams for all levels of the series: entire books, units within books, chapters within units, and lessons within chapters. They also construct design diagrams across different media: student edition, teacher edition, ancillary products such as computer software or video disks, and assessment. The top panel in figure 7.1 depicts the diagram for the design of the table of contents at the whole book level. The middle panel shows the diagram for the design of instructional activities at the lesson level. The bottom panel diagrams the comprehensibility design across the different media of the series.

The entire production team of writers, illustrators, software developers, and so on writes the prose and develops the activities according to both overall and specific design pictures, accompanied by prototypes prepared by the in-house staff. The first draft of the series reflects the original design pictures. Textbooks for each grade level are organized hierarchically with three units: physical, life, and earth science. Note that the top-level organization is similar to the design of many current science textbooks. Where this design deviates dramatically is at the chapter level, where chapter designs reflect disciplines: zoology and botany; physics and chemistry; geology and meteorology. Contemporary textbook offerings customarily use a topical net design to subdivide life, physical, and earth science almost capriciously, failing to reflect the organization in the domains. Student activities in the textbook draft adhere to the linear string design: observe, analyze, report. Whether youngsters classify living and non-living objects or conduct experiments, the activities consistently follow the same basic sequence.

Across all media of the new series are characteristics of comprehensibility. All levels of the student edition, from whole books to individual sections, connect with student background knowledge, are organized according to coherent design patterns, and enhance interest. These same features appear in ancillary materials. Likewise, the teacher edition *as a text* connects with *teacher* background knowledge, is coherently organized, and enhances teacher interest.

Drafts in hand, the staff collects teacher and student evaluations during review and try out. Teachers complain about the new hierarchical design, explaining that they liked the old topics arranged as a topical net better (note the hierarchical and topical net designs in the third cell of the top panel in figure 7.1). A new chapter design means that they would have to replan many of their lessons to match important topics in the domains of zoology, botany, physics, chemistry, and so on. However, during try out, the publisher discovers that students working with the new drafts remember more content than other students using the topical net version. Publishers share these results with teachers. Teachers are impressed and admit that the try out data have changed their minds.

Publishers also collect review and try out on the instructional design (the third cell of the middle panel of figure 7.1). Originally, they aim to keep their plans simple by using a single linear string to design student activities in which students observe, analyze, and report. In other words, all activities use one example. Some staff members suggest that it makes greater instructional sense to design activities according to branching trees with several different examples. Otherwise, children will have few opportunities to reflect on patterns and extend the patterns to new phenomena. Other staff members note that the original instruction plan ignored group work. Classrooms that are true communities of inquiry often divide up the work, with each group focusing on one aspect in depth and subsequently teaching the rest of the class, so that each student eventually learns everything.[1] They suggest that a matrix pattern best depicts the design of this type of group work. During review and try out, teachers in focus groups like a combination of all three designs (note the linear string, branching tree, and matrix in the figure). During piloting, youngsters who engage in all three types of activities learn more content, can identify patterns better, and are more able to extend their learning to new situations than children who only work with one type of activity.

Review and try out also reveals problems with the comprehensibility design. Teachers in urban areas note that, while the materials are all clearly organized, both the student text and the teachers' manual ignore the experiences and interests of their students. Furthermore, students in urban schools perform less well during piloting than students from other types of communities.

You can see from figure 7.1 that publishers take review and try out to heart. Textbooks in the final series are organized hierarchically. Instructional activities follow linear string, branching tree, and matrix designs. And some examples explicitly build on the interests and experiences of children living in cities.

State adoption

Next, we focus on a state adopting several textbook series, screening the choices available to districts (the middle row of all three panels). They begin, as most adoption committees currently do, by specifying a set of goals. In this scenario, committee members create a design for the goals, much as the publishing staff did. With one exception, their goals match those of the publisher. From the beginning, committee members are aware that instructional activities must present more than one example to enhance student reflection and extension (see the middle panel of figure 7.1). Otherwise, the publisher and the state construct the same curriculum and comprehensibility goals (see the top and bottom panels of figure 7.1). Once publishers submit their materials, committee members search for and diagram the design for each series and compare it with the original goals. Is the content organized hierarchically? Do all parts of the series exhibit features of comprehensibility? Are instructional activities sequential (observe, analyze, report) using more than one example? In their analysis, they discover important differences among textbook series. Some books have a topical net design, the one with which teachers are most familiar (see the top panel of figure 7.1). Some series offer a variety of instructional designs, including one that would support group work particularly well (see the linear string, branching tree, and matrix in the middle panel). Some series are comprehensible across all media, some series have comprehensible student materials but less-well-organized teachers' manuals, and the different media in some series are almost unrelated (see the matrix, topical net, and list in the bottom panel of the figure).

To conduct review, committee members share their analysis at public meetings, exhibiting design diagrams to support their recommendations. At first, teachers and parents in the state are unconvinced that curriculum designed to match the important topics and linkages for scientists will enhance student learning and understanding. They prefer the traditional topical net design (note the hierarchy and topical net diagrams in the top panel). Furthermore, they see no reason to reject otherwise good series because not all of the media are organized, familiar, and interesting (the matrix and topical net in the middle panel). The committee supports its recommendations by pointing to differences in the diagrams and explains that by studying important content in science, children will be gaining the understandings that they will need to make academic progress as well as to become informed citizens. Furthermore, comprehensibility is the minimum requirement for learning to occur; teachers will be able to teach more effectively and children will learn more meaningfully if all of the materials in a series are comprehensible. Most teachers and parents change their minds and support the committee recommendations. Subsequently, school districts throughout the state choose from among the adopted textbooks.

District selection

Finally, we turn to a district selecting a textbook series. Their work is pictured in the third row of each panel in figure 7.1. In our scenario, a district committee has decided that the needs of their youngsters may be better met by a textbook series that is organized thematically rather than hierarchically. They specify a matrix design whereby life science, physical science, and earth science are subdivided into Evolution, Stability and Equilibrium, Determinism, and Form and Function (see the matrix in the top panel). They decide, furthermore, that this curriculum plan would lend itself well to group work and construct an instructional plan that has a matrix design as well (depicted in the middle panel). For example, different groups of children could study evolution in life science, physical science, or earth science, and teach what they have learned to the rest of the class.

Knowing, however, that their state has limited the adopted list to textbooks with a hierarchical design, committee members decide to search for both hierarchies and matrices (pictured by the hierarchy and matrix in the top panel of figure 7.1). Their search also identifies books with a variety of carefully designed instructional materials (branching tree, linear string, and matrix in the middle panel). The selection committee decides to choose between these different designs by the results of review and try out. Piloting teachers report that the thematic version with a variety of instructional designs promotes student enthusiasm, reflection, and extension. In fact, without teacher prompting, students begin to notice the themes spontaneously in their social studies and literature activities. Various comprehension measures indicate that youngsters learn more from the thematic series as well. However, teachers find the thematic version to be quite a bit harder to teach. Many report that their background knowledge in science is too weak for them to be able to do justice to the themes. They also note that while using a matrix to design group work was successful with the theme of evolution, it did not work as well with a more abstract theme like determinism. Teachers feel uneasy deciding on their own when to use each of the instructional possibilities pictured in the middle panel of figure 7.1. The district decides to request a waiver from the state, order the thematic series, and provide extensive teacher inservice to give teachers the support that they need. The district also shares their analysis with publishers, explaining why they chose one series over the others.

This scenario adds a purposeful theme to the original task model: publishers, state adopters, and district selectors use the same lenses to place into the hands of teachers and students well-designed textbook series. When the overall design is working well, tasks completed by separate participants are guided by similar curricular, comprehensibility, and instructional themes. Participants "speak the same language." The tasks completed by one group of participants can inform and support the work of the others. The work of adopters and selectors provides guidance to publishers, and textbooks improve. Better textbooks support in turn the work of adopters and selectors, who are in the enviable position of choosing among a collection of equally wonderful products.

This brief scenario, we trust, suggests the power of the design rubrics to improve textbook publishing, adoption, and selection. In the following section, we flesh out the model, focusing in some detail on the work of a fictional district selection committee. In order to demonstrate what we consider to be the breadth as well as the depth of our rubrics, we portray this district conducting a far more ambitious set of tasks than might be either practical or sensible. For example, to demonstrate how a publisher, an adoption state, or a district – or, for that matter, a professional organization – could construct a well-designed curriculum, we picture the district specifying a curriculum so detailed and innovative that it would fail to match any current textbooks on the market. Our purpose is to demonstrate our ideas, not present an algorithm for anyone to follow. On the other hand, while we have fabricated the plot to *demonstrate* what could be, the setting and characters are based on our experiences with real districts and district committee members. We think that professionals working in publishing houses to produce textbooks or on state adoption and district selection committees can extrapolate from this story, adapting what is useful for their situation.

A District Committee Uses Design Rubrics to Select a Textbook Series

The School Board of the Elysian Fields Unified School District has decided that it is time to select a new social studies series for students in grades 5–8. The district's textbooks are old. Responding to recent state adoption policies, publishers have developed new materials designed to be more interesting for children, to be better written, and to address topics typically ignored in older books, such as religion and the histories of many ethnic groups. The board appoints the district curriculum coordinator, Dr Carole Clark, to oversee the selection, and two classroom teachers with strong history/social science backgrounds, Mary Mathews and Tom Taylor, to serve as her assistants. The Board gives the three a free hand with two stipulations: (1) materials selected must meet the needs of the diverse student population in the district, and (2) the basis for the final selection must be clear to all, particularly the board members themselves.

This textbook selection is not the first that Dr Clark has supervised. Two years earlier, she directed a district committee that was choosing a basal reader series. At that time she relied heavily on two approaches for selecting textbooks. Before even gathering together a committee, she attended a workshop led by Connie Muther, director of Textbook Adoption Advisory Services (TAAS).[2] At the workshop she learned how to appoint a committee representative of the needs of her district, essential jobs to fill, a workable sequence for the selection tasks, and how to plan and conduct meetings. She also learned to prepare materials for analysis, being careful to disguise both publisher names and glitzy features, such as eye-catching but uninformative illustrations. The TAAS materials provided her with useful charts to record and summarize the committee's findings. However, the training did not help her to analyze the calibre of the basal readers. The committee developed several general goal statements, which the school board subsequently approved, but members were unsure about how to recognize the goals in the materials once they had prepared them for review. Even with her training, Dr Clark was unable to give them much guidance.

The second approach, *A Guide to Selecting Basal Reading Programs*, developed by the Center for the Study of Reading at the University of Illinois, helped to fill the gap.[3] The *Guide* contains a leader's manual and eight booklets, each on a different topic:

- Beginning Reading and Decoding Skill
- Comprehension I: The Directed Reading Lesson
- Comprehension II: Skills and Strategies

- Reading and Writing Instruction
- Selections in the Basal Reader
- Tests in Basal Reading Programs
- Vocabulary Instruction
- Workbooks

Each section in the *Guide* begins with an explanation of current reading theory. A second section presents guidelines to help selectors to examine materials according to the theory. These guidelines focus on instructional suggestions in the teacher edition, student activities, and the selections included in the student edition. For example, a section on the directed reading lesson defines reading comprehension as a constructive act. The next section demonstrates how to evaluate whether pre-reading activities, comprehension questions, and follow-up activities would help youngsters to construct the meaning of a text. Examples and exercises give selectors practice with the guidelines. The section ends with a sample chart for summarizing the analysis. Members of the committee found this approach to be valuable as they analyzed in detail the instructional approaches for each series and compared one series with another. While the Guide was developed specifically for reading, Dr Clark decides that it could be particularly helpful in evaluating some of the instructional activities in social studies series as well. After all, comprehension, vocabulary, and writing are important in content areas, too.

However, neither the TAAS training nor the *Guide* helped the committee focus on the *design* of the series. Were the separate parts of the series coherent and therefore comprehensible to teachers and students alike? Were the reading selections related according to important literary themes? Were they interesting, well written, and important? The committee tried to address these issues, preparing and completing lengthy checklists to supplement the TAAS and *Guide* work sheets. But in the end committee members were vaguely unhappy with their selection and unable to justify it to the board. In the intervening years, teachers have abandoned the reading series and turned to trade books. While Dr Clark supports this change, both she and the board members are discouraged by the large investment in books that have not been used. This time Dr Clark is determined to apply notions of design to guide both what her committee does and how they evaluate textbook series. In the current adoption, they will adopt the TAAS notions to organize the selection process and the *Guide* to analyze some of the instructional guidance in the series. To guide both their tasks and their analysis, the district will also apply design rubrics. Our depiction of their work focuses on how they use these rubrics.

Clark and her assistants appoint a selection committee. Members come from both the school and parent community. The committee includes teachers who are knowledgeable in social studies curriculum and instruction, from a diversity of ethnic backgrounds, and with training and experience teaching student populations with special needs. Parent members represent the diversity within the student population.

A committee reflecting the characteristics of the students in the district and with expertise in curriculum and instruction is likely to reach an equitable, well-reasoned decision. But Clark, Mathews, and Taylor have a second, equally valid, reason for constructing the selection committee with care. This group will be creating a design to guide the entire process, from establishing goals to choosing a new series. A designer's product is only as well-crafted as the resources at hand. Someone will need knowledge about the *content domain* (e.g., prominent historical eras and the basic features of major societies and cultures), the *background knowledge* of typical students (they know about contemporary sports and show business figures; they probably do not know very much about contemporary or historical political personages), the *developmental trends* in content and writing patterns (younger students handle concrete content presented as a story better; older students can handle more abstract content presented as exposition), the *conventions of good writing* (tell them what you are going to say, say it, tell them what you said), and a variety of *instructional strategies* (teacher talk versus small group discussion). As they design their tasks, members of the committee will find themselves drawing on what they already know about the domain, typical students, well-crafted writing, and instruction.

Establishing goals

All districts that develop a textbook selection process establish goals. The committee begins by surveying the goal statements of neighboring districts. Members discover two extremes. Some of the districts specify goals that are actually behavioral objectives (e.g., students will be able to name the state capitals; students will know the early exploratory voyages made by John Cabot, Ponce deLeon, and so on). These goals are clearly testable. Their presence in the materials can usually be easily spotted, and whether students reach the goals is readily measurable. Unfortunately, behavioral objectives do not address whether students will acquire major understandings. They also do not question the characteristics of the materials themselves. How comprehensible is a textbook series? How well does it reflect the curricular domain? What type of instruction will the series support?

At the other extreme, some neighboring districts adopt global statements (e.g., "The younger generation needs to understand our history, our institutions, our ideals, our values, our economy, and our relations with other nations in the world"; "Whenever appropriate, history should be presented as an exciting and dramatic series of events in the past that helped to shape the present."[4] Such statements remedy some of the problems of behavioral objectives. They address the larger issues, but at a price. They are not readily observable in the units, chapters, sections, and paragraphs of a student textbook or the accompanying teacher edition and ancillary materials. They are not easily testable student outcomes. Somehow such global goals need to be linked to specifics.

Under Dr Clark's guidance, the committee decides to combine these two approaches by progressively breaking down global goals into increasingly specific subgoals. They choose an overarching goal. The textbook series that they select must nurture the minds of *all* children in their district. They decide on three subgoals that are necessary for reaching the overarching aim:

- the series must have a coherent curriculum that reflects the lens of social scientists
- the series must meet comprehensibility standards
- the series must support student-centered instruction.

Committee members suggest that they begin by specifying several subsubgoals under each of these three major subgoals.

Carole Clark suspects that breaking down general goal statements may be a more difficult task than the committee members realize. Their initial subgoals must be powerful *generalizations* that nonetheless can link to a set of progressively more detailed subgoals. To be able to specify both the generalizations and the specifics, committee members must know the territory well. She realizes that most people were not taught according to a few generalizations that give order to their knowledge. Even her committee members who know a lot about social studies, or writing, or children, or instruction, are unlikely to have a handful of goal statements at their finger tips that can subsume progressively specific subgoals.

Dr Clark also knows that choosing goals will be the most significant, and probably the most difficult, decision that committee members will make. Potent goal statements can clearly suggest what the design of the textbook series should look like, what parts should be tested during review and try out, and how data should be summarized to guide the final selection.

To help them prepare, Clark encourages committee members to divide into study groups. One group surveys curriculum frameworks, such as the History–Social Science Framework[5] from California, the *Proclamations*[6] from Texas, and *Academic Preparation in Social Studies*[7] from The College Board. A second group focuses on comprehensibility goals and reviews recent research on the characteristics of comprehensible text. And a third studies the CORE instructional model proposed by Robert Calfee and his colleagues at Stanford University. Each group searches for no more than five large generalizations and specific subgoals to share with the rest of the committee. These goal statements will become the themes guiding the entire design.

The committee members reconvene for feedback and commentary on their work. On large pieces of butcher paper, each group has listed goals and subgoals and has drawn pictures of the design implied by the goals. The curriculum group had the largest, most difficult job. Nonetheless, since the goals for curriculum in many ways shape comprehensibility and instructional goals, the committee considers curriculum goals first.

Because Mary Mathews chairs the curriculum group, she agrees to report on their work and asks her cohorts to post their butcher-paper charts on one side of the room. As they work, members of the subcommittee complain. If only the experts could agree on a design for important content and how it should be organized, they would not have had to remake the curriculum wheel. They explain that integrating various curriculum frameworks into a simple, coherent design had not been easy.

Ms Mathews begins her report. The initial task, she explains, had been to specify the historian/social scientist lenses that the group wished the curriculum to convey. Their chart, pictured in figure 7.2, displays the two goals and two subgoals that they identified. These goals combine nicely into a coherent design, displayed in figure 7.3. To guide the design, the group identified four broad categories that social scientists use to understand societies and cultures. They next specified domain themes for each of the categories (note the column headings in figure 7.3). They also divided world and US history into major historical periods linked by the passage of time (see the row headings in figure 7.3). The design implies that textbook series are to present each of the time periods according to its culture, geography, economy, and political institutions. Likewise, each of these categories will have a history over time according to an overarching theme.

The next task had been to break down this design. According to Ms Mathews, group members first considered assigning major time periods to each grade level, as advocated by California in their History–Social Science Framework. Mathews explained that this alternative had been doubly appealing because at least one major series, the only one adopted for the California market, chunked the historical sequence accordingly. The group had developed several grade level designs before members began to express dissatisfaction. The designs looked far too familiar – marches through time that would fail to captivate youngsters' attention, increase their understanding, or be memorable. Members were also concerned about the match between these designs and youngsters' cognitive development. High-school students have the background to understand historical events with far more sophistication than elementary-school children. If students consistently study early history in elementary school, early modern in middle school, and the twentieth century in high

Curricular Subgoals

A textbook series that would nurture the minds of __all__ children must have a curriculum that reflects the lens of the historian/social scientist.

1. Major societies and cultures can be understood according to their culture, geography and environment, economics, and politics.

2. History can be divided into periods of major events and movements according to significant historical turning points.

> *2.1 World history can be divided according to Ancient World (through the fall of classical cultures), Medieval and Early Modern World (to industrialization) and Modern World (to present).*

> *2.2 U.S. history can be divided according to Making a New Nation (through the end of the revolutionary war), U.S. Growth and Conflict (to the beginning of Industrialization), Becoming an Industrial Nation (to the beginning of World War 2), and Becoming a World Power (to present).*

Figure 7.2   Curricular subgoals that reflect historian/social scientist lenses.

school, their levels of knowledge and understanding of each of these subsequences would differ substantially. Is sixth grade the best time to study about the development of classical civilizations around the world? Is eighth grade the best age to study in depth the *Constitution* or the Civil War? Are elementary and middle-school children to be given no knowledge about or understanding of events close in time to their own experiences? Members argued these questions vigorously.

Ms Mathews explains that several group members reached the same insight simultaneously. Why not break down grade level designs *thematically*, rather than chronologically? Fifth-graders could learn about the development of cultures over each of the major time periods in US history. Sixth-graders would use the same lens to study the historical development of cultures of the world. Seventh-graders could study the influence of geographic characteristics on the major historical periods of world history. Eighth-graders could use the same geographic themes to study US history. High-school students would trace themes from economics and political science across world and US history. Mathews notes that such a design would be a new twist on the old notion of the spiral curriculum, with subsequent years recycling back through major historical events according to the lens of the anthropologist, geographer, or economist and political scientist, rather than focusing on an ever-expanding environment.

Group members became excited about this design, particularly its brand of "spiralling." Youngsters begin with the concrete; with a study of culture that they can easily link to their own experience (family life, language, religion, education, and so on in the early beginnings of the major cultural groups that founded the United States, for example, through the founding and development of the country, up to the last decades of the twentieth century). This study of culture can lay a strong foundation for subsequent sweeps through history, which become progressively more abstract and removed from students' daily lives.

Ms Mathews asks group members to post designs for each grade level on the wall. The work for grade 8 is shown in figure 7.4.

The design is controlled by an overall geography theme: People are influenced by the geographic region in which they live, and in turn people have an impact on the environment. The design has two sets of elements. First, it divides into the same four time periods that chunk the fifth- and eleventh-grade designs as well. Second, it divides either regionally (for the first two time periods) or causally (for the third and fourth periods). Ms Mathews explains. Geographic characteristics of a region have always had a potent effect on the culture that people create, how they make a living, and their relationships with inhabitants of other regions. For example, geographically based regional differences among the North, South, and West can help explain how the country could become so divided that civil war seemed inevitable. Studying the effect of geography on the history of regions up through the Civil War makes sense. However, with industrialization and accompanying technological advances, the relationship between people and geography changed. People's impact on the environment (the second half of the theme) became equally powerful. People used technology to blur many natural regional differences. Extensive water-conservation systems brought water to deserts, which now had the natural resources to support farming. Areas formerly unconnected by natural transportation links such as navigable waterways became joined by rail lines, roads, and airlines. People flattened hills and filled in valleys. In important ways, geographic characteristics became less deterministic, and regional differences less striking. Nonetheless, the geography of the nation as a whole has played a potent role in the development of the United States as both an industrial nation and a world power. One way in which to understand this role is to distinguish between the impact of geography on people and the influence of people on geography.

Figure 7.3   A diagram to represent the curriculum design.

	Culture — 6th Grade	Geography and Environment — 7th Grade	Economics	Politics — High School
World History				
Ancient World (Full of Classical Cultures)	Theme: The world is composed of people with different cultures all satisfying the same basic human needs: food, clothing, shelter, self-expression, and the need to make sense of the world.	Theme: People are influenced by the geographical region in which they live and in turn, people have an impact on the environment.	Theme: The principles of supply and demand drive people to trade and explore, fostering cultural exchange and conflict.	Theme: All societies have rules for people to live by and have ways of governing. In turn, government influences society.
Medieval and Early/Modern World (Industrialization)				
Modern World (To Present)				

	Culture — 5th Grade	Geography and Environment — 8th Grade	Economics	Politics — High School
United States History	Theme: The world is composed of people with different cultures all satisfying the same basic human needs: food, clothing, shelter, self-expression, and the need to make sense of the world.	Theme: People are influenced by the geographical region in which they live and in turn, people have an impact on the environment.	Theme: The principles of supply and demand drive people to trade and explore, fostering cultural exchange and conflict.	Theme: All societies have rules for people to live by and have ways of governing. In turn, government influences society.
Making a New Nation (Through End of Revolutionary War)				
US Growth and Conflict (To Industrialization)				
Becoming an Industrial Nation (To World War 2)				
Becoming a World Power (To Present)				

Figure 7.4   A diagram to represent the curriculum design for grade eight.

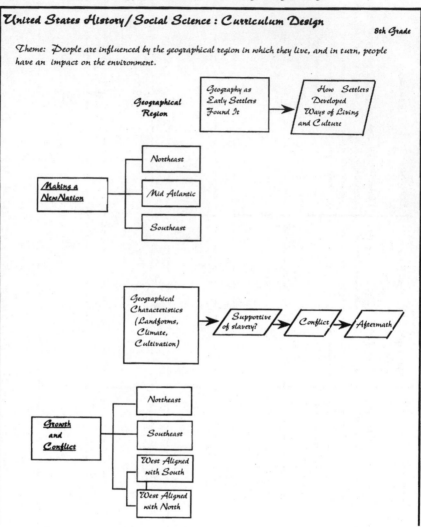

The two sets of elements in the eighth-grade design are linked sequentially. One could picture a textbook with four large parts matching the four historical time periods and progressing from "Making a Nation" to "Becoming a World Power." Each of these parts would have a branching tree design, with subsequences defined by meaningful geographic characteristics. Units within the parts could cover the subsequences. Chapters within units could present the events within the subsequences.

Figure 7.4 contd.

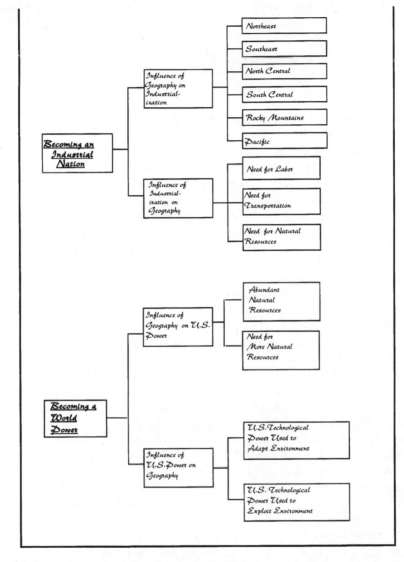

At this point, other members of the committee break in with questions: "What about multicultural and multiethnic histories? Might not this curriculum give short shrift to the histories of those people who have traditionally been under represented or stereotyped in historical treatments?"

Ms Mathews explains. Group members tried to be highly sensitive to the historical accounts of underrepresented people. One of their primary reasons for having youngsters begin with culture was to address this concern early on; to give fifth- and sixth-graders an anthropological lens for studying culture and knowledge about the major cultures of the United States and the world that they could use in subsequent years.

"Where are citizenship and ethical goals in the design?"

Ms Mathews explains. To bring overall coherence to the curriculum, the group decided to use the lenses of social scientists and historians. Historians and social scientists study citizenship values and ethics as elements of culture, geography, and sociopolitical institutions. The themes for these lenses suggest how citizenship and ethics are to be treated. To be sure, a history/social science curriculum could be designed quite differently, and in many cases as effectively. This particular design seemed to the group to simplify and bring coherence to the curriculum frameworks they viewed.

"How will the committee use these goals and their designs?"

Ms Mathews continues. The selection committee will use the goal designs as curriculum standards against which to evaluate textbook series. In other words, the curriculum group would like to see a series with three design features: (1) books across grade levels divided into roughly the same broad time periods; (2) fifth- and sixth-grade books that reflect a multicultural lens; and (3) seventh- and eighth-grade books that reflect the lens of the geographer. Series do not have to match the curriculum design exactly. The group knows that textbooks have been crafted according to the specifications of large adoption states. The curriculum goals represent an ideal. The selection committee will be searching for series that best match the curriculum design.

"Just how detailed does the curriculum group intend to get?"

According to Ms Mathews, the curriculum group pondered whether to specify goals for every textbook unit, chapter, and lesson at each grade level. They decided not to break down the design to the level of specific details. If they were a group of editors, they would probably create goal designs for every textbook unit, chapter, and lesson at each grade level. However, as members of a selection committee, they are more interested in developing general goals that nonetheless are specific enough to be used to evaluate the units, chapters, and lessons within a grade. Ms Mathews' answers satisfy the committee, and they approve the curriculum group's work.

The comprehensibility group reports next. Wonderful as the curriculum of a textbook series may be, if the materials are not comprehensible, any effects will be substantially compromised. Tom Taylor, chair for this group, asks the members to post their goals and designs on the wall adjoining the curriculum designs. He explains that his group, like the curriculum group, began by developing a handful of goals and subgoals and linking them into a goal design. According to Taylor, the group's review of the research suggested two overall text characteristics that affect how well youngsters comprehend textbook

Comprehensibility Subgoals

A textbook series that would nurture the minds of <u>all</u> children must meet comprehensibility standards.

1.   Comprehensible textbook series use a familiar interesting style.

    1.1   Examples, illustrations, and analogies are familiar, based on what readers already know or can readily experience.

    1.2   Style enhances interest by using vivid vocabulary, action, and examples and illustrations with absolute interest.

2.   Comprehensible textbook series have a well-designed structure.

    2.1   Functional devices (introductions, transitions, and conclusions) link the separate parts into a whole.

    2.2   Wherever possible, series are organized with strong linkages (hierarchies, branching trees, arguments or explanations.)

Figure 7.5   Comprehensibility subgoals based on the features of text that enhance comprehension.

materials. First, young readers will better comprehend a textbook series that is structured with strong linkages. Second, reader comprehension is improved by textbook writing that connects with reader knowledge and understanding and enhances reader interest. The comprehension group identified a third goal to extend the comprehensibility features to all parts of a textbook series.

Mr Taylor explains that the group composed a matrix design to link the two types of text characteristics with the parts of a textbook series. He explains the implications for textbook selection. Whether the focus is on the student edition, teacher edition, or ancillary materials, textbook materials should be coherently structured and written to enhance familiarity and interest. Taylor directs his audience's attention to two charts, the Comprehensibility Subgoals and the Comprehensibility Design, which are depicted in figures 7.5 and 7.6.

Comprehensibility evokes less controversy than curriculum. The committee accepts this design with virtually no discussion.

The final report comes from the instruction group, chaired by Carole Clark.

Comprehensibility Design

	Style		Structure	
	Familiar (examples, illustrations, analogies)	Interesting (vivid vocabulary, action, and absolute interest)	Functional Devices (introductions, transitions, and conclusions)	Strong Linkages (hierarchies, matrices, branching trees, arguments, and explanations.)
Student Edition				
Teacher Edition				
Ancillary Materials				

Figure 7.6   A diagram to represent the comprehensibility design.

Well-designed curriculum in comprehensible text is dependent on strong instructional possibilities. Dr Clark's group posts their butcher paper on a third wall, adjacent to the work of the comprehensibility group. She begins her report by describing the CORE instructional model to other members of the committee: the importance of connections and organization; the necessary opportunities for students to reflect and extend. Referring to the goal chart reproduced in figure 7.7, Dr Clark explains that the instruction group specified a goal for each facet of the model. For each goal, the student edition can support instruction in the characteristics of the prose that students read and the tasks they complete. Teacher editions and ancillary materials can present both teacher and student tasks. Wherever the student edition fails to offer instructional support, the teacher edition and ancillary materials must pick up the slack. The group linked the instructional elements into a matrix design displayed in figure 7.8, not unlike the comprehensibility design.

Committee members begin to raise a few questions: "Isn't the CORE model rather vague?" "Don't teachers need more guidance?" "What about important instructional issues like cooperative learning groups or the constructive nature of learning?" "What about issues specific to history/social science, such as the

---

Instructional Subgoals

A textbook series that would nurture the minds of __all__ children must support principles of strong instruction.

*1. Both the prose and tasks in an instructionally strong textbook series **C**onnect reader experience and understanding with textbook content.*

> *1.1 The same familiarity and interest-enhancing features that make a textbook comprehensible also contribute to its instructional power.*

> *1.2 If connections are not present in the student edition, they must appear in the teacher edition or ancillary materials.*

*2. An instructionally powerful textbook series uses strong linkages to **O**rganize content.*

> *2.1 The same linkages that make a textbook comprehensible also contribute to its instructional power.*

> *2.2 If the linkages are weak, strong organizational strategies must appear in the tasks in the student edition, teacher edition, or ancillary materials.*

*3. Both the prose and tasks of an instructionally strong textbook series must explicate models and principles that students can discover during **R**eflection.*

*4. An instructionally strong textbook series provides opportunities for students to **E**xtend models and principles to new situations.*

Figure 7.7   Instructional subgoals based on the CORE model.

use of literature or primary source materials?" "How will we use these goals to evaluate textbook series?" Dr Clark explains that design within flexibility is one of the strengths of the CORE model. It does assume that the teacher acts as a professional who creates instruction according to the general features of the model. The model also assumes that learners construct their own knowledge by building on, or connecting with, what they already know. They construct by comprehending, reflecting, and extending. All three activities are enhanced in social interaction and using a variety of powerful materials. Therefore, the CORE model implies such instructional features as cooperative learning groups, source materials, and literature. Textbook materials that connect, organize, and support reflection and extension using a variety of types of materials would be a potent resource for the teacher designing CORE instruction. Committee members shift restlessly in their seats. Their questions persist:

Instructional Goal Design

	Connect (*Link student experience and knowledge to text*)	*Organize* (*Link separable elements into a design*)	*Reflect* (*Identify models and principles*)	*Extend* (*Apply models, principles to new situations*)
Student Edition *Prose*	*See Comprehensibility Goal Design*	*See Comprehensibility Goal Design*	*See Curriculum Goal Design*	*See Curriculum Goal Design*
Tasks				
Teacher Edition *Teacher tasks*				
Student tasks				
Ancillary Materials *Teacher tasks*				
Student tasks				

Figure 7.8   A diagram to represent the instructional design.

"We still don't see how we will use these goals in our analysis. How will we *recognize* tasks that support the model?"

Dr Clark explains that the group anticipated these questions and prepared a set of example tasks for each element in the model. She posts the last sheet of butcher paper (see figure 7.9). Group members used three criteria to choose these examples. Each activity supports the overall geographic theme, scaffolds one element of the CORE model, and encourages students to construct their knowledge rather than regurgitate unrelated facts. The examples will help the selection committee use the goals to evaluate the instruction in student editions, teacher editions, and ancillary materials. Finally satisfied, committee members approve the instructional support goals.

Analyzing textbook design

Several weeks later, the selection committee reconvenes. In the meantime, Carole Clark has ordered and received complete history/social science series

Tasks to Support the CORE Model
'Becoming An Industrial Nation' Examples

Connect   Students identify a major industry where they live and contact people working in the industry to discover why the industry is located where it is. Other students search for a major change in their environment that was engineered and speculate on how that change has altered the geography where they live.

Organize   Students use graphic organizers to highlight the causal relationships between geographical characteristics and the development of industrialization in different sections of the country. They also use graphic organizers to highlight the causal relationships between industrialization and changes in population centers, transportation, and types of natural resources, such as electrical power sources.

Reflect   Students begin by pinpointing geographical conditions that did/did not support industrialization. They speculate about different ways in which people altered geographical conditions to support industrialization. They conclude by composing a list of geographical principles, such as 'What an industry has to have to thrive,' 'What you can do to fix the geography,' and 'Why the US could become an industrial nation.'

Extend   Students choose one industry that interests them and write a report about the history of the industry answering the questions, 'In what ways was the geography just right for this industry to develop?' 'How did the geography have to be changed?' 'In what ways has the geography been helped by the industry and in what ways has it been harmed?'

Figure 7.9   Examples of textbook tasks for each element in the CORE model.

for grades 5–8 from five publishers. She has removed student editions, teacher editions, and ancillary materials from their cartons and stacked them on the floor. The piles, each at least three feet high, line the walls of the room.

Committee members are overwhelmed and angry. "Why did we go to all the work of constructing goal designs," they ask? "We will never be able to make detailed analyses of so many materials." "We should have created a simple checklist instead that we could complete by searching through the scope and sequence charts in the front of each teacher edition." "Even better, why can't we order the new version of our old series? The old books weren't so bad. At least they are familiar."

Dr Clark steps to the front of the room where a chart rests against an easel (see figure 7.10). Remember, she admonishes her committee, how excited they were with the goals they established for themselves. And how discouraged they have been with the uninspired, disorganized writing and tasks in the old textbooks. They have the opportunity to make a difference; to flex their muscles as an important part of the marketing community. Checklists will

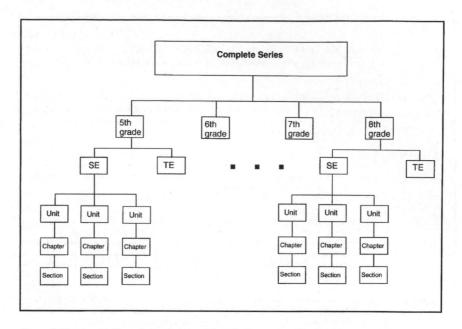

Figure 7.10   A sampling plan to improve the efficiency of textbook analysis.

encourage them to make their selection blindly. They will have only a superficial notion of the strengths and weaknesses of the series that they choose and little ammunition to influence change. Fortunately, they can *design* their analysis to capitalize on their individual strengths and keep each task within reasonable bounds. Clark points to the figure on the easel.

It is true, Dr Clark explains, that the analysis could be overwhelming if not approached planfully. Therefore, they will handle the analysis tasks by sampling. Most of the analysis will focus on the student edition. The analysis will begin with the design of a series across student textbooks and proceed through the whole-book level and each unit within each book. Having considered the units, committee members as a group will choose a single chapter within each unit and a single section within each chapter. Wherever possible, they will select content that is similar across series (e.g., chapters on industrialization immediately following the US Civil War and sections on the growth of cities that resulted). Once student editions have been completely analyzed, committee members will turn to the teacher editions and ancillary materials, to search for tasks that compensate for any shortcomings in the student materials.

Members of the three study groups, already experts in their particular areas, will divide up responsibility for the actual evaluation. The comprehensibility group will start by schematizing the designs for each level of the student editions. They will be trained to identify and picture the elements, linkages, and themes in textbook materials. The curriculum, comprehensibility, and instruction groups will use the design pictures to make their separate evaluations. In addition, the instructional support group will search the tasks in the student edition for evidence of the CORE model.

Group members will summarize these initial evaluations to highlight problem areas in the student editions. As a final task, groups will search teacher editions and ancillary materials for teacher and student tasks that will remedy any lacks in the student editions. Once the analysis is finished, the selection committee will have design pictures and summary charts for each series.

Dr Clark's explanation reassures committee members. However, Mr Taylor, the chair of the comprehensibility group, suggests one revision to increase the efficiency of his group's work. Rather than initially conducting a complete analysis of each series from whole book to section, the comprehensibility group could begin by depicting the designs at the whole-book level of each series before they consider units, chapters, and sections within individual books. They could share these "big pictures" with the rest of the committee. Committee members could use them to identify the series that best match curriculum, comprehensibility, and instructional goals. Such screening could cut down on the amount of detailed analyses that committee members would have to complete and focus their efforts on series that matched their goals on a global level. Members decide to proceed accordingly and set their next meeting for six weeks hence.

When the selection committee reconvenes, the comprehensibility group has completed its diagrams of tables of contents for student textbooks in each of the five series. Members post pieces of butcher paper around one half of the room. The task for the session is to screen out all but two or three series for detailed analysis. Dr Clark reminds selection committee members that the design pictures are to be compared with the original comprehensibility, curricular, and instructional designs posted on the remaining two walls.

Mr Taylor reports on his group's work by asking the committee to focus first on the chart in figure 7.11 as an example. This figure depicts the whole-book level design of an eighth-grade US history textbook. The box at the top of the figure signifies that the book starts with an introduction. The dark lines connecting boxes indicate transitions. Places where the boxes overlap represent overlapping time spans. For example, the time span covered in unit 2 begins and ends later than the time span for unit 1, but the bulk of the unit covers the same time period as unit 1. The time span for unit 8 actually begins and ends earlier than the time span for unit 7. Several pairs of units begin at the same time (e.g., units 3 and 4). Diagrams for all other books follow the same format.

Selection committee members discuss whether each whole-book design

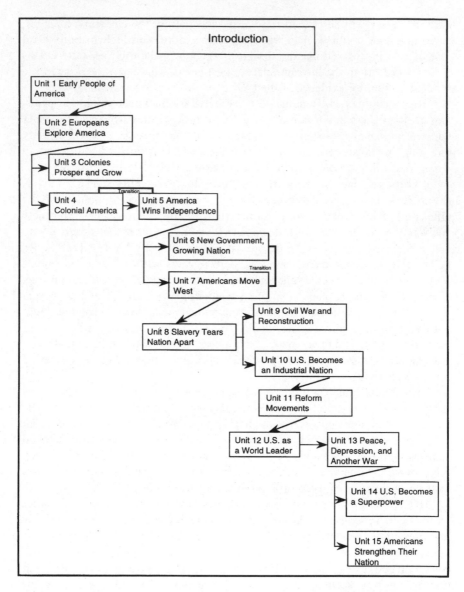

Figure 7.11 The whole book level design of an eighth-grade US history textbook.

matches the curriculum, comprehensibility, and instructional goals. They are concerned about many of the books. For example, committee members remark that while the eighth-grade book depicted in figure 7.11 does cover the time period in their goal design from the early explorers to modern US history, it fails either to chunk the historical sequence into a few periods defined by major historical shifts or to reflect a geography theme. The design looks very different from the curricular design that they constructed for eighth grade (see figure 7.4). To summarize committee comments, Taylor begins to fill in the chart depicted in figure 7.12. On a three point scale (+, √, −) members assign this design a − for domain match; it does not come close to matching their initial curriculum goals and would require extensive reorganization and supplementation by classroom teachers. Based on the discussion of comprehensibility, they give the design all minuses for failing to connect with student understanding, being poorly organized, and having boring titles and subtitles. For example, while children might already know something about pioneers, the title "Americans Move Westward" gives no hint that the topic might be familiar. The organization of the book is list-like – *15* separate units is far too many to qualify for teaching a few major ideas well. And titles like "The U.S. Becomes An Industrial Nation" are unlikely to spark the interest of 13-year-olds. Instructional support depends on comprehensibility and domain match, all of which receive minuses accordingly. The book replicates so few of the goal designs that committee members agree to reject it for further analysis.

Fortunately, other books fit more closely. The committee chooses two series for further analysis. They discuss which chapters and sections to sample for each grade level. For eighth grade, for example, they notice that both books have chapters on the causes of the Civil War and industrialization. They search for evidence of geography themes within the chapter sections, and notice that both books chronicle the regional differences that led to the Kansas–Nebraska Act, the violence in Kansas that resulted, and the country's growing realization that a peaceful solution to the conflict over slavery was not going to be possible. They also notice that both books present the growth of cities as an outcome of people migrating from rural America in search of work in the newly emerging industries. Recognizing that both of these sections could develop important geography themes, the committee chooses these chapters and sections for close scrutiny. Before the next meeting, the comprehensibility group completes the unit, chapter, and section diagrams for student editions in these series. In addition, the instructional group analyzes student tasks according to the instructional support goal designs.

Design charts decorate three of the four walls at the final session. Committee members spend several minutes before the meeting circling the room and studying the new designs. They notice that analyses begin with the whole-book level and proceed with analyses of units, one chapter within each unit, and a section within each chapter. The committee marked with bold face the elements in the design that they subsequently analyzed in detail. Designs for two eighth-grade books are displayed in figures 7.13 and 7.14. We have included the analyses of two units as examples (the buildup to the Civil War

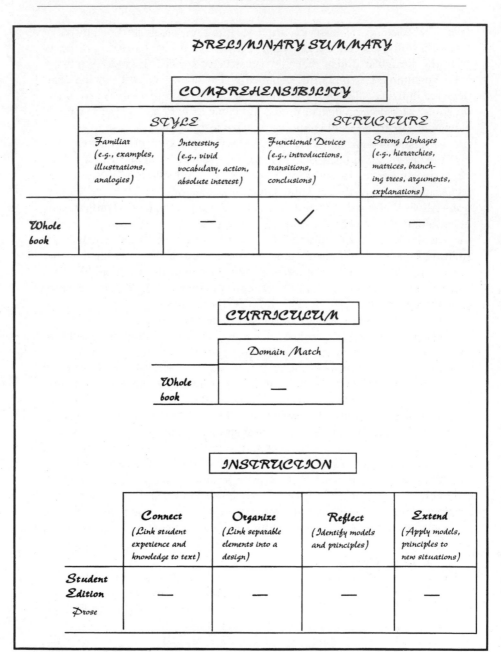

Figure 7.12 A chart to summarize committee discussion of an eighth-grade US history textbook.

Figure 7.13   The design of an eighth-grade history/social studies textbook: Book 1.

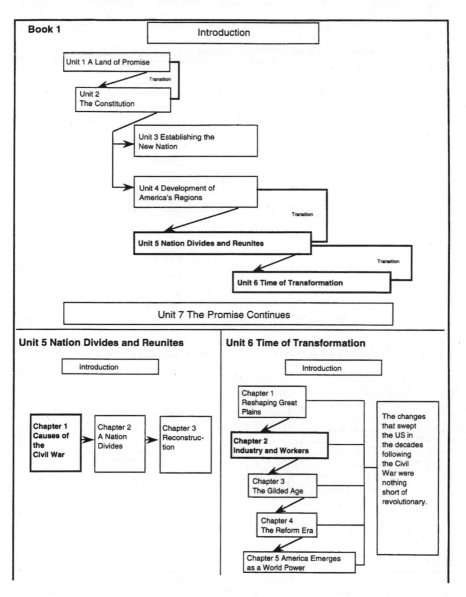

Figure 7.13 contd.

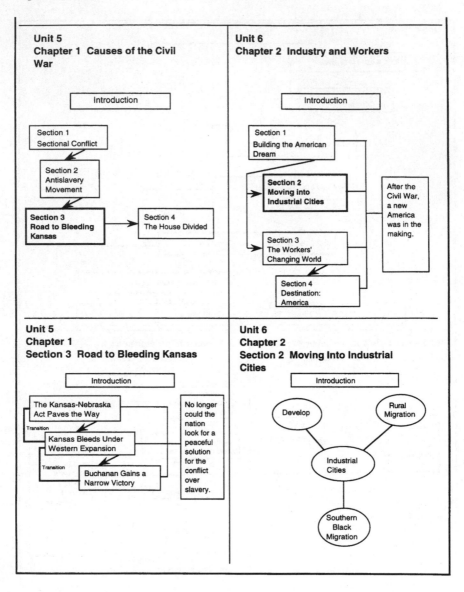

and the changes that occurred following the War), one chapter from each unit (more immediate causes of the Civil War and industrialization), and one section from each chapter (battle over Kansas and urbanization). For the whole book, units, and chapters, we have marked with bold face the elements in the design that we subsequently depict in detail. So, for example, in figure 7.13, the design diagram for the whole book shows in bold face the titles "**Nation Divides and Reunites**," and "**Time of Transformation**." The analyses for these two units is immediately below the whole-book design. Note that in an actual analysis, the designs for all units would be considered, increasing the number of units, chapters, and sections for these two books to seven. Since we must fit our design pictures on to a standard piece of paper, the figures display only part of the analysis.

As committee chair, Dr Clark leads the discussion, beginning with a consideration of curriculum and following with comprehensibility and instruction. She fills in summary charts to create a record of the discussion. We report on the consideration of the two eighth-grade books as an example of the entire discussion. The summary charts are presented in figures 7.15 and 7.16. Both figures report ratings for the whole-book level and units 5 and 6 with their chapters, and sections.

Committee members' first impression is that, at the whole-book level, the two designs look somewhat like their whole-book curricular goal designs. Both books chunk into major periods linked according to time (albeit with a significant amount of overlap and a heavy focus on the period from the beginning of the Revolutionary War to the beginning of World War I). In addition, selected titles in Book 1 show evidence of regional topics (e.g., "Development of America's Regions," "Reshaping the Great Plains," "Sectional Conflict"). Because of these titles, the committee decides that Book 1, at the whole-book level, matches the curriculum goals better than Book 2, and Dr Clark marks the summary charts accordingly. At the unit, chapter, and section level, however, they decide that both books depart from the committee's curricular designs, because neither regional differences nor environmental issues consistently chunk the basically sequential treatment, although committee members note that in many cases the content covered offers the pieces that alert teachers could use to develop the themes. They also note that Book 1 seems to match their original geographic theme slightly better than Book 2. For example, the section "Moving into Industrial Cities" has two sections that appear to deal with the effect on cities of geographic migration while "The Growth of Cities" only has one section. Carole Clark completes the summary charts accordingly.

Next, committee members discuss differences in comprehensibility. They note that Book 1 seems to be more comprehensible than Book 2. To be sure, Book 2 is more likely to use familiar examples and illustrations than Book 1, but

Figure 7.14   The design of an eighth-grade history/social studies textbook: Book 2.

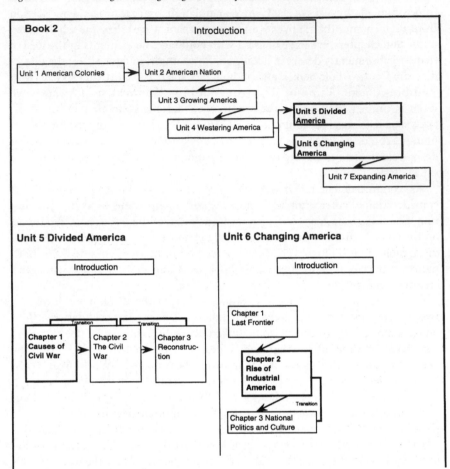

the committee found the style of Book 1 to be consistently more interesting and the structure to have stronger linkages. The group is particularly impressed with the use of argument structures in the unit "Time of Transformation," the chapter "Industry and Workers," and the section "Road to Bleeding Kansas."

Finally, committee members turn to the instructional design. Members of the instructional support group report on both the prose and student tasks for both books. They explain that to consider how well the prose of the books would connect with student learners, they combined how familiar and interesting each book was. To consider prose organization, they combined linkages

Figure 7.14 contd.

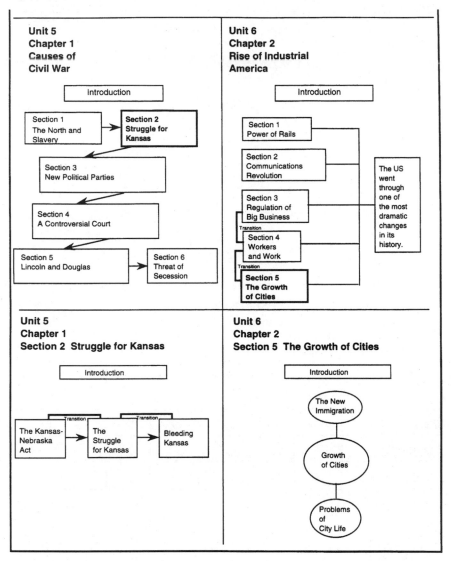

and functional devices. As the comprehensibility analysis suggests, they find Book 1 to connect and organize better than Book 2. However, they judge the prose of neither book to enhance reflection and extension, primarily because geography themes do not guide the design of either book at the unit, chapter, or section level. How could children and teachers be expected to reflect about the

Figure 7.15   A chart to summarize committee discussion of Book 1.

SUMMARY BOOK 1

CURRICULUM

	Domain Match	
Whole book	+	
	#5	#6
Units	✓	✓
Chapters	✓	✓
Sections	✓	✓

COMPREHENSIBILITY

	STYLE		STRUCTURE	
	Familiar (e.g., examples, illustrations, analogies)	Interesting (e.g., vivid vocabulary, action, absolute interest)	Functional Devices (e.g., introductions, transitions, conclusions)	Strong Linkages (e.g., hierarchies, matrices, branching trees, arguments, explanations)
Whole book	—	✓	+	+
Units	#5 — #6 —	#5 ✓ #6 ✓	#5 ✓ #6 ✓	#5 ✓ #6 +
Chapters	— —	✓ ✓	✓ ✓	✓ +
Section	— —	+ +	+ ✓	+ ✓

relationship between geography and the major periods of US history if there is no evidence of a book having been designed around this relationship? What understandings would children and teachers have that they could extend to new situations?

Next, the instructional support group reports on student tasks for both books. Other committee members note that the design of these tasks is crucial.

Figure 7.15 contd.

	Connect (Link student experience and knowledge to text)		**Organize** (Link separable elements into a design)		**Reflect** (Identify models and principles)		**Extend** (Apply models, principles to new situations)	
INSTRUCTION								
Whole book								
Prose	✓		+		—		—	
Tasks	N/A		N/A		N/A		N/A	
	#5	#6	#5	#6	#5	#6	#5	#6
Units								
Prose	✓	✓	✓	+	—	—	—	—
Tasks	N/A	N/A	N/A	N/A	N/A	N/A	N/A	N/A
Chapters								
Prose	✓	✓	✓	+	—	—	—	—
Tasks	—	✓	✓	—	—	✓	—	✓
Sections								
Prose	+	+	+	✓	—	—	—	—
Tasks	—	—	—	—	—	✓	—	—

Regardless of the design of the prose, the tasks that children complete could help them to reflect on the geography themes and extend their understanding to new situations. The instructional support group begins. They note that neither book has any tasks for the book as a whole or for individual units. Tasks occur at the ends of chapters and sections. The group notes that many of the tasks in both books are innovative and could support student learning. However, their job was to search for tasks that would help children acquire understandings about the relationship between geography and US history. Unfortunately, they found few tasks in either book that would help children make connections, organize, reflect on, or extend these causal relationships.

Having discussed and summarized their impressions of student editions, committee members focus on teacher editions and ancillary materials to search

Figure 7.16 A chart to summarize committee discussion of Book 2.

SUMMARY BOOK 2

CURRICULUM

	Domain	Match
Whole book	✓	
Units	#5 ✓	#6 ✓
Chapters	✓	✓
Sections	✓	—

COMPREHENSIBILITY

	STYLE				STRUCTURE			
	Familiar (e.g., examples, illustrations, analogies)		Interesting (e.g., vivid vocabulary, action, absolute interest)		Functional Devices (e.g., introductions, transitions, conclusions)		Strong Linkages (e.g., hierarchies, matrices, branching trees, arguments, and explanations)	
	#5	#6	#5	#6	#5	#6	#5	#6
Whole book	—		—		✓		✓	
Units	—	✓	—	—	+	+	✓	✓
Chapters	✓	+	—	✓	✓	✓	✓	+
Sections	—	—	+	—	✓	—	✓	—

for instructional activities that would complement the designs of student textbooks. To illustrate the analysis, figure 7.17 reports the results for the teacher edition of Book 1. Notice that the instructional support group has listed activities that fit within the comprehensibility and instruction designs. For example, the teacher edition suggests activities that can help children form connections and organize what they are learning. One activity in the section,

Figure 7.16 contd.

INSTRUCTION

	Connect (Link student experience and knowledge to text)		Organize (Link separable elements into a design)		Reflect (Identify models and principles)		Extend (Apply models, principles to new situations)	
Whole book								
Prose	—		✓		—		—	
Tasks	N/A		N/A		N/A		N/A	
Units	#5	#6	#5	#6	#5	#6	#5	#6
Prose	—	✓	✓	✓	—	—	—	—
Tasks	—	—	—	—	—	✓	—	—
Chapters								
Prose	✓	+	✓	+	—	—	—	—
Tasks	—	—	✓	✓	✓	—	—	—
Sections								
Prose	—	—	✓	—	—	—	—	—
Tasks	—	—	—	—	—	—	—	—

"Industrial Cities," could help students to extend their understanding about the growth of cities to their own state or community. As a final task, the committee creates an overall summary that combines the analyses of the student book and teacher edition for every grade level in each series. The overall summary prepared for Book 1 is shown in figure 7.18. Committee members conclude that the teacher edition does offer suggestions that would render the units, chapters, and sections more comprehensible, but unfortunately adds little opportunity for students to reflect about or apply geographic themes.

At the end of the session, both design diagrams and summary ratings ring the room, clustered according to series. Committee members express frustration.

Teacher Edition Book 1

COMPREHENSIBILITY

	STYLE		STRUCTURE	
	Familiar	Interesting	Functional Devices	Strong Linkages
Whole book		#6	"Looking Back" and "Looking Forward" provide transitions between units.	"Understanding Chronology" helps clarify sequential overlap among units.
Units	#5 #6	#5	#5 #6 "Looking Back", "Looking Forward," and "Understanding Chronology" introduce and provide transitions.	#5 #6 "Understanding Chronology" helps clarify sequential overlap among chapters.
Chapters			"Looking Forward" and "Understanding Chronology" introduce. "Bulletin Board" concludes.	
Sections	"Access Strategy" connects.	"Access Activity" enhances interest.	"Introduce" introduces. "Close" summarizes.	

	Connect	Organize	Reflect	Extend
Whole book		"Looking Back" and "Looking Forward" provide transitions between units. "Understanding Chronology" helps clarify sequential overlap among units.		
Units	#5 #6	"Looking Back," "Looking Forward," and "Understanding Chronology" introduce and provide transitions. "Understanding Chronology" helps clarify sequential overlap among chapters.	#5 #6	#5 #6
Chapters		"Looking Forward" and "Understanding Chronology" introduce. "Bulletin Board" concludes.		
Sections	"Access Strategy" connects. "Access Activity" enhances interest.	"Introduce" introduces. "Close" summarizes.		"Research" Find out about major cities in state or region.

Figure 7.18   A chart that combines the analyses of the student and teacher editions for Book 1.

Figure 7.18 contd.

	INSTRUCTION							
	Connect (Link student experience and knowledge to text)		**Organize** (Link separable elements into a design)		**Reflect** (Identify models and principles)		**Extend** (Apply models, principles to new situations)	
Whole book								
Prose	✓		+		—		—	
Tasks	—		+		—		—	
Units	#5	#6	#5	#6	#5	#6	#5	#6
Prose	✓	✓	✓	+	—	—	—	—
Tasks	—	—	+	+	—	—	—	—
Chapters								
Prose	✓	✓	✓	+	—	—	—	—
Tasks	—	✓	+	+	—	✓	—	✓
Sections								
Prose	+	+	+	✓	—	—	—	—
Tasks	+	+	+	+	—	✓	—	✓

Most of the materials do not closely match the original goal designs. Should they continue with their task? Perhaps it would be better to turn to trade books and construct their own series. Carole Clark responds. She acknowledges that she, too, wishes that one of the series had emerged as a stellar example of the committee's goals. Whichever series the district eventually chooses, district teachers will have to choose, organize, supplement, and omit content. However, because the books cover so much, they are potentially a rich resource for teachers.

In addition, the committee's work thus far will be a powerful tool for teachers, Dr Clark explains. Their analysis describes the series' designs clearly, highlighting both strengths and weaknesses. Because of their work, the district will know exactly where the curricular, comprehensibility, and instructional mismatches are, and can offer teachers the professional support to design powerful instruction that will enhance student learning. Teachers will be able to use the goal designs as standards, compare the textbook design pictures, and plan their instruction accordingly. Furthermore, by sharing these analyses with publishers, the district might be able to influence textbook materials of the future.

Perhaps the outcome of the committee's analysis is not surprising, she muses. After all, textbook publishers designed the books to match curriculum frameworks from California and proclamations from Texas. Neither of these documents creates goal designs guided by clear, explicit themes.

Not hearing any more discussion, Dr Clark explains that the next task will be to distribute the two series for public review and classroom try out. She suggests that her two assistants help her to design this task, since she sees no need for the entire committee to be involved. Committee members agree and adjourn for several months.

Conducting Review and Try Out

During earlier textbook selections, the district became overwhelmed by the logistics of conducting useful public review and classroom try out. Two years before, Dr Clark had despaired at the number of participants and the amount of data. While she sensed the power of public and teacher input, the magnitude of the task had negated any potential benefit. Clark knows of districts that refuse to complete review and try out because the results are too confusing. She suggests to her assistants four overarching themes:

- review and try out shall be guided by the goal designs
- review and try out shall build on analyses conducted by the committee
- review and try out shall be representative, following standard sampling techniques
- review and try out shall be standard across all participants

Clark, Mathews, and Taylor agree to use their new design tools to create an approach that will carry out all four themes.

The overall design for review and try out is displayed in figure 7.19. Whether the public is reviewing series or teachers are trying them out, all participants will experience three events: preparation, tasks, and measurement. The elements for the design are linked into a sequential matrix. Review will build on the analytic work of the selection committee. Try out will supplement the committee's analysis by focusing on the comprehensibility and instructional support of the two series. This design will standardize tasks for all participants

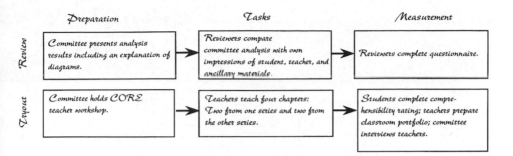

Figure 7.19 A diagram of the overall design for review and try out for the public reviewing series and teachers trying them out.

and ensure that review and try out builds on both the goal designs and committee analyses.

The overall design does not address the issue of representative sampling. Elysian Fields School District has 30 classes for grade 5, two classes in 15 elementary schools, and 90 classes for grades 6–8, nine classes in ten middle schools. If every teacher participated, the district would have data from 120 teachers and over 3,500 students! The mind boggles at the logistics of distributing materials and collecting results from the entire district. Dr Clark and her assistants create a representative and manageable sampling design to guide classroom try out. The result is displayed in figure 7.20.

To construct the design, the committee of three considers classrooms and materials. Classrooms can be classified by school level (elementary or middle), school test scores (high or low), and grade level (5–8). To enhance any comparisons, the committee decides to have two classrooms at each grade level from each school. Materials can be classified by series (1 or 2) and chapters, four for each series.

Clark and her assistants link classrooms and materials into a hierarchical design that reduces the number of classrooms from a potential high of 120 to 16. Two elementary schools and two middle schools will participate. One elementary school and one middle school will have test scores that are low for the district as a whole. The other two schools will have scores that are high. Within each school, the committee will randomly select two classrooms for each participating grade level: fifth grade for the two elementary schools and sixth, seventh, and eighth for the middle schools. Each participating classroom will use four chapters, two from each series. One classroom for every grade level will start with two chapters from Book 1; the other classroom will begin with Book 2. Halfway through the try out, classes will switch books. The value of this design is that it reduces the number of classrooms substantially without

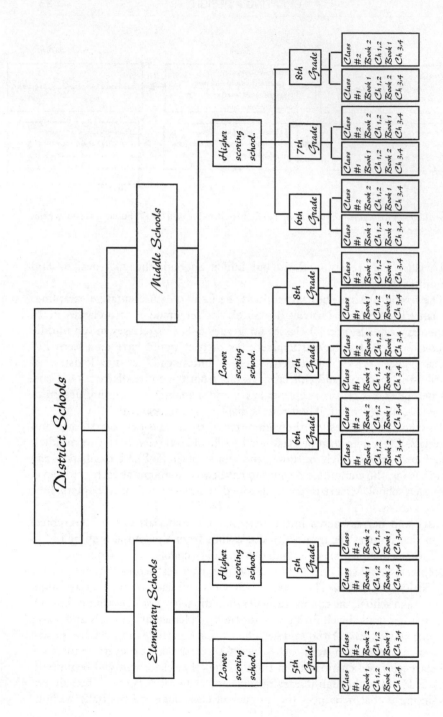

Figure 7.20 A representative sampling design to guide classroom try out.

biasing the results. Neither book is tried out more than the other, is used at a particular grade level more often than the other, is used with high scoring students more than the other, or is used first more than the other.

Having constructed their two designs, Clark, Mathews, and Taylor conduct the review and try out. They choose and publicize review sites around the district. Each site has a visual display to prepare the public for the review task. One wall is covered with curriculum, comprehensibility, and instructional goal designs. The remaining walls display the design pictures and summary charts prepared by the selection committee. On tables in the room are the student editions, teacher editions, and ancillary materials for the two series. An instruction sheet asks reviewers to study the analysis in light of the goals, skim through the materials, and note on a questionnaire where their impressions support or disagree with the analysis. The committee of three summarizes the results on summary charts similar to those used during the larger committee's analysis.

At the same time, Clark and her assistants recruit the 16 try out teachers specified by the sampling design. To prepare teachers for the try out, they conduct several workshops to teach participants the CORE model and give them practice using it to design instruction. At the final session, teachers meet in grade-level groups to work out instructional designs for the eight chapters for their grade level, four from each of the two series. Together they design CORE lessons, using suggestions and tasks from the series as much as possible. Whenever a series has no suggestions, the group designs its own approach, but any plans are based directly on the materials in the series and are uniform across teachers and classes.

Teachers return to their classrooms, integrating the try out chapters into their instruction over the course of the next few months. To measure the success of the instruction, teachers collect a portfolio of student work. Their goal is to provide the best demonstrations of students completing connect, organize, reflect, and extend tasks. At the end of the try out period, Clark and her assistants interview the 16 teachers, asking them to assess how well each of the two series supports the CORE model.

Besides assessing a series' instructional strength, try out is also a time to focus on comprehensibility. While the selection committee analyzed the comprehensibility of textbook sections, it neglected subsections of a few paragraphs. The comprehensibility group had explained that, while they would certainly expect a textbook editor to be concerned about the comprehensibility of paragraphs, a paragraph-level analysis requires greater text analysis skills than they had. A workable alternative to text analysis is to ask students to assess the comprehensibility of several small sections from a textbook. Clark and her assistants choose a small section from each of the chapters in the two series used in the try out. Immediately prior to teachers beginning a round of instruction, children read two sections on the same content and compare them. For example, eighth-graders read two five-paragraph subsections on problems that new immigrants had with city life. One subsection is from Book 1; the other from Book 2. After reading, all youngsters complete a paper/pencil rating, assessing which version is easier to understand, which is better organized, which is more interesting, and which they would include in a textbook. Results supplement the committee analysis.

After review and try out is finished, Dr Clark meets with her two assistants. Their task is to evaluate the data. Posted on the wall are the summary sheets from their analysis. The three search for evidence that disconfirms the selection committee's work. Do teacher interviews and student portfolios suggest that the materials support the CORE model better than the analysis indicated? Do student ratings demonstrate important differences in comprehensibility at the paragraph level? The committee of three prepares new overall summary sheets that integrate the try out data, the review data, and the selection committee's text analysis.

Selecting a textbook series

Although we have not mentioned the school board until now, throughout the selection, Carole Clark has been reporting to them regularly in anticipation of the moment when the selection committee would have enough data for the board to make a decision. As soon as the committee had completed its goal designs, she shared the diagrams with the board, explained the basis for the designs, and elicited official approval from the board members. Once the committee had completed its analysis of the student textbooks and teacher editions, she again returned to the board to present a detailed report. Dr Clark explained why the committee had eliminated all but two of the series for close scrutiny as well as the committee's conclusion that, while neither series fitted the original goal designs closely, one series was a closer match to both the curriculum and comprehensibility designs than the other. To support her conclusions, she displayed both the design pictures and the summary sheets that the committee had prepared.

Members of the school board were impressed with the work of the committee. They asked Dr Clark to clarify some of the design diagrams and to explain some of the committee's summary ratings. They asked her to propose how the district could help teachers learn to capitalize on the strengths of either series to design instruction that would reach the original goals. Satisfied with her answers, they passed a resolution to support the work of the committee thus far.

Dr Clark returned to the board a third time to present the designs that she, Ms Mathews, and Mr Taylor had prepared for review and try out. She asked for the board's help in publicizing the review sites and invited each member to participate in the review. She also explained the sampling plan for classroom try outs, stressing both its efficiency and its lack of bias. Board members asked several questions of clarification, but passed a resolution approving the two plans.

Now Elysian Fields School District finally has enough data to make a decision. The data are pictured and summarized. Dr Clark reconvenes her selection committee, they evaluate both their earlier analyses and the last of the overall summary sheets, and they choose one series over the other. Dr Clark makes her final report to the school board, displaying again all of the charts that support the recommendation of this one series. The board accepts the recommendation with little hesitation. Elysian Fields schools have a new textbook series. Clark completes her work by sharing the same subset of diagrams and charts with publishers who had submitted their series for consideration.

Our depiction of this final task is admittedly skimpy. In addition to textbook design, textbook selection involves considering political pressures. Such considerations are outside the realm of our work. If a selection committee has completed the first three tasks with care, and has communicated throughout with the school board, the final decision should be straightforward and supportable. In chapter 9, we return to the issues involved in public decision-making and discuss them in greater detail.

The Versatility of the Lenses

Our purpose in this chapter has been to demonstrate how a small set of rubrics can bring "design" to the development, adoption, and selection of textbooks. To make our point, we have focused heavily on a fictional district committee establishing goals, analyzing the text, conducting review and try out, and making a final choice. Our scenario suggests that considering the elements and linkages according to a theme, sketching a picture of the design, and evaluating the picture according to a set of criteria is a powerful approach with versatility. Indeed, we propose that the same set of lenses can be used by states adopting and publishers developing textbook materials.

Suppose that we were forced to choose whether publishers, adopters, or selectors could make best use of the rubrics. Who would we pick? During the past few years, as we have become acquainted with presidents, vice presidents, editors-in-chief, editors, and field consultants from textbook publishers of various sizes, we have repeatedly been impressed with their expertise. And we suspect that they are in the best position both to appreciate and apply the design rubrics. If textbooks were well-designed from the level of entire series to subsections of a few paragraphs, selection committees would be able to recognize and evaluate the design with ease. Only when materials are poorly designed does the analysis become difficult and tedious. Order is simple to identify and analyze; chaos is far more difficult.

In chapter 9, we explore what textbook publishing, adoption, and selection could look like if publishers, states, districts, and professional organizations each were to assume an appropriate leadership role. Publishers point out that they are providers, and as such must respond rather than lead. Perhaps. Nonetheless, we argue that if publishing staffs used the lenses that we have proposed at each stage of textbook development, many of the current textbook problems would be solved, regardless of whether the marketplace ever assumed a leadership role.

Notes

1   Brown et al. (1993).
2   Textbook Adoption Advisory Services, 25B Esquire Drive, Manchester, CT 06040; telephone (203) 649-9517.
3   Adoption Guidelines Project (1990).
4   Actually from California State Board of Education (1988), pp. 3–4.
5   California State Board of Education (1988).
6   Texas Education Agency (1991).
7   College Entrance Examination Board (1986).

Part III

STEPPING INTO THE FUTURE

8

A NEW APPROACH TO TEXTBOOK DESIGN: INSTRUCTIONAL SUPPORT SYSTEMS

Up to this point, we have traced a path in which the goal of educational publishing is to create the best possible student textbook, the focus of adoption and selection committees. Accordingly, we have focused on text comprehensibility, curriculum coherence, and instructional effectiveness. The teacher's job has been to "get the kids through the book," the better the book, the better the outcome. In this chapter we propose a strategy for reform of instructional materials that retains the advantages of the current approach. We describe an integrated package developed by educational publishers. This package satisfies the needs of a diverse marketplace reflecting both state and local decisions, but also addresses an educational future that meets the challenge of higher achievement standards, while accommodating variations in students and situations. The strategy entails a shift in focus from the *student textbook* toward what we are labeling the *instructional support system* (ISS).

We present a system designed to support the teacher in creating a community of inquiry within the classroom, a learning environment that opens access to a wide range of resource materials, in which curriculum goals are reached by alternate routes, and mileposts ensure that progress is monitored. The *teacher's guidebook* is the centerpiece of the instructional support system. The teacher, rather than moving students in lock step fashion through the student textbook, employs the guidebook to make professional decisions that shape instruction throughout the school year. The instructional support system, in short, is a strategy for achieving fundamental change in education without a major upheaval in the existing structure of schools and the other institutions that currently undergird that structure. Student textbooks remain part of published materials, but as anthologies and reference sources more than paths through a fixed curriculum. Teacher "manuals" are retained as an essential feature of the publisher's system; not as detailed instructions on using the textbook, but as a professional resource for designing the school year within a curriculum domain – CORE for the teacher.

Admittedly, publishers have explored various alternatives to the conventional textbook. One technique entails stand-alone modules that can be used "off the shelf" in whatever order the teacher chooses. When California moved toward literature-based learning several years ago, small (and not-so-small) publishing houses offered inexpensive paperback versions of standard children's classics such as *Charlotte's Web*[1] and *Roll of Thunder, Hear my Cry*,[2] most on state-approved lists. The result for schools and teachers was a bewildering embarrassment of riches: what books to buy, for what grade levels, and what to do once you had them. Publishers responded with study guides for approved stories, in essence creating mini-basals. Similar modules have emerged in science ("magnets and electricity," "volcanoes and earthquakes') and social studies ("the Constitution and the Declaration of Independence"). These materials permit considerable flexibility, in that individual teachers can decide which modules to use and when to use them. They are not necessarily adaptable, because the directions can be as prescriptive as a regular textbook. Scattershot movement through unrelated topics is unlikely to promote the development of expert lenses suggested in earlier chapters. Thematic relations that bring coherence to literary works are easily lost in the shuffle.

Another contemporary development is the teacher handbook, a resource manual with numerous student projects and activities. It is left to the teacher to decide on the progression and to identify appropriate student materials. Again, the result ensures flexibility, and the teacher is forced to be adaptable at some level. But coherence becomes a major challenge, because most teachers lack needed time and energy to design their own curriculum almost from scratch.

The dilemma, then, is between curriculum coherence and instructional efficacy. The front-to-back textbook offers a solution of sorts to the first problem, but instruction is neither flexible nor adaptable. Using the terms of the CORE model, there is little likelihood that students will *connect* with the ideas and information, *organization* will be neglected in the rush to cover the material, and time is not available to *reflect*, nor for the project-based activities that *extend* student understanding and transfer.

A different resolution of this dilemma is possible when the classroom teacher has a conceptual understanding of the curriculum domain, possesses an overarching structure and starting points for lessons, activities, and projects, and knows how to organize resources and schedules to invite experimentation and student-centered inquiry. This answer turns the CORE model on its head and applies it to teachers.

Today's teachers have implicit ideas about curriculum, instruction, and assessment, often based on their experiences as students. Innovations in the design of published materials must connect with this background. (a) Teachers are accustomed to scope-and-sequence charts that cover the material, and they feel a responsibility for comprehensive coverage. We propose a new model that provides a road map with clear starting and ending points, along with a handful of mileposts along the way. (b) Teachers are accustomed to teacher-directed instruction, with occasional excursions into small group activities and individual assignments. We propose a new model that begins with teacher-guided activities, but then turns to a progression in which students take on increasing responsibility. (c) Finally, teachers are accustomed to curriculum-embedded assessment, pre-tests that allow them to place students in ability groups, and end-of-unit tests that tell them which students have learned the material and which ones need a rerun. We propose a new model that incorporates assessment into the fabric of instruction, encouraging and supporting teachers to rely increasingly on their own judgments about patterns of student growth.

The primary organizational challenges for teacher decision-making are the management of time and students. Current series treat the school year as a steady progression of texts, lessons, and activities. Our model employs assessment activities as "bookends" to begin (Connect) and end (reconnect) the year, with direct instruction (Organize) based on the initial assessment results, and a move toward larger thematically oriented student projects (Reflect and Extend). Skills are the focus early in the year, and integrated activities toward the end. This plan provides teachers a broad framework within which adaptations are not only encouraged but are impossible to avoid.

Reflection comes about in two ways in this design. First, because the series does not provide sufficient "work" to fill the available time, the teacher must introduce complementary texts and activities along the way. Today's textbooks leave students and teachers out of breath trying to complete the coverage; there is no time to think. The design that we propose starts with the principle that "less can be more," by leaving time for reflection, and for bringing in ancillary materials and assignments that are appropriate to student interests and current events. These adaptations often take shape as thematic projects that extend skill and knowledge into the "zone of proximal development,"[3] assignments that stretch students to achieve beyond their grasp. Such adaptations can be supported by instructional materials, but cannot be completely prepackaged.

Second, to focus on a small number of outcomes that are linked across grades opens the way for professional dialog among teachers. For example, literature – stories, fairy tales, narratives – is important for the development of literacy in the elementary and middle grades. Story analysis can be based on four building blocks across this entire span: character, plot, setting, and theme. These four curriculum elements appear during assessment, direct instruction, and student projects, but also offer a technical vocabulary for teachers across the grades to enter into a professional dialog that is largely missing today, and that is the essence of genuine reflection.

To illustrate the concept of an instructional support system, we will rely on the textbook series with the greatest influence on education in the United States – the basal reader. The next section describes the contemporary basal reader system, as a backdrop for the instructional support system.

Current Systems for Teaching Reading

Reading textbooks have an enormous influence on literacy instruction. Publishers invest far more resources in basal readers than in the social studies and science textbooks described in previous chapters, and elementary teachers spend more time on reading instruction than any other domain. Citizens gauge the success of schools by reading test scores more than any other indicator.

Current reading series have their origins in the nineteenth-century McGuffey's Readers.[4] McGuffey personally assembled these bare bone collections, and also handled promotion and sales. There was little competition, and the series became an instant commercial success, although it was soon mimicked by a dozen clones. McGuffey's comprised a graded series of 4 × 6 inch student books, 150–250 pages in length, with 60–80 selections of fables, stories, poems, each a few pages long. Each lesson included a vocabulary list, a selection with several questions, and a phonics exercise. At the front of each book were a few prefatory comments for the teacher concerning educational philosophy and instructional practice: "More difficult words are often repeated, as this is the only method of learning anything thoroughly."[5] The series included group practice in oral reading and spelling practice. Moral education was emphasized: "The reading lessons are derived from the purest fountains of juvenile literature."[6] Much was left to teacher judgment. The lessons were insufficient to cover the entire school year, and so had to be supplemented by other sources. The series contained no explicit guidance about instructional format and procedures, leaving the teacher to prepare lessons.

Today's basal reading series are much changed from McGuffey's. First appearing in the 1930s and burgeoning after World War II, large and intricate basal readers have dominated the textbook market for the past half-century. These programs handle the entire reading program from kindergarten through eighth grade. The influx of inexperienced teachers during the post-war baby boom were provided with detailed scripts, with the assurance that these incorporated the expert precepts of contemporary reading experts. Basals included *consumables* such as student workbooks and worksheets, more than enough to keep students busy practicing skills for the entire school year. Publishers offered workshops to client districts, partly to explain the proper use of the materials, but also to sustain an ongoing business relationship. Basal series were revised every five years or so, and repeat business was critical.

Basal readers became the flagship of the major elementary publishers. Reading is the focal point of the K–8 curriculum. Standardized reading tests became commonplace in the 1950s, and newspaper reports pressured school administrators to "increase those test scores." School principals responded by mandating time and materials, sometimes designating a third or more of the

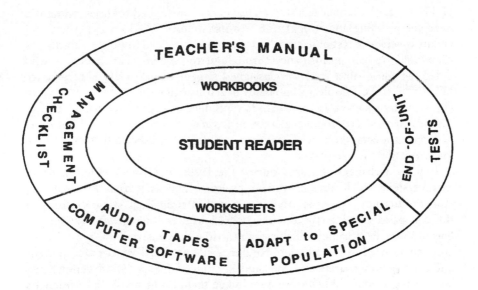

Figure 8.1 The design of contemporary basal reading series.

school day to basal reading in the early grades, especially in schools with low test scores. Other curriculum areas – social studies, science, mathematics, art and music, and even writing – had to make do with the time that was left.

The student reader or anthology is the centerpiece of the basal design (figure 8.1). Student workbooks and worksheets are closely linked to the reader, the teacher's manual serving as the "glue" that connects the other elements. The overriding theme in this design is steady progression through the textbook from beginning to end in fixed order, with repeated practice on work sheets ensuring that students become proficient in the behavioral objectives incorporated in each lesson. From an economic perspective, the high-cost items are the student materials: texts and workbooks. Other components, including the teacher's manual, are often giveaways.

As we have already noted, readability, indexed by word familiarity and sentence length, became an important consideration for design of the student textbook in the 1940s.[7] Vocabulary control became more important than content; hence the advent of "Dick and Jane" stories written specifically for basals. Passages repeating a few short and familiar words presumably eased students into fluent oral reading. Story substance and interest were downplayed; students first needed to learn to read aloud with fluency and skill. Appreciation of genuine children's literature could wait until later.

The teacher's manual accustomed teachers to prescribed routines, with little need for planning and preparation. Administrators relied on the manual to ensure coverage of test objectives. Curriculum-embedded multiple-choice tests monitored student performance throughout the school year. Students who failed the end-of-unit tests were assigned remedial worksheets to re-practice failed objectives. Simple technologies began to enter the picture. The Ditto copier, an inexpensive way in which to reproduce student materials, became an essential part of classroom management; while the teacher worked with one group of students, the rest of the class completed worksheets that came to be known as the "purple plague."

Important changes appeared during the 1960s. Publishers added management systems to document student progress, and as a basis for assigning students to ability groups. Audiotapes helped individual students through difficult passages while the teacher worked with another group. Computer-based programs became available for individualized instruction, typically for students in need of remediation. Resource kits provided word-practice cards and overhead transparencies, video and computer software. These components were optional, and publishers seldom linked them to the textbook or teacher's manual. They did help with classroom management: "While I'm working with the 'robins,' the 'blue jays' can finish their workbook assignments, and the 'cardinals' can move to the listening (audiotape) station."

In the 1980s, largely in response to the Whole Language movement,[8] some publishers moved away from readability formulas and the skills emphasis of the post–Sputnik era toward genuine children's literature. The student reader was supplemented by "big books" in the early grades (super-sized editions of classics such as *Three Little Pigs*) and "chapter books" in the middle grades (e.g., *Charlotte's Web* and *James and the Giant Peach*[9]). Two core components remained constant during this transformation: the student reader and the teacher's manual. We will now look at these elements from two recent series: *Silver Secrets* (fourth grade) by Silver Burdett & Ginn,[10] and *Literary Readers: Book 4* by Houghton Mifflin.[11] Both were bestsellers; both reflect excellent models of current practice. SBG tends toward skill development while HM highlights a literary tradition – a valuable contrast.

The Student Readers

This central element of the basal reading series takes shape as an attractive anthology, around 250–300 8 × 10 inch pages for fourth-grade students. Selections range from 1–2-page excerpts through 6–10-page short stories, with an occasional work of greater length. The selections are mostly narratives – stories, fables, and personal anecdotes. Today's series feature award winners by top-ranked authors, assurance of literary quality and freedom from censorship (good writers seldom allow their works to be edited, although they do permit excerption). Vocabulary control and readability formulas play a minor role in textbook design by this grade level, and stories are chosen with an eye to developmental appropriateness. The anthology also includes poems, playlets, and expository snippets, most only a few pages long.

The books are attractive, richly illustrated with full-color pictures covering a half-page or more. They are of sturdy construction, designed to serve multiple students for 5–7 years between adoptions – the only national standards for textbooks are those of the Association of American Publishers that define physical features. Today's publishers also offer "separates," stand-alone paperback trade books. The anthology prepared for each grade contains material sufficient for the entire school year. Each student is issued a reader at the beginning of the year, which he or she returns when school ends, hopefully only slightly the worse for wear.

Responding to increased interest in literary themes and thematic projects, publishers now organize student anthologies into topical segments rather than the lesson-by-lesson sequence typical of earlier series. HM's *Literary Readers*, for example, lead students through Nature, Sharing, Challenges, Dreams Come True, Facing the Truth, and Self-Discovery. Each section includes a few stories along with some poetry and an occasional essay. SBG's *Silver Secrets* organizes the fourth-grade experience around four themes: imagination–fantasy, nature and the environment, words and communication, and entrepreneurship.

Current designs for thematic segments are only partly successful, in our judgment. For instance, SBG's second theme, Hidden Worlds, focuses on environmental issues. The major selections include two Native American stories (one a fable, the other contemporary), an excerpt from Laura Ingalls Wilder's *Little House in the Big Woods*, describing a visit by two bears, a short story by Isaac Bashevis Singer about a family parakeet, an immigrant tale by Betty Waterton (the grandmother's seeds are lost during a wagon trip, but bloom the following year), a lengthy poem on the desert experience by Byrd Baylor, and a modern fable, *The Mountain that Loved a Bird*, by Alice McLerran. Scattered along the way are several other short passages, a little poetry, and a few expositions. The teacher's manual suggests an array of activities – keep a diary like Wilder's, transform McLerran's piece into a puppet show. However, the segment lacks coherence. The environmental theme is not emphasized at the beginning of the unit, nor is it reviewed at the end of the unit, neither in the teacher's manual nor the student textbook. Student activities are embedded within individual passage-lesson sets, with no explicit connection from one passage to the next. Selections and activities are disconnected and lack integration.

The HM Self-Discovery segment includes excerpts describing a young girl's encounter with George Washington (Fritz' *The Cabin Faced West*), a retelling

of the Paul Bunyan fable by Malcomson, a day in the life of a young boy playing
hooky while chasing sheep (Krumbold's *And now Miguel*), and a dramatization
(*The Arrival of Paddington* by Bradley and Bond). The unit ends with a
comment to the student that "you have just read [how] a pioneer girl, a giant
lumberjack, and a young boy all discover who they truly are."[12] Expecting
young students to appreciate this generalization seems a bit of a stretch. Like
the SBG series, HM focuses students on the individual selections, offering
little connective tissue in either the anthology or the teacher's manual. The
student's text has a title page for the unit, but lacks an introduction. The
teacher is encouraged to "discuss with students what the characters discover
about themselves, and what they might discover about themselves in similar
situations,"[13] but the anthology provides no support for teacher or students for
pursuing this goal.

The anthologies are mostly text and decorative art. SBG begins each
selection with a brief synopsis and concludes with a Follow-Up page of
discussion questions and writing exercises. At the end of *The Mountain that
Loved a Bird*, for example, students are asked "Why did the bird have to leave
the mountain; what happened when the mountain's heart broke; how did the
mountain change during the story?"[14] The parallel to McGuffey is remarkable,
except that McGuffey provided no answers in the teacher's manual. The HM
anthology is virtually all text, with no student activities along the way, a trend
that publishers have increasingly adopted in recent years: a reading book is for
reading, not studying.

The material is generally fun reading. Unlike the 1960s "Dick and Jane," the
stories are real literature – and indeed mostly narratives. What are the learning
objectives for these passages? For "Dick and Jane," the stories were an occasion
to practice reading aloud, but current designs clearly have something else in
mind. Our previous chapters focused on expository passages, which are typical
of science and social studies. The goal in these materials is to learn the content:
the causes of earthquakes and volcanoes, geographic landmarks, biological
taxonomies, and so on. The obvious challenge in textbook design is to ensure
that the content is comprehensible and memorable. The use of high-quality
children's literature in reading anthologies ensures that the text design is
coherent and comprehensible. Stories that are disorganized and difficult to
understand will not sell, will not win awards, and will not be selected. A good
starting point! But the question remains: How can students acquire the expert's
lens for viewing narratives? Our suggestion is that they could learn how stories
are constructed, a student-friendly introduction to the analysis of text structures. The point is that, since the stories are so well designed, why not use them
to help students learn how to look behind the scenes of a "fun story" to gain a
deeper understanding of narrative design, including the literary themes that are
the hallmark of good literature?

How are stories typically built? We extend our discussion of narrative structure in chapter 2. The structural analysis of a narrative is primarily sequential but, unlike the string of events that explain the water cycle or present the history of California, narrative episodes reflect human motives and respon- ses.[15] Stories are slices of life that can lead the reader to empathize with the characters. Story analysis builds on four design elements: character, plot, setting, and theme.[16] The typical narrative challenges the characters with an overriding problem, and the plot then moves toward the resolution of this problem – for better or worse. The setting positions the characters in time and space, within a situation that engages the reader by its novelty and intrigue. In all but the simplest stories, action occurs in a sequence of episodes, each with its subplot. Situation comedies and soap operas illustrate the idea, as does *The Three Little Pigs*. As one fourth grader put it, "When an episode ends, that's where you can put a commercial." Although sequence is fundamental in story analysis, other structures serve a role. The matrix, for instance, provides students with a graphic organizer to compare and contrast characters within a story, or to bring together two or three related stories.

We will illustrate story analysis with Laura Ingall Wilder's *Two Big Bears*, a story within a story within a story that appears in both the SBG and HM fourth-grade anthologies. Clearly a popular choice, this ten-page extract is an intricate but engaging piece of writing, which consistently captures the imag- ination of ten-year-olds – the question is, how to help students "see" the author's craft in building it. As figure 8.2 shows, the tale begins on a winter day in the North Woods, the father off to trade his furs, the family left to fend for itself – the implicit "initiating" problem, as story grammarians label it. The story continues with three episodic events that build tension, when, finally, the first bear appears in the barnyard. This threat is resolved when Laura and her mother manage to make it back to the house. The father's return home closes out the problem raised by his absence, and then he tells his own "bear tale," after which everyone goes to bed. The graphic analysis of this beguiling story suggests that its underlying structure may account for its attractiveness – just when the reader thinks everything is working out, a new problem arises. The intertwined plot structure of the two bear tales offers an opportunity to compare and contrast different approaches to story development. In one instance the threat is real; in the other it is not. In one instance the protagonists solve the problem by a judicious retreat; in the other the father launches an audacious attack.

From our perspective, a fundamental question is how instructional materials can help the teacher to lead students through an analysis of the story structure to achieve a particular curriculum goal. Learning about plot structure is one obvious possibility; one can also imagine contrasting the characters, or delving into the thematic issue of how to handle a threatening situation. How should we

ANALYSIS OF STORY STRUCTURE

Winter in the Big Woods, icicles on the little house	**SETTING-- STORY A**
Pa has to go to town to trade furs	INITIATING PROBLEM A
Pa sets off with a big load and no gun; Ma and Laura are worried	EPISODE 1
Sunset, Pa's not back, time for chores Ma and Laura go to barn to milk Sukey	EPISODE 2

In grey light, Laura sees dark shape by
  barn gate -- looks like Sukey has
  escaped from the barn
	EPISODE 3

	STORY B

Ma pushes open gate and slaps the cow,
  then realizes that this animal has
  shaggy fur and glittering eyes -- a bear!
	INITIATING PROBLEM B

Ma tells Laura to turn around and walk
  back to house -- slowly at first, then
  dashing for safety to the house, where
  they are safe behind the heavy logs
	RESOLUTION B

The night goes on, no sign of Pa, the girls go to sleep	EPISODE 4
Morning, Pa arrives with candy and calico, everyone is relieved and happy	RESOLUTION A

Later, after supper, Pa gathers girls to
  tell his bear story. Trading furs took
  longer than Pa thought, so it was dark
  when he started home. Lots of bear
  tracks, only star light to see by
	SETTING -- STORY C

Suddenly, in open space ahead, a big black bear raised up on hind legs	INITIATING PROBLEM C

No gun, the bear unmoving, no turning
  back, so Pa started running straight
  at the bear, shouting and waving arms.
  The bear didn't move
	EPISODE 1

Pa picked up a large branch and charged ahead, striking bear with all his might	EPISODE 2
Wood against wood -- the "bear" was a large stump!	RESOLUTION C
Both Pa and Ma had shown their bravery --time for the girls to go to bed	FINAL CONCLUSION

Figure 8.2   Story analysis of Wilder's *Two Big Bears*.

lay out for the teacher some "big picture" possibilities without stultifying the process? The student readers are silent on this point; they simply present the stories. We look next at how the SBG and HM teacher manuals answer this question.

The Teacher's Manual

Walk into almost any elementary classroom in the United States during the reading lesson, and you are likely to see the teacher's manual in action. Surveys show that more than 75 per cent of fourth-grade teachers rely on basal readers, and assign weekly worksheet activities.[17] The teacher sits before a group of 8–12 students, each with his or her reader open to the assigned page, the manual spread imposingly across the teacher's lap, the other 15–20 students busy at their desks completing workbook exercises. The manual influences curriculum and instruction more strongly than perhaps any other educational force, yet outside the classroom it has remained virtually invisible for more than half a century. Scarcely any research or scholarship has focused on this accessory, nor on the mechanisms that sustain it: pre-service preparation of teachers (including textbooks on reading methods), professional services provided by publishers, principals' evaluation of teachers, and standardized tests.

Today's basal manual is physically impressive – a brightly illustrated, 2–5 pound volume of 400–700 oversize 10 × 12 inch pages, spiral-bound to open easily on to the teacher's lap. The first section of the manual contains general prefatory material: a statement of the reading philosophy and instructional strategy, a scope-and-sequence chart of learning objectives, cross-references to ancillary resources available in the series, and a list of the expert consultants who designed the program. This introduction is typically overlooked by the busy teacher, whose job is to get on with the business of instruction. The bulk of the manual comprises the sequence of scripted lesson plans that guide the teacher from beginning to end of the school year through the student anthology and associated worksheets and assessments. Procedures are standardized throughout the school year and over grades. Lessons during October and March, in first grade and in sixth, are virtually identical. The content varies – stories are longer and the vocabulary more demanding – but the routines remain the same.

The *lesson* is the basic building block of the basal design: the sequence of activities before, during, and after the reading of the selection. The teacher determines how to manage time and students, but otherwise follows fairly explicit instructions about the lesson introduction, questions to raise along the way, directions for skill development, and activities to support story comprehension. The format begins with *preparation*; questions around the general topic covered by the selection, and introduction of problematic words.

Preparation may take only a few minutes or may last for two or even three 20-minute periods. Students next open their books to the story; the teacher moves them one page at a time, asking questions from the manual at the bottom of each page. Depending on passage length and student facility, reading the passage may take one or more class periods. The lesson postlude entails additional discussion and analysis, focused on development of specific skills (infer, analyze cause–effect, evaluate character).

The SBG format has four elements: bridging (or preparation), vocabulary, passage comprehension, and skill development (figure 8.3). The two preparatory segments in *Silver Secrets* are quite elaborate. The Bridge is two pages on "Word Study" linked to a previous selection on Eskimo life, where the task is to figure out how to handle strange words such as *mukluk* and *parka*: "Explain that students can use context clues to define unfamiliar words . . . . Why are context clues important? [Answer: They help readers figure out the meanings of words.]"[18] Vocabulary preparation goes on for two more pages, including a segment on concept development, and memorization of 16 "critical words" from the upcoming story (e.g., *trembling*, *quivered*, *bargain*).

The preparatory segments end with exercises that "build background" ("What would you do if you were walking along by yourself and suddenly right in front of you was an enormous bear?"[19]) and "develop purpose" ("Explain to students that they will apply the strategy of making thought circles to represent characters' thoughts."[20]). The manual then proceeds page by page through the passage with detailed questions ("What is the dark shaggy animal that Laura sees . . . ? Answer: A bear."[21]). The passage reading ends with follow-up questions in the student anthology, the manual spelling out questions and answers ("Why did Ma slap at a bear at the barnyard gate? Answer: She could not see well in the dark and thought the bear was their cow."[22]). The questions are somewhat redundant.

The final lesson segment is a hodgepodge of activities. Workbook pages provide students with further practice on the vocabulary words and on skill objectives from the preparatory period. Other activities are optional (e.g., students act out scenes from the story, draw character sketches, and compare the two bears). These supplementary tasks, some quite imaginative, require significant preparation, and teachers seldom include them in the lesson.[23] They take additional time and effort, and they are not tested.

The HM manual, although more casual and open-ended, has a similar lesson structure. The preparatory lesson segments include a brainstorming exercise ("Write the word Pioneers on the chalkboard. Then ask students to think of words they associate with pioneer living"[24]) and vocabulary practice (*lantern, faint, quivered*). Reading of the selection is organized in two segments. The primary segment directs the teacher to cover the concepts of plot and prediction; the secondary segment poses specific questions and answers ("What did

Day 1: **THE BRIDGE**
        Introduce topic -- Context Clues
        o   Teacher uses several sentences from previous story on Eskimos to
                instruct about sentence-level clues: 'The snow crunched under the
                mukluks on their feet.'
        o   Worksheets for skill practice

Day 2: **VOCABULARY STRATEGIES**
        Story and Support Words
        Strategy -- Semantic Mapping
                Sixteen words from <u>Two big bears</u> are taught by direct instruction, study
                predefined 'map,' and worksheet practice

Day 3: **GUIDING COMPREHENSION**
        Build Background
                'What would you do if you were walking . . ., and suddenly right in front of
                you was an enormous bear?'
        Set purpose
                Make 'thought circles' to imagine characters' thoughts
        Guide the Reading Process
                Detailed questions at bottom of each page: 'When does the story
                happen? How do you know?' 'When Pa doesn't return home, how do
                the girls feel?'

Day 4: **SELECTION FOLLOW-UP**
        o   Several questions similar to previous ones, plus a diagram showing
                how the bears were alike and different
        o   Optional 'creative' questions: 'What kind of person could live on a
                frontier?'
        o   Suggestions to dramatize, sketch characters

Day 5: **EXTENDING SKILLS** [worksheets]
        Introduce Alphabetic Order [to four places]
        Practice Context Clues
        Practice Classification
        Maintain suffixes <u>-en</u>, <u>-ous/ious</u>

ENRICHMENT [Optional]
        Create a Diorama
        Keep a Journal/Diary

READING FICTION [Optional]
        Context Clues [final lesson and worksheet]

Figure 8.3   The design for the Silver Burdett & Ginn lesson on *Two Big Bears.*

Laura and her mother see when they went to milk the cows? Answer: A bear at the barnyard gate."[25]). The manual includes a variety of post-reading projects: skill development ("Help students categorize similar feelings"[26]), dramatizing the story, and writing a personal narrative.

In these two series and others, the teacher's manual provides an integrated program that supports every facet of curriculum and instruction. The page-by-page directions script the teacher about what to teach, when and how to teach it, and how to arrange for practice and testing. The SBG manual includes page replicas from the student anthology and the workbook. The teacher literally finds *everything* needed for the reading lesson spread out on his or her lap. The HM manual, which relies on passage synopses rather than page replicas, is less scripted, but the routines are quite similar to those used by SBG. The structural uniformity from one series to another means that teachers can move between series with relative ease.

The manuals give less attention to several matters of critical importance in the management of classroom instruction: allocating time, organizing groups, and dealing with individual differences in student interest and achievement. These issues tend to be handled by local customs and district mandates, although advice from publishers' consultants can be helpful. As noted earlier, some districts mandate a daily time allocation for reading, especially if test scores are low. Teachers are told how much time to spend in the reading series, and sometimes even which pages to cover on a given day.

Most series fit naturally into weekly chunks: five sessions of 20–30 minutes for preparation, the actual "reading," and follow-up activities. Pacing varies with student ability, to be sure. The manual standardizes the teacher's actions, but one student responds briefly to a question about *aliens*, while a second strains for an answer, and a third talks forever about his favorite Saturday astronaut cartoon. Confronted by large and diverse classes, elementary teachers often divide the class into three homogeneous groups based on reading test scores. The midstream group progresses at one passage per week, slower students take longer or are placed in a lower-level anthology, and the fast group receives enrichment experiences. Three groups, half an hour each, time to exchange places and bathroom trips – reading instruction easily fills two hours a day in the typical classroom.

If teachers had to prepare three different lessons each day, the burden would be overwhelming. In fact, teachers handle the task by shifting to different places in the manual. The format follows the same routines; only the passage and questions differ. Workbooks and optional worksheets ensure an abundance of activities to occupy students at their desks. The manual assigns a basic set of worksheets for a lesson, and the teacher adds complementary worksheets as necessary: "They only made three workbook pages for this story, and my first group is fast. Better make copies of three extra 'worksheet masters' to keep them busy while I work with the slow group." Teachers often set up workstations with audiotapes and computers. In the later elementary grades, students who finish their work early are allowed to read library books of their own choosing.

Although adoption committees concentrate on the student anthology, the manual is what matters most to teachers. In addition, even though it is a "freebie," publishers invest considerable development effort and market research in the manual. Publishers typically offer professional development workshops as part of the package, generally at little or no cost. Workshops focus on "How to use the manual," along with ancillary tasks such as management of time and students. These follow-up services are critical for effective implementation of the reading series. Both publisher consultants and district administrators have told us that publisher reading in-service programs are often the major source of professional development for many teachers in both instruction (cooperative learning) and curriculum (literary themes).

What is the design?

What elements, linkages, and themes comprise today's basal reading series? As noted earlier in this section, the major elements in figure 8.1 form a topical net with the student textbook at the center. The main goal is to move students through the anthology following directions that spell out the routines and highlight the specific objectives for each lesson. The linkages among the elements depend almost entirely on the manual, which moves students from easier objectives toward more difficult ones.

Not apparent in the figure are several implicit themes of fundamental importance for understanding how reading is taught in today's elementary classrooms:

- The *routinization* of instruction – the assembly-line character of basal systems simplifies classroom planning and management. The lesson format remains virtually unchanged from the beginning of the school year until the end, from kindergarten through the middle-school years. The content shifts from an emphasis on phonics in the early grades toward text comprehension in the later years.
- Reading as *skill development* – the fundamental outcomes of reading instruction in the basal system are that students learn to read aloud with fluency and accuracy, to define words in decontextualized settings, and to answer questions about passage details. Reading is not primarily about concept development in this model.
- The *narrative* as the primary genre – today's student anthologies are mostly stories. Narratives tend to be more comprehensible than technical expository material; they are inherently more interesting, they have a relatively straightforward and familiar structure, and the "real literature" in today's series is actually fun to read! Exposition, especially as it appears in science and social studies textbooks, tends to be less comprehensible – less engaging, less well structured, and less "fun." Although the narratives are engaging, the comprehension instruction provided in the teacher's manual is rather superficial. Newer series attempt to promote thematic

understanding, but we have found few instances in which appreciation of thematic issues rises above routine literal questions.

- Activities to support *management* – the elementary teacher's main challenge is to keep students busy. The basal lesson design meshes with this theme. The panoply of workbooks, worksheets, and optional activities guarantees that teachers never lack for activities. To be sure, teachers also seem compelled to "do everything," and frequently express concern that they may "miss a skill."

Today's basal series are solidly pragmatic. They fill the needs of a marketplace in which teachers rely on detailed guidance for controlling large groups under difficult circumstances, with strong demands for accountability. The series make few if any professional demands on the classroom teacher (some manuals include professional articles, but these are not essential to the daily routines, and appear to attract limited attention). The series set out a fixed curriculum route for mainstream students, and youngsters who complete all of the assignments for a given year will usually show a year's growth on standardized tests. Differences in student background, development, ability, and interest are mentioned here and there in the manual, but it is left to the teacher to adapt activities to accommodate these differences; the manual is fundamentally designed as "one size fits all." Motivation is also seldom included as part of the system. Materials are brightly colored and attractively illustrated, and many activities are described as "games." But despite the earnest efforts of the program developers, the sameness of the lesson routines can become boring with the passing of months and years. Teachers often introduce variety by adding trade (library) books to the diet, arranging for drama and art events, taking field trips, and so on.

The bottom line is that the system works; most students become reasonably competent readers by the end of elementary school. On the other hand, many students develop little interest or understanding about literacy, and a significant proportion fail altogether. The next section proposes a design for a reading system that fosters an educational experience that is more appropriate to the needs for critical literacy of future graduates, a system that incorporates what we know about social–cognitive learning, and that fosters the teacher's role as a professional responsible for making informed decisions.

The Teacher's Guide: Centerpiece of the Instructional Support System

In a world of accelerating change, effective instruction is flexible instruction. Today's textbooks are still oriented toward daily schedules printed on millions of chalk boards. The clock strikes 8:00, the school bell rings, students start their reading lessons; two hours later, the clock strikes 10:00, the school bell rings, time for recess and then the math lessons. Imagine instead school days organized around the flow of students' interests and investments in a task, weeks during which the allocation of time varies over subject matters. Today's textbooks lead to a school year in which September differs little from June. We imagine a differentiated school year, in which instruction moves from direct instruction toward larger thematic projects.

Effective instruction for tomorrow's graduates will mean social interaction, a classroom permeated with materials that promote cooperation and discussion, that support the development of "group intelligence." Students need to learn skills, but these need to be connected to purposeful outcomes – "Why am I doing this task? What do I need to know? Where can I find the information? Where can I find help? How can I help? How well are we doing the job?" This goal entails project-driven rather than activity-driven instruction, school tasks that take shape as genuine problems, where students are responsible for finding, framing, and exploring issues that connect with their situations. It means student-guided rather than teacher-directed activities. Materials to support this scenario will set forth genuine assignments that require time, that demand both individual and group investment, that incorporate an element of uncertainty (the answers are not in the back of the book), and that lead to significant outcomes that warrant public presentation.

Comprehensible texts will be the backbone of future systems. Video images and computer networking may seem to transcend mundane matters such as literacy, but the capacity to handle text is likely to be even more important in tomorrow's world, both for understanding complex data systems and also to gain access to the cheapest and oldest of information technologies – books and libraries. The coming generation of instructional systems will need to support students' capacity to handle reading and writing across a broad range of genre. For publishers, the challenge of comprehensibility will be to design "meta-texts" that provide students in the middle years of schooling with anthologies that offer choice while ensuring structure and interest. Perhaps the greatest challenge for publishers is to design a replacement for the teacher's manual that retains the best features (a rich array of activities) while moving away from today's lockstep.

Our recommendations for such a replacement are laid out in figure 8.4. The Teacher's Guide is the hub of an Instructional Support System. The other elements in the plan are linked into a matrix of sorts, whereby materials for teachers and students alike consider curriculum, instruction, and assessment. For example, under curriculum the ISS would provide text anthologies, reference books, magazines, technological resources, and so on for the student, and content updates, links to technological resources, tradebooks, magazines,

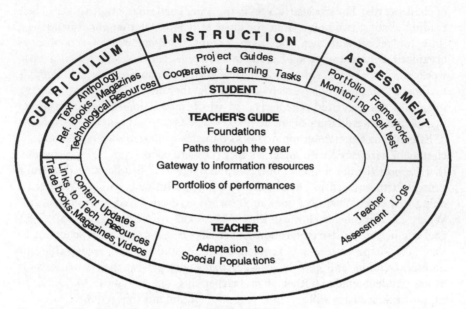

Figure 8.4   The design of an Instructional Support System.

and videos for the teacher. Central to the ISS concept is the notion that the teacher's role is critical for deciding what should be taught, and when and how to teach it. The challenge for publishers is to create a professional resource book that supports teachers in adapting a basic curriculum to variations in students and situations, and to provide a flexible array of student materials and resources – including a student textbook – for implementing this curriculum. The system offers a set of strategies rather than a fixed itinerary, a conceptual map rather than a list of directions, suggestions and models to coordinate resources rather than a "programmed instruction" manual. The basic components of the ISS model all have counterparts in the changes that we described above in many contemporary series. While our proposal is consistent with these trends, we emphasize the need to accelerate the pace of reform, particularly the task of "de-scripting" the teacher materials.[27]

Before turning to the Teacher's Guide, we offer a few words about the student materials at the top half of the figure. The student anthology in the ISS model remains a significant resource for introducing students to high-quality literature. Many of today's publishers provide classroom library sets; we urge even greater efforts to include contemporary works and offer greater variety – the tendency is to sell kits with 15 copies of eight titles (120 books), whereas two copies of 60 titles would provide greater coverage and choice. Expository works also need to be added to the mix. Science and history books are primarily expository, but these cover "serious" topics. Books about dinosaurs, earth-quakes and volcanoes, space travel, and other popular topics offer students the opportunity to acquire comprehension strategies for expository text.

The remainder of this chapter sketches a design and specifications for the ISS Teacher's Guide. For practical purposes, we assume that the Guide takes shape as a "book." Because the Guide is dynamic rather than linear (it bounces around rather than moving from beginning to end), and because the teacher's role is active rather than passive (creating plans rather than following prescriptions), a computer-based multi-media format offers many advantages. Nonetheless, we begin with today's "paper" realities. We also envision a future in which elementary teachers rely on a single system that integrates all subject matters, where reading, writing, and problem-solving are interwoven with literature, social studies and science, the arts, and even mathematics. Again, for practical reasons we will use a reading–writing series to illustrate how the Guide functions as part of the Instructional Support System.

The Guide is organized in four segments: *Foundations* lays out curriculum concepts and instructional strategies; *Pathways through the Year* presents practical sketches for organizing the school year, developing units, and conducting lessons; *Gateways to Information* describes the resources available in the series and elsewhere; and *Portfolios and Exhibitions* offers techniques for assessing student progress and program effectiveness. Each of these sections is described in greater detail below.

Foundations: Curriculum Concepts and Instructional Strategies

This section of the Guide provides the teacher with a professional cornerstone for adapting the core curriculum to local conditions. The Guide begins not with "the first lesson," but with a plan for designing the school year. Every grade level has its own Guide, but the Foundations section places each grade within a broader developmental perspective. The fourth-grade Guide, for example, links to third-grade outcomes and fifth-grade expectations. The teacher's vision is guided not by a fixed sequence of activities and outcomes, but by a developmental perspective that attends to variations in students' previous backgrounds and present interests. CORE runs throughout this plan as a way of supporting the teacher's efforts: *connecting* with the teacher's previous experiences and present situation, *organizing* the array of tasks confronting the teacher, scaffolding the difficult job of *reflection* during action, and offering attractive opportunities to *extend* instruction beyond the specifics provided in the Guide.

The plan incorporates the concept of the *differentiated school year* shown in figure 8.5, a functional scheme in which curriculum and instruction vary depending on needs and opportunities. Highest priority early in the year is

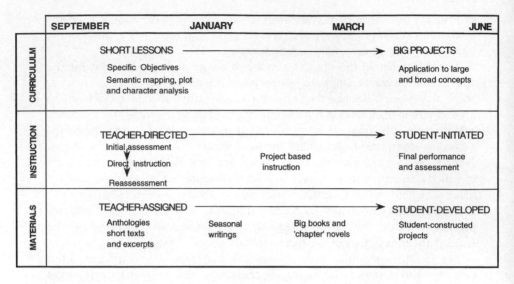

Figure 8.5 A plan for a differentiated school year.

"teaching for assessment." Short, coherent, familiar, high-interest student materials – comprehensibility is critical – allow the teacher to assess student competence in handling basic tasks. How well can students decode and spell? How do they handle the comprehension of words and tasks? What are their tactics and strategies for analyzing and interpreting stories and reports, for composing and comprehending? Later in the fall come the celebrations – Halloween, Thanksgiving, and the holidays of the winter solstice. The plan of action encourages teachers to cultivate literacy skills in a systematic but engaging manner during these seasons. Because they disregard the calendar, current manuals are blind to the passing of the seasons and holidays. Teachers are expected to teach "reading" even when children are absorbed with Halloween! January is a time for reassessment, and to set the stage for long-term thematic projects that span the fruitful months that stretch to the end of the school year. The year closes with assessment, a matching bookend to September's opening.

The *Foundations* section is primarily conceptual. Two major tasks confronting the elementary teacher at the start of the school year are *organization and assessment* – the creation of a literate classroom community and the appraisal of the skills, knowledge, and interests of the children who will be his or her charges for the next nine months. Teachers are left largely on their own to manage these responsibilities. How should the classroom be arranged for the first day of school? What should it look like? How should we make the best of opportunities and limitations? What if you are a fifth-grade teacher with 20 middle-class students, a part-time aide, and two computers, in rural New Hampshire – or fifth-grade teacher, with no assistance, serving 35 students from an impoverished community in South Central Los Angeles? We are not suggesting stereotypical answers. To the contrary, in each of the two preceding contexts, we imagine a Guide organized around alternatives that the teacher can adapt depending on his or her style and local contexts. For example, most contemporary classrooms blend whole-class, small-group, and individual activities. The teacher is in the best position to decide on the most appropriate mix of these patterns. The Guide should support the teacher in considering the options, and in designing the classroom environment accordingly. *Foundations* raises these issues and sketches responses that are described in greater detail in later sections of the Guide.

Classroom management is of paramount importance to all teachers. The safe alternative follows a military model; the teacher takes charge, sets the rules, and deals with the class as a "troop." Whole-class direct instruction meshes well with this philosophy. Most elementary students follow the rules and do as they are told, more or less willingly. For students to learn initiative, self-responsibility, and teamwork, however, the teacher must employ other management models: cooperative learning, conflict management, and student-selected activities. The Guide lays out various models with suggestions about how to construct a community of learners that is responsible and mutually supportive. Today's teachers may hear about such ideas in college courses and after-school workshops. The Guide incorporates the techniques as an integral part of the system.

The *Foundations* section also describes important features of the *literacy curriculum* undergirding the series. Reading is a highly politicized domain; some experts insist on precise specification of testable skills while others emphasize the holistic character of literacy. The key is to construct a workable middle ground; figure 8.6 describes progress from fourth through eighth grade by a developmental curriculum for narrative comprehension and composition that incorporates skills along the way.

Instructional strategies appear in the Guide as prototypical lessons: examples might include a 40-minute teacher-directed exercise, a one-week small-group activity, and a three-week thematic project, each exemplifying instructional strategies along the lines of the CORE model. The idea is to provide rich examples of prototypical lessons along with variations, potential problems, and opportunities – to promote professional reflection on the development and implementation of a lesson concept. The lesson designs are templates for planning rather than prescriptions for action.

The *Foundations* section of the Guide differs in significant ways from contemporary teacher manuals. It is a reference to which the teacher returns throughout the school year for guidance and ideas, a resource for supporting a

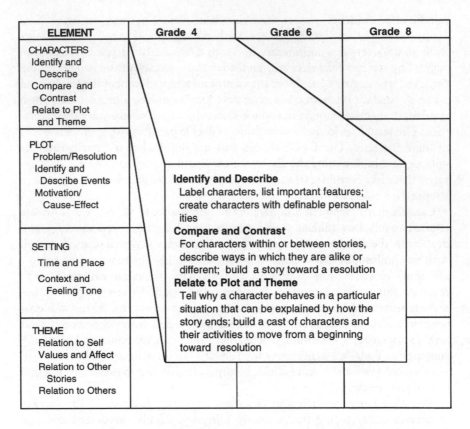

ELEMENT	Grade 4	Grade 6	Grade 8
CHARACTERS Identify and Describe Compare and Contrast Relate to Plot and Theme			
PLOT Problem/Resolution Identify and Describe Events Motivation/ Cause-Effect	**Identify and Describe** Label characters, list important features; create characters with definable personalities **Compare and Contrast** For characters within or between stories, describe ways in which they are alike or different; build a story toward a resolution **Relate to Plot and Theme** Tell why a character behaves in a particular situation that can be explained by how the story ends; build a cast of characters and their activities to move from a beginning toward resolution		
SETTING Time and Place Context and Feeling Tone			
THEME Relation to Self Values and Affect Relation to Other Stories Relation to Others			

Figure 8.6 An example of a developmental curriculum matrix for describing standards of progress in narrative comprehension and composition during elementary grades.

level of professional development that is unfortunately rare in today's schools. Educators seem not to recognize the importance of publishers as a resource for professional development. In fact, publishers routinely provide consultants as a "perk" to districts that adopt their series, a continuing service to customers. We propose a Guide that provides a foundation for ongoing professional development at a time when curriculum, instruction, and assessment are all undergoing major change. We also suggest that publishers offer professional development services to consumers, not as a "perk," but as a valuable and valued part of the series, part of *Foundations* and part of the purchase price.

Pathways Through the Year

Following the conceptual introduction to the Guide, the "bread and butter" comes in the three following sections. The first of these, Pathways, concretizes the differentiated school year, zooming in from the broad strokes of the Foundations to more focused views. Included, for instance, are detailed plans for one- or two-week segments or *lesson blocks* centered around a particular curriculum goal and instructional function. The blocks serve as frames or templates, starting points to assist the teacher in planning a coherent unit of substantial duration, while indicating alternatives and encouraging adaptability. *Pathways*, following the layout in figure 8.5, includes segments that emphasize initial organization and assessment, instruction of specific objectives, and the development of student-constructed projects.

The basic lesson-block concept is presented in figure 8.7. We have chosen a two-week plan as the starting point not because two weeks is magical, but to suggest the importance of spending sufficient time to engage with a topic. Practically speaking, a two-week segment also recognizes the reality of weekends, the possibility that young students may forget, and the value of review and extension. Lesson-block designs build explicitly on the CORE model. The opening event connects with student experience. Direct instruction emphasizes organization. By the end of the first week, the groundwork has been laid for activities during the second week that stretch student learning and give opportunities for presentations and assessments. The emphasis in this design is on depth rather than coverage.

We suggested in the previous section that the first few weeks of the school year be devoted to developing a classroom community and assessing the students. Classroom assessment is in the midst of a major paradigm shift, a change from curriculum-embedded multiple-choice tests toward reliance on teacher-based judgments of student competence. Portfolios and performance tests are "hot items." What do these terms mean, and how can they be connected to the reading–writing curriculum? The Guide, as we conceive it, approaches this matter developmentally, providing models that describe how the teacher can assess through instruction. It is easy to create conditions that lead to failure. The challenge is to create situations that optimize student performance.

The initial lesson block, accordingly, lays out a structure for organizing student teams and assessing achievement levels, interests, and styles (figure 8.8). The example, designed for sixth grade, begins on day 1 with the topic most on adolescent minds – themselves. The "Me and my summer" web introduces the students to one another and to the teacher, and provides assessment opportunities. One component of the reading–writing curriculum is the capacity to comprehend and compose in the narrative genre – to

WEEK 1

INTRODUCTORY LESSON [15-25 minutes, either whole class or small groups]

C   CONNECT: Use semantic mapping and brainstorming to introduce topic, concept story theme, and link to students' background knowledge and experience. Also serves as a basis for assessing students and adapting instruction.

SECONDARY LESSONS [Three or four sessions of 25-45 minutes, usually including one whole-class direct-instructional unit]

O   ORGANIZE: Depending on topic, use appropriate visual graphics to display main ideas and relations. Provides record of original experiences and understandings, information gained from reading text, and foundation for writing and project activities.

          PREVIEW: Set stage for culminating activity.

          PRACTICE: May include re-reading passages, looking at related material, and cooperative-group exercises.

WEEK 2

REVIEW LESSON [15-45 minutes, usually whole-class, to bridge weekend and restart the block projects]

          RE-ORGANIZE: Look back over graphics, vocabulary, passage content

R   REFLECT: Look forward to completion of project activity

SECONDARY LESSONS [two sessions of 30-60 minutes, mostly individual or small-group activities]

E   EXTEND: Main idea during the second week is to 'stretch' students in applying knowledge and skill introduced during first week. Additional readings, library research, field trips, all directed toward completion of student projects.

          PROJECT PRESENTATIONS

          TRANSFER ACTIVITIES: Another form of practice

FINAL LESSON [generally following project presentations, 15-20 minutes. May include brief whole-class discussions, interviews with individual students, or written assignments]

          REFLECT:

          ASSESSMENT: Mention self-assessment

Figure 8.7   A design for lesson blocks built around a variation on the CORE model.

understand and to tell stories. Character, plot, and setting are important design elements undergirding this capability. Day 2 suggests a strategy for exploring this domain, with two contrastive short stories. The rest of the week is spent on this topic, partly to engage students but also to collect evidence on skills and styles. Week 2 builds on this foundation to develop a class management system; the topic shifts to social studies, but reading and writing strategies remain critical curriculum goals, and the task is still grounded within the narrative genre.

The initial assessment block contrasts sharply with the corresponding block

Figure 8.8 An example of lesson-block design for the beginning of the school year.

WEEK 1 -- Preparation -- The first week of school -- setting the stage for development of a learning community.

Day 1 -- **CONNECT/ORGANIZE** -- Teacher-led whole-class activity. Goal is for students to get to know each other through personal experience, using webbing to generate words and organize into categories.

"Who are you?' Ask each student to write one or more self-descriptive words on a Post-It card; generate additional words from categories. Check for vocabulary extent and fluency, classification skills, interests, and styles.

"How did you spend your summer?' Repeat webbing process. Small groups compare and contrast summer experiences.

Day 2 -- **REVIEW AND REFLECT; READ** -- Teacher-led whole-class activity. Goal is to assess reading skills and ability to analyze and organize text information.

Read short story on summer, like 'Last days of summer', adapted from <u>Snow shoe trek to Otter River</u>, by David Budbill. Ask students to discuss character, plot, reactions to story. Check for knowledge of narrative terms.

Check knowledge of concept strategies -- webbing and weaving -- to organize information in passage.

Day 3 -- **RECONNECT** -- Small-group activity. Goal is to go from text to personal experience.

Each student has learned something about others. "If you were to imagine the best summer possible, what would it be like, and who would be there. What would happen? Write it or draw what comes to mind.' Collect segments and post around room or hang from 'clothesline.'

Days 4 and 5 -- **EXTEND** -- Goal is to bring together previous work into a new project through group collaboration.

Construct draft of 'Best summer' with whole class using segments.

WEEK 2 -- Preparation -- The second week of school -- present students with a genuine problem: How to develop a plan for managing themselves as a community.

Day 1 -- **CONNECT/ORGANIZE** -- Teacher-led whole-class activity. Goal is to review previous week, and build on that experience toward a class management plan, incorporating language development strategies as part of the task.

"We've started building 'Best summer,' and we'll come back to that. But this week the job is to build 'The best school year.' What makes you feel good about a day in school? What makes you feel unhappy about a day in school?" Record on cards, compare and contrast.

Day 2 -- **REVIEW AND REFLECT; READ** -- Teacher-led whole-class activity. Goal is to assess reading skills and ability to analyze and organize text information.

Lead students through Bill of Rights, in a format appropriate to the group. The Constitution tells citizens what the country had decided to do; the Bill of Rights protects citizens' rights. The School Board and the principal tell students what they have to learn, but each class has to decide how to make sure that everyone has a chance to learn.

The teacher is in charge now -- the job is to develop a Constitution and a Bill of Rights for the school year. "Responsibilities and Rights" as starting categories.

Day 3 -- **RECONNECT** -- Small-group activity. Goal is to go from text to personal experience.

"When you are on the playground or in the neighborhood, how do you work out problems so that everyone has a fair chance in the game? What are the playground rules? What about other games that you see on television -- basketball, football, the Olympics?" Student teams compile ideas and report back.

Days 4 and 5 -- **EXTEND** -- Goal is to bring together previous work into a new project through group collaboration.

Build a Constitution and Bill of Rights. Start with "good class," then "Rules, rewards, penalties, and protection."

at year's end, when assessment is again the focus but serves a very different purpose. The aim in the final "exhibition" block is summative evaluation, based on student performance and self-assessment. The perspective here is retrospective rather than prospective. In what areas has each student shown growth? What are individual strengths and limits, interests, and turnoffs? Which expectations for progress in the following grade remain in question?

The lesson blocks immediately after the opening segment are designed as models for *direct instruction* in various literacy domains. There are times when teachers should teach: they should present information, confirm student understanding, and test transfer of learning. The experienced teacher continually monitors the progress of a class, deciding when and what to teach. The Guide explicates this expertise. It lays out methods for "kid-watching," assuring that teachers do not fritter away time teaching students what they already know, and do not advance new ideas when the time is not right. Lesson blocks are designed as coherent packets of curriculum objectives, big ideas that embed ancillary skills and knowledge within a supportive and engaging context. For example, if the instructional objective is to develop a sense of plot, then it makes sense to spend several days examining a variety of stories in which plot is an essential element.

The *Two Bears* excerpt offers an opportunity to analyze a complex but well-designed narrative, with two intertwined plot structures that are transparently episodic but also contrastive. The teacher, following the CORE model, needs a connection; presentation of a video of a segment from *Little House on the Prairie* will do the job. Educators often see television as "the enemy," but it also offers important opportunities. Written text in the literature anthology continues this opening. The instructional block design for the segment is laid out in figure 8.9. The block opening lays out a range of questions, a schema for organizing one or two additional lessons that focus student attention on the concept of plot episodes over the two-week span. During these two weeks, students analyze other short stories with easily accessible episodic structures. The teacher places increasing responsibility for text analysis on students' shoulders, and the task moves from comprehension (the texts serving as models) to composition (the models serving as frames for student writing). The Guide lays out a plan of action, the student anthology offers options (the library offers others), and the teacher orchestrates the scenario. The closing presents a framework for a student assignment (extension in the CORE model), and an opportunity for the teacher to assess students' acquisition of the concept. This example features *Two Big Bears*, but many other stories might serve the same purpose. And while students are actively engaged in significant tasks, this lesson block centers around direct instruction in a clearly defined curriculum objective – episodic analysis of a narrative text.

Direct instruction is most appropriate in the fall of the school year following

INSTRUCTIONAL SUPPORT SYSTEM -- LESSON BLOCK DESIGN FOR TWO BEARS

WEEK 1 -- PREPARATION

Day 1: **CONNECT**

Construct a web on "The scariest things that have ever happened to me." Brainstorm on words, phrases, images, stories; write responses on slips of paper to make a 'messy web.'

Begin a list of 'horror stories, ' including books, fairy tales, televideos, and movies.   Add to web.

Day 2: **ORGANIZE**

In small groups, create categories for ideas and stories from Day 1. Aim is to come up with several classification schemes: problem, characters, events, feelings and behaviors, resolution.

Day 3: READING OF THE STORY

Following the basal model, and assuming that this lesson block is designed for early part of the school year, teacher would be advised to read through Two big bears for instruction in close analysis of the story. Later in the year, the same lesson block design could employ multiple stories and small group reading and reporting.

Begin with a quick reading of the story aloud by the teacher to the class. 'Today we're going to read a scary story about life on the American frontier. After I've read the story, we'll go back and analyze the story -- which is really two stories.'

On rereading, ask students to separate the two stories, and to identify the major events in each, using the story structure for guidance.

Day 4: **REFLECT**

The stories in Two big bears have similar themes, and offer an opportunity to compare and contrast. Lay out a matrix like the one below for whole-class discussion:

	Ma's Bear	Pa's Bear
Problem		
Characters		
Events		
Feelings		
Resolution		

WEEK 2 -- **EXTEND**

The second week can be designed around any of a variety of project options like those sketched below, depending on the class makeup, the time in the school year, and the instructional outcomes. The most natural extension of the first week emphasizes plot structure, and it is probably most sensible to stay with this concept. The main thematic element in the two stories is the importance of staying 'cool' in a threatening situation; other familiar stories appropriate to this theme include James and the giant peach and Stone fox.

Dramatize the two bear stories -- divide the class into two groups to prepare the scripts, scenery,etc.

Extend the Day 4 matrix to include other elements and stories, using the earlier brainstorming.

Compose individual or small-group stories on the theme of 'meeting monsters.' Begin with the characters (including the 'monster'), so that the overall design is in place. This type of story lends itself well to cartooning, a form of composition that appeals to many young students.

Figure 8.9   A lesson-block design for *Two Big Bears*.

initial assessments. Direct instruction in the ISS model has several features. First, it is *adaptive*. The teacher determines what students need to know preparatory to large-scale curriculum domains and authentic projects, and focuses instructional effort on these outcomes. Second, it focuses on *clearly defined outcomes*. Wilder's stories are memorable, and it is tempting to simply revel in her talents as a story-teller. Students can appreciate the stories while also exploring the reasons for their appreciation. Her stories are also engaging because they are placed in exciting contexts – who wouldn't want to read a story about encounters with wild and crazy bears! While the content is beguiling, the process for analyzing and synthesizing the substance is what endures and transfers to students' understanding and appreciation of a broad range of literary works.

Instructional blocks in the direct-instruction segment of the Guide incorporate many elements found in contemporary teacher manuals: the teacher *introduces* a learning objective, students *practice* the objective, and the teacher *assesses* student mastery. The block concept gives the teacher control over curriculum decisions, but within a framework that guides planning once the decision has been made. The Guide for a given grade level sets forth a small collection of significant curriculum outcomes that are plausible for that grade. By third grade, for example, students should be able to move developmentally beyond the concept of plot as "beginning, middle, and end," toward the idea of a sequence of episodes linked by characters' motivations and an overarching problem. *The Two Bears* example shows how a block of lessons lasting for two or three weeks can support the introduce–practice–assess model, while allowing the teacher to adapt instruction to local contexts. Practice is purposeful and assessment is contextualized.

The lesson-block strategy for direct instruction has several advantages. It assures that students cover prescribed curriculum objectives, and that teachers can document student achievement in these domains. But the block design also offers flexibility about when and how students move through these objectives, and it frees the teacher to select substantive content that is appropriate and opportune for students. For sixth-graders, *Charlotte's Web* is a marvelous story about friendship, but so is *Bridge to Terebithia*,[28] as well as a host of other narratives old and new. Friendship takes many forms. If the teacher's goal in a given lesson block is to help students understand the development of character through the establishment of enduring (and perhaps thwarted) friendships, he or she can choose selections appropriate to this purpose rather than depending on an editorial staff far removed from the situation. The Guide provides teachers the scaffolding needed to make wise choices in the face of today's diverse array of students and situations.

This point has far-reaching implications. One class may need more work on narrative comprehension while another is having problems with informational text. The first teacher can embed stories in the Thanksgiving activities while the second selects histories and recipes; lesson-block designs support direct instruction in both of these contexts. The student anthology in the ISS design provides short excerpts as entry points, along with recommendations for correlated selections, some of which will be available as part of the series, many others to be found on library shelves.

The final segment of the Guide presents the teacher with frameworks for designing *thematic projects* during the stretch of time between January and June. Again, the frameworks take shape not as prescriptions but as models. The purpose is less instruction on specific objectives such as plot analysis or persuasive essays than showing that students in the class have learned to apply previous learning to new problems where they have a genuine voice in the framing of the problem. But if the teacher judges that additional instruction is needed on particular objectives, block designs allow embedding instruction within a project. If a teacher's eighth-graders are struggling with persuasive essays (national writing tests suggest that many are), then a project on "Saving the environment" may include letters to local businesses and politicians that incorporate the elements of an argument. To help students compose these letters, the teacher calls on a lesson block for comprehending and composing arguments. Rather than "covering" persuasive texts at random intervals and in disjointed ways, the Guide allows the teacher to decide when and how to handle the objective, while ensuring that the skill is on the curricular agenda, and offering instructional guidance for approaching the task.

The Guide contains examples demonstrating how projects can provide opportunities for students to practice skills and knowledge in genuine contexts. For instance, imagine an eighth- grade project built around *Roots*,[29] the Alex Haley autobiography celebrated in an acclaimed television series. A traditional series might provide the raw materials for the project: excerpts from Haley's book in the student anthology, segments of the television program available as a video option, and a "project workbook" that directs students toward the writing of individual autobiographies. This approach solves the teacher's preparation problems by providing all of the project materials, but it also limits the learning options.

A strategy more in the spirit of the Instructional Support System lays out a basic plan of action, along with suggestions for alternate routes and pointers toward other resources available in the series and elsewhere.[30] The project begins by exploring the theme of heritage: people understand themselves by understanding their ancestry. Today's students often lack a sense of personal history; families no longer sit on the front porch and tell tall tales from their past. The idea is not to rattle skeletons in family closets, but to help students reflect on their heritage. Haley provides one starting point for the project, but the Guide suggests alternatives – Alice Walker's *The Color Purple*,[31]

Wojciechowska's *Shadow of a Bull*,[32] and Lash's *Helen [Keller] and Teacher*.[33] The school or neighborhood librarian offers contemporary resources. The teaching strategy, made explicit in the Guide, builds on one or more forceful narratives that capture students' interest in the personal origins of an individual who is significant to this group of students, a person or people whom they can identify.

For a large project such as *Roots*, the lesson-block concept serves as a metaphor rather than a detailed script. Two weeks is clearly insufficient for a serious project, and a detailed structure such as that in figure 8.9 is too constraining. But the CORE model provides a flexible design while ensuring responsibility for academic outcomes. The opening task, for instance, might focus on analysis of character and plot in the initial selections. A second step might call for exploration of students' autobiographies, drawing on social science methods. Studying history may be dull, but studying your own history can be a different matter. The Guide lays out for the teacher a broad-based design that suggests a variety of strategies and materials for this part of the project. Some of the most important elements take shape as student questions. How can you learn about your origins? Where can you search for information? How can you interview relatives and friends? How should you analyze the data? How do you report the results? Such questions transcend the specifics of how to "do a project." The answers cannot be printed, because these are unique and unpredictable. But illustrations of thematic projects in the Guide can offer teachers workable models for a "first run," inviting adaptations that capture the spirit of the *Foundations* section of the Guide.

The *Pathways* curriculum is partly sequential; the teacher is directed during the year from assessment to instruction through projects and back to assessment. But *Pathways* is far from lockstep. The initial assessments are linked to later segments, with suggestions to the teacher about particular objectives and lesson blocks, and possible choices for holiday topics and thematic projects. The various instructional blocks can be employed throughout the school year in various guises; eventually they become "macro-routines" for both teacher and students, but as tools rather than prescriptions. This design has a cost, of course – the teacher has greater freedom and flexibility, but also greater responsibility for planning and decision-making.

Gateways to Information

The Instructional Support System employs the student anthology as one resource, but relies for the most part on other resources – children's trade books, video and computer programs and packages, magazines and newspapers, and products and projects created by other students throughout the country. In an information age, standard print materials will be an important resource, but knowing how to access information is an equally critical objective for tomorrow's graduate, probably as important as knowing what to do with information once in hand. Like the McGuffey readers, the ISS series must be supplemented by other resources.

This section of the Teacher's Guide, a looseleaf binder, comprises two continuously updated segments. The first segment describes general strategies for locating information. Strange as it may seem, many teachers lack systematic means for contacting libraries, museums, business and government, and other sources of information outside the classroom. The information highway is quickly becoming a reality, an event that will make many of us novices for the next decade. Libraries and museums are generally ahead of schools in modernizing techniques for handling information, but bringing classrooms online is critical if all students are to acquire the skills and strategies needed for gaining access to the highway. It is not enough to install telephone lines, computers, and modems in classrooms, a Herculean undertaking in its own right. Nor, in our judgment, will it suffice to provide teachers with a one-day workshop on Prodigy or America Online. Rather, lesson guides must offer guidance: not as an ancillary option but as an integral part of the system; not as a collection of activities but as part of a strategic enterprise.

The second segment of the resource section comprises a resource catalog. Few teachers have current information about titles in children's literature and tradebooks, and most lack connections to support groups such as public television and producers of innovative curriculum projects. A small band of frontrunners attends conventions and visits book stores; they join computer networks and subscribe to professional magazines. But such affiliations are rare for most teachers. They work hard every day, and unlike other professionals have few built-in opportunities to attend meetings and network with others. This section of the ISS is designed to make it easy for every teacher to be a frontrunner.

Portfolios and Exhibitions

As noted earlier, assessment methods are undergoing enormous change. End-of-unit multiple-choice tests are inadequate in the "new standards" age.[34] Today's reading series include portfolio-like repositories for student assignments, but the real challenge is to assist teachers in developing assessment strategies adaptable to local conditions, where teacher judgment serves for appraisal of student achievement. More is needed than a manila folder. Authentic assessment requires innovative technologies for collecting, analyzing, and reporting student achievements, but the teacher's evaluation is critical. And perhaps the most significant shift will come as teachers help their students to develop the capacity to self-assess their individual and collective accomplishments.

Supporting teachers in the transition from prescriptive testing to dynamic assessment, from multiple-choice items to thematic projects, will depend less on new materials than on innovative ideas and strategies. The research on teacher-based assessment shows a clear need to provide practical information about technical matters such as reliability and validity, as well as political issues such as the tensions inherent in assigning student grades. This section of the Guide supplements the curriculum section with concrete models of assessment tactics and methods spanning a range of formal and informal assessments. Portfolios of student work can demonstrate progress from the beginning of a task to its completion. Unlike the architect or photographer, however, the idea is not to assemble "best works" in a large folder, but to construct a developmental record of progress. Performances and exhibitions (e.g., dramatic declamations or science fair projects) display accomplishments, but also motivate students and excite parents. The assessment section of the Guide provides models for these events, along with guidelines to support teachers as trustworthy judges.

Valid information about student achievement comes not only from product-based sources, but from the teacher's observations and interactions with students. Most teachers rely on these sources of information, but as "informal" activities. Relatively few teachers are prepared for serious "kid-watching," for the tasks of documenting and reflecting about those on-the-fly events that are crucial for instructional decision-making and for gauging progress. This section of the Instructional Support System concept builds such elements into the core of the teacher's daily schedule, and provides technical assistance to ensure adequate and defensible validity and reliability.

An essential feature of the assessment section is the inclusion of a developmental scale for judging student progress, a scale offering teachers a view of achievement not from "bad to good" but from "novice to expert." Today's assessments often take shape as a checklist of grade-level micro-objectives; the fifth-grade teacher marks a student's success in distinguishing fact from opinion. Imagine, instead, a multi-year strand of accomplishments such as that in figure 8.6. Students within any given class will span a broad continuum in both level and quality. Fourth-graders may reasonably be expected to distinguish between solid facts and blatant opinions; eighth-graders should appreciate shades of gray. But the fifth-grader who on the surface mentions shades of gray may not do this very well, while a classmate who struggles to find the right label for fine distinctions may be closer to grasping the concept. The aim is not to penalize the first student for her sloppiness, nor unreservedly commend the second student for his effort but, rather, to aid the teacher in assessing this achievement for a particular age–grade cohort, and in laying out profiles of students' strengths and areas of need. A developmental assessment scale also provides teachers with a common language for discussing student progress with colleagues, thereby encouraging professional dialog and connectedness.

The Teacher's Guide as Centerpiece of the ISS: A Practical Idea?

A century ago, McGuffey's Readers and their clones were the primary resource for guiding teachers in helping students to acquire literacy. We are by no means proposing a return to McGuffey as a model, but we do think that the series offers some lessons for today. First, these texts provided a developmental sequence of activities and outcomes to teachers of the day. In an era of one-room schoolhouses, teachers were forced to adopt a developmental perspective, because students in their classrooms ranged from early childhood through adolescence. Second, the texts were clearly insufficient to provide everything needed to teach reading and writing. The books were small, designed as a starting point for students and teachers, an opening to a broader array of literature and readings. Third, and related to the previous point, the books treated teachers as professionals. The preface to the McGuffey was quite explicit about the importance of moving through the brief text quickly, and then on to other sources. The Readers were also quite explicit about the fact that the classroom teacher was best positioned to decide how to manage this transition. We are struck by the parallels with the textbook series in other countries – Japan, the UK, Australia and New Zealand – which are also abbreviated and adaptable. The explicit assumption in these countries is that teachers possess a conceptual understanding of national curriculum frameworks, and that student textbooks are a starting point for local adaptations, rather than serving as the entire curriculum.

The Teacher's Guide described above as part of an Instructional Support System is a cost-effective way of providing teachers with the resources needed to function as full-fledged professionals. The quality of the Guide would be a focal point during the selection and adoption of a textbook series, even more so than the content of the student anthology and the coverage of curriculum objectives. A significant corollary would be the publisher's commitment to follow-up services for professional development, and to sustained and continuing consultation. This commitment would take shape as an explicit contract for the publisher to provide active and ongoing assistance. In fact, many publishers currently provide such benefits, but these promises tend to be incidental to the main purpose of "selling books." Because the arrangements tend to be informal, individual schools and teachers may not know how to take advantage of them. In the ISS model, the Guide offers a foundation for establishing a genuinely professional relation between teachers and publishers.

The proposal will entail major changes for publishers. Current economic relations between publishers and school districts depend on the sales of student books and "consumables." The educational relations between publishers and boards of education, state and local, hinge on the assumption that every student is "exposed" to a predefined curriculum framework if teachers follow directions. The Instructional Support System shifts the economic relations from products to professional services, and the educational relations from directions to professional guidance. Both of these moves start from the assumption that classroom teachers are in the best position to make informed decisions, and can best conduct themselves as professionals when provided adequate guidance and support. The future well-being of American schools is likely to depend on our capacity to realize this ideal.

Notes

1   White (1980).
2   Taylor (1976).
3   Vygotsky (1978).
4   Venezky (1992, 1994).
5   McGuffey (1867), p. v.
6   Idem.
7   Chall and Dale (1995) and Klare (1984).
8   Goodman (1986), Weaver (1990) and Pressley and Rankin (1994); also Hoffman et al. (1994).
9   Dahl (1961).
10 Silver Burdett & Ginn (1989).
11 Houghton Mifflin (1989a).
12 Ibid., p. 435.
13 Houghton Mifflin (1989b), p. 187.
14 Silver Burdett & Ginn (1989), p. 424.
15 Trabasso and Magliano (1996).
16 Lukins (1990).
17 Miller, Nelson and Naifeh (1995
18 Silver Burdett & Ginn (1989), p. 424.
19 Ibid., p. 258
20 Ibid., p. 260
21 Ibid., p. 260
22 Ibid., p. 265
23 Drum and Calfee (1979) and Fraatz (1987).
24 Houghton Mifflin (1989a), p. 29
25 Ibid., p. 243

26 Ibid., p. 33
27 Apple and Christian-Smith (1991).
28 Patterson (1977).
29 Haley (1976).
30 Calfee and Patrick (1995).
31 Walker (1992).
32 Wojciechowska (1964).
33 Lash (1997).
34 Resnick (1987).

9

BRINGING ABOUT THE IDEAL: LEADERS AND COLLABORATORS

Instructional Support Systems will not come about without substantial changes in publishing, adopting, and selecting. Educational historians such as Larry Cuban and David Tyack describe how schools appear at times to undergo pendulum swings, but these are actually superficial, with fundamental shifts occurring only rarely.[1] In fact, our visits to exhibit halls at teachers' conventions during the past decade have persuaded us that instructional materials are changing. Today's basal readers differ in many respects from the days of "Dick and Jane", and we think that most of these changes are for the better. The question is whether "better" will be good enough to meet the needs of tomorrow's teachers and students. As we described in chapter 6, the textbook enterprise builds on an interplay among publishers, policy-makers, administrators, and teachers. Each group is an intricate entity in its own right. How might this complex array of individuals and collectives transform the system to place instructional support systems in classrooms? Can anyone tweak the system at some point and promote widespread change? Past experience and common sense both suggest that such tweaking is unlikely to have much effect. In chapter 7 we described a plan for well-designed publishing and selection of instructional materials. This chapter pushes the argument farther, considering a leadership strategy for transforming the entire enterprise.

Three steps are essential for the changes that we propose. First, participants must exploit the power of the design lenses explicated earlier in this book. Second, everyone in the enterprise – publishers, states, districts, professional groups, trade groups, university faculty, and interested public – must build on these design notions toward leadership positions. Third, participants must collaborate, relying on the design rubrics as a foundation for a common language and focused approach. In the sections that follow, we suggest the shape of each of these steps, which are summarized in figure 9.1.

LEADERSHIP

	Goal Designs	System Design	Review & Try Out	Final Steps
Publishers		Design system whereby elements are linked according to themes. Use graphics to guide work.		Use design rubrics to sell product from a position of strength.
States & Districts	Use curricular, comprehensibility, and instructional themes to design the elements and linkages of frameworks. Use graphics to communicate.	Analyze system design to be sure elements, linkages, and themes match goals. Rely on graphic depictions to guide work.	Use design rubrics to guide public review.	Use design rubrics to justify adoption decisions to publishers and public.
Professional Organizations	Use curricular, comprehensibility, and instructional themes to design the elements and linkages of frameworks. Use graphics to communicate.	Train practitioners to consider system design.	Review designs of instructional support systems. Use graphics to communicate.	Disseminate reviews widely.
Researchers and University Faculty	Use scholarship and research to suggest curricular, comprehensibility, and instructional goals.	Train preservice teachers to consider system design.	Use scholarship and research to verify efficacious system characteristics.	

COLLABORATION

	Parties work together to establish goal designs.	Parties use the same design lenses to publish and analyze systems.	Parties share useful review and try out information.	Parties work together to design adoption cycles.

Figure 9.1 A chart summarizing leadership roles for publishers, states and districts, professional organizations, and university researchers, and tasks on which they could fruitfully collaborate.

The Potential of Design Lenses

The design lenses presented in earlier chapters may appear deceptively simple – a handful of diagrams. We have claimed that publishers can use these diagrams to design student materials. We have shown how elements and linkages based on such diagrams can be scrutinized for evidence of curricular, comprehensibility, and instructional themes. We have described how a variety

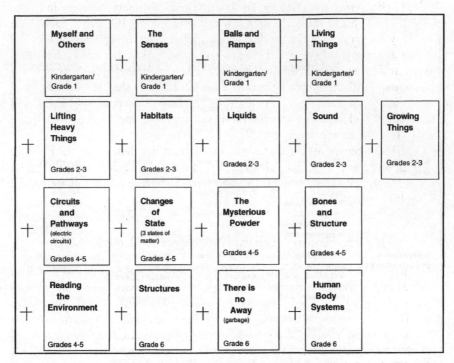

Figure 9.2 The design of a recent science series for kindergarten through sixth grade (Education Development Center, 1992).

of participants might apply such diagrams to guide goal setting, system design, review and try out, and adoption and selection. The graphics can link the plethora of tasks and bring coherence to textbook publishing and selection so that when instructional materials reach the hands of students and teachers, they fulfill the intended goals.

We are convinced that design lenses are particularly critical to the design of Instructional Support Systems. One problem reoccurs across all of the latest programs that we have examined, whether in science, social science, or language arts. While we have found chapters and even multi-chapter units that meet the criteria of curricular coherence, instructional effectiveness, and comprehensibility, serious problems still appear when we look at the level of the textbook as a whole, and at higher levels of the system – the mesh between the teacher's manual and the student book, and the transitions from one grade to another. At levels of the system higher than the chapter or unit or broader than the student edition, the design tends to break down. The design of a recent science series for kindergarten through sixth grade is depicted in figure 9.2.

Indeed, the series qualifies as an Instructional Support System in some respects. It is made up of 17 smallish modules (about 100 pages each) that generally progress in difficulty but are intended to be used flexibly, with no particular order within grades. However, when we look at this series, the pieces do not fit well together. We search in vain for a clear rationale for many choices. We cannot find compelling themes. Publishers have shared with us their frustration in the need for improving the coherence of a series. Publishers, and the adopters and selectors who choose their wares, seemingly have problems in controlling the enterprise as a whole.

Our design lenses may seem simple, but therein lies their strength. Finding a way to represent the various elements and linkages by a schematic that can be scrutinized for thematic coherence can be an invaluable tool for monitoring and controlling complex programs.

All Participants Exhibit Appropriate Leadership

Fundamental reform will require leadership by publishers, states and districts, professional organizations, policy-makers, and university researchers. The change process builds on a variety of roles and actions. Textbook editors conceive a new vision. States try to bring about educational reform through textbook revision. Professional organizations publish curriculum standards that demand textbook reform. University researchers push for textbook materials that meet criteria supported by their research. Leadership comes from a variety of sources. To bring about transformational change, all leaders must take on a common yoke, or at least agree to head down the same path.

Leadership from Publishers

Publishers play a pivotal role, despite their occasional disclaimers about being at the mercy of market forces. "We are producers, not leaders," they demur. Because publishers actually produce textbook series, their expertise in maintaining the design across the various elements is crucial. The most carefully designed goal statements that can be shaped by professional groups, states, or districts depend on the competence of editors, authors, writers, graphic designers, and illustrators to come to life.

System design. Design lenses will be particularly critical to publishers in the development of Instructional Support Systems (see Figure 9.1). Instead of scope-and-sequence charts that bean count all content and skills, the strategy is to represent graphically the elements, linkages, and themes for the entire system: teacher guide, student textbook, computer programs, CD-ROMs, and so on. Within each of these products, graphics can also link overall themes to particular passages and lessons. Editors, authors, writers, graphic designers, and illustrators can rely on the diagrams to tie together tables of contents, text outlines, activities, video disks, computer software, and so on. The diagrams link all the diverse pieces to common themes of content domain, comprehensibility, and instruction.

Publishing staffs are up to this leadership role. The editors, authors, and writers with whom we have talked have been extraordinarily knowledgeable and capable. Despite incredibly tight adoption schedules, they have greater incentive and more resources than any other players for dealing with system design.

Final steps: Selling the product   Publishers who decide to create Instructional Support Systems will have a tricky sales problem. Publishers must sell new designs to their staffs and to the marketplace. The front-line "troops" in publishing are the sales staff, who need convincing when it comes to innovations. Schools and teachers tend to be wary about change for the sake of change, and so publishers' representatives generally prefer the tried and true. Otherwise, they know that they will have a tough time making the sale. In chapter 6 we mentioned an executive editor who proposed two requirements for successful change within a publishing house; a dream and a team. We would add: a carefully designed dream and a team that thoroughly understands the design.

Publishers may convince their staffs, but how can they persuade adoption states and local school districts to invest millions of dollars in what might appear a risky experiment? Even the best designed series will not have an impact unless it makes its way through adoption and selection. While completing this book, we watched one publisher develop an innovative history/social science series to match the equally innovative 1988 California framework. The series fared less well in other states. Might the publisher have done a better selling job outside of California? Suppose that the publisher had shared the story of visions and goals that the staff related to us, and highlighted the story with clear design pictures and examples, approaching other states and districts from a position of strength? Such a strategy might have impressed other markets with both the vision and the actual series. To be sure, the California framework has a unique organization and covers content underemphasized or omitted in other social studies textbooks (e.g., the histories of minority groups and religions). The point is that publishers can take a stronger leadership role by telling their stories and highlighting the design features of their product along with examples.

Publishers have other opportunities to sell the market on textbook innovation. Every professional conference has an exhibition hall in which textbook publishers advertise their wares. Each booth features examples of student textbooks, teacher editions, and ancillary materials. Posters highlight features in the materials or depict groups of children gathered around teachers, teachers in focus groups, or educational experts whose names are on the series as authors and consultants.

We are convinced that good design can support effective advertising. Peters and Waterman point out, in their book on successful businesses, the importance of the KISS principle – "keep it simple, sweetheart" – as the foundation of effective design.[2] Imagine, for instance, a display that depicts the series design, the handful of themes that guide its development, along with supportive examples. Suppose that the display proclaims the goal "Our science materials are organized thematically: *Change* in grade four; *Structure and Function* in grade five; *Conservation* in grade six." In fact, several recent series have moved in this direction – but the important next step is to show how the design actually works to integrate the various elements. Imagine a graphic portraying the design of the entire series, linking tables of contents, typical lessons, student activities, and multi-media activities, and showing how each theme appears at each program level. The publisher who uses design rubrics will be well-prepared to create displays that focus attention on the curricular, comprehensibility, and instructional features of an entire instructional support system. By the way, design coherence need not threaten the entrepreneurial spirit. In Japan, textbooks must meet national curricular design criteria, but competition thrives among Japanese publishers.[3]

We do not mean to minimize the problem faced by publishers who attempt innovations in the textbook arena. As shown in figure 9.1, other participants must shoulder leadership roles as well. For instance, in California, publishers followed the lead provided by then Superintendent Bill Honig and professional associations in the development of the social studies framework. But publishers brought the visions into reality.

Leadership from Adopters and Selectors

Adoption states and districts often embrace opportunities for leadership, and you will recall from figure 9.1 that we suggest leadership roles for them across all four tasks. As potent market forces, adoption states and large districts can exert leadership by the materials that they choose and the process by which they make these choices. As we explained earlier, publishers report that they would make major changes if as few as 10 per cent of districts requested them.

State and district innovators also face a marketing challenge. They must first convince publishers to match their vision, then influence local clients to purchase the materials, and finally persuade the public of the educational benefits. In chapter 7 we described how design lenses can support adopters and selectors as they establish goals, analyze system design, conduct review and try out, and influence how school boards make final decisions. How can the committee that has learned to apply the design lenses to instructional support systems assume a leadership role that places improved materials in the hands of teachers and children? The following sections address this question.

Goal designs   A well-designed array of state or district goals would go a long way toward providing publishers with direction for the development of Instructional Support Systems that are attractive to the textbook market. States and districts should not overestimate the leadership potential that they possess at this stage of the enterprise, particularly if they can demonstrate that their choices will be guided by the goal designs.

System design   Districts and states could exert strong leadership by focusing on overall system design. Instructional Support Systems have several defining characteristics: the elements convey a coherent curriculum, are comprehensible, and support student-centered instruction, a coherent design integrates the various parts, and the design is held together by the teacher guide. Districts and states searching for well-designed Instructional Support Systems could hold publishers to these standards.

Rather than focusing on the student textbook, selection committees would consider how the various elements of a package are linked by a consistent set of curricular, instructional, and comprehensibility themes. Committees would also have a way to examine the design of the teacher guide for supporting teachers' decision-making.

Review and try out   During review, states and districts have a continuing leadership role. For fundamental change in the textbook arena to take hold, parents, classroom teachers, and students must see immediate benefits in the redesign effort. During review and try out, states and districts who approach the task should be prepared to demonstrate *local* evidence of substantially enhanced achievement, sufficient to persuade all stake-holders to embrace the program.

A commercial analogy may be appropriate. Think about the release of a new computer system such as Windows 95 or the Apple Newton. Cable TV brings the announcements of such releases into people's homes around the world, not just as advertisements but as "news." Spokespersons enter press conferences armed with carefully crafted charts and accompanying commentary to explain the new design to the world, but also to persuade the audience of the new system's virtues. A successful advertising campaign works from a *plan* with all the hallmarks of a systematic design. Before answering the press's questions, the spokesperson presents a rationale, customarily "pictured" in some way, to guide the subsequent discussion.

Imagine a comparable scenario in which the work of the adoption boards is a well-orchestrated series of events, each providing opportunities for input from publishers, educators, policy-makers, and the public. Review committees and publishers have time during the initial meetings to lay out their work. A well-designed agenda that sets reasonable time limits and encourages presenters to put their ideas on to paper guarantees a fair hearing for all participants.

After such preparation, the official adoption "meeting" can now open with informed presentations by both the committee members and publisher representatives. Committee members show their goal design pictures along with the design pictures for each of the selected series. They explain how each series does and does not match the goal designs. Publishers provide their own commentary, complete with the design as they envision it. They explain what they were trying to accomplish and the challenges that they faced. The presentation ends with goal designs for the hearing itself (complete with accompanying charts). Speakers are asked to address curricular, comprehensibility, and instructional issues ranging from the specific to the global. The state or district that wants to convince its constituents of the merits of a particular instructional system can employ design lenses established early-on, to focus the public debate and communicate the strengths of the programs that it has chosen.

Final steps: Adoption or selection After attending a range of hearings and observing the process from beginning to end, we (and others) are amazed at the frequent "disconnect" between the initial mandate, the hearing process, and the final decisions. The criteria seem to be made of rubber at times. To be sure, democracies encourage debates and disputes, and uncertainty is one price of freedom. On the other hand, the lack of a clear and rational process does have undesirable consequences. For instance, publishers have to anticipate the range of requests and banishments, and so they try to cover the territory while protecting themselves from blindside tackles. The result is that no one is really satisfied. The committee that establishes a clear and consistent rationale for its choices, and that communicates this rationale to publishers, is more likely to find the latter responsive to their requests. Fixing small problems is easy; some publishers now offer "tailored texts" in which small segments can be added or deleted on request. But such piecemeal efforts do not deal with the larger design issues that have been the focus of this book.

Imagine the committee that looks at textbook series to see how well they function as Instructional Support Systems. While analyzing the system design, the committee relies on graphic representations of parts, linkages, and themes for depicting their initial goals and the systems that they evaluate. Now they present their analysis to the publishers who submitted materials, and explain the rationale for their decisions by reference to these graphics. By communicating their rationale more clearly, the district or state provides publishers with feedback that they can use in preparing future systems. The present process is a source of interesting "war stories," but these offer little for improving the process for the future. The alternative that we have suggested seems likely to improve the present situation, and we think that most publishers would welcome a more level playing field.

Leadership from Professional Organizations

Professional organizations play a different role than either textbook publishers or educational practitioners. Their efforts fall under the rubric of "advisement." They are at least one step removed from final decisions, and seldom either produce or choose instructional materials. Since they influence rather than determine outcomes, they have the freedom to recommend sweeping revisions without the responsibility for worrying about practicalities. This freedom extends to professional organizations a potent leadership role, as long as they can connect their advice with practical realities.

We can imagine ways in which the contributions of professional organizations might be more far-reaching. Policy spokespersons such as Harriet Tyson-Bernstein, and university researchers such as Roger Farr and Michael Tulley, have offered policy advice directed toward professional organizations: "The first prerequisite to good textbooks is a coherent national curriculum – or at least a medley of coherent alternative curricula in each discipline."[4] "We do not recommend in-service training in the teaching of reading, but we do strongly recommend training for reviewers in the review and evaluation of reading textbooks."[5] "Foundations should support independent, critical reviews of textbooks in general circulation magazines and newspapers."[6] These recommendations speak to all four tasks in figure 9.1.

Goal designs   Who should establish the goals for Instructional Support Systems in science, social science, and language arts? This question is more problematic in the United States than in countries with a strong, centralized ministry of education. Education is reserved to the states in this country, and so national consensus is difficult to achieve.

Professional organizations offer an opportunity for establishing design goals to guide publishers, states, and districts in the development and implementation of Instructional Support Systems across the country. Probably the strongest impact of professional organizations at present is emerging from the efforts to define nation-wide *standards* for student accomplishment. Virtually every subject-matter organization has developed standards in one form or another. Some of these standards seem to have fairly obvious implications for textbook design, although none of them address the issue directly.[7] Other standards seem less applicable to textbook series.[8] Nonetheless, as a lever for influencing what is taught and how, standards documents offer promise as a way in which to connect professional groups with other parts of the enterprise.

Whatever frameworks they develop, however, professional organizations face the task of selling others on their expertise. They must convince publishers, state and district policy-makers, and classroom teachers that their frameworks will work with today's teachers and students. They must demonstrate the expertise to *design* frameworks that can guide the work of both those who produce instructional materials and those who adopt and implement them. A hierarchical framework in which a handful of overriding goals are successively decomposed could be used to link the various parts of an entire Instructional Support System. Furthermore, the orderliness of the design, as depicted by coherent graphics, would allow a professional organization to communicate its ideas to the rest of the education and publishing communities.

System design   Professional organizations could also assume leadership by training adopters and selectors to recognize and characterize Instructional Support Systems – the elements, linkages, and domain, comprehensibility, and instructional themes. Harriet Tyson-Bernstein has suggested that the National Education Association and the American Federation of Teachers, through local affiliates, organize subject-matter study groups to train teachers in state-of-the-art approaches to selecting textbooks.[9] The Association of Supervision and Curriculum Development already sponsors workshops for adopters and selectors. The design lenses described in chapters 5 and 7 could be an important part of such professional preparation.

Teacher training need not always take place in such formal settings. The Association of American Publishers, whose members comprise most of the major textbook publishers along with smaller niche firms, could play a unique role. Suppose that the AAP were to take leadership in developing a set of industry-wide comprehensibility, curricular, and instructional standards. Imagine a public relations campaign directed toward classroom teachers and policy-makers at the district and state levels. AAP-sponsored booths at professional meetings could "advertise" these standards through the use of design diagrams and supportive examples from existing materials. Imagine advertisements in professional newspapers (such as *Education Week* and *Reading Today*) and professional journals (such as *Science Teacher*, *Reading Teacher*, and *Social Education*). This suggestion may appear far-fetched, and we know that AAP members will be quick to point out problems of implementation. However, let us suggest a parallel with how the dairy association promotes the benefits of milk drinking: What's wrong with promoting the virtues of well-designed instructional materials?

Besides informing the market, such a campaign might also change public perceptions of textbook publishers. Talking with state administrators, district curriculum specialists, and classroom teachers, we have heard a frequent refrain: "Textbook publishers can't be trusted. All they are interested in is making money. They will tell us anything in order to make the sale." An AAP-sponsored public relations campaign could demonstrate that publishers as a group possess professional competence for improving instructional materials, and that they share aspirations about quality education with many others in the community.

Review and dissemination   The third important leadership role that professional organizations can play is to review instructional materials critically, and to disseminate their reviews widely. A few scattered attempts can be found along these lines. As we write, the American Textbook Council publishes *Social Studies Review*, a critique of social studies textbooks, and the California Textbook League publishes *The Textbook Letter*, an analysis of social studies and science texts. Until 1992, the National Center for Science Education, Inc. reviewed science textbooks in a newsletter called, *Bookwatch*.

While many of these reviews mention text design, current work has two limitations. First, the reviews are not widely disseminated. During our conversations with state and district administrators as well as classroom teachers, no one mentioned any of these reviews. Publisher representatives *did* refer to them, reinforcing our impression that publishing staffs are better informed than many others. Second, the reviews do not follow a format that permits easy comparisons among different materials. Reviews are typically presented in article format, each considering whatever features strike the reviewer as particularly interesting. For example, each *Bookwatch* issue offered three reviews of the same textbook. Reviewers approached the book from their own perspective; one reviewer might highlight the treatment of evolution, another might complain about turgid writing, while the third might applaud the laboratory exercises. Reviewers did not work from a common set of criteria (e.g., comprehensibility, curriculum, and instruction), which made direct comparisons among textbooks virtually impossible. Furthermore, all of the reviews we have read focused on the student edition, and gave little attention to the teacher's manual and ancillary material.

A different model, one that might be a regular feature of periodicals reaching a practitioner audience, would employ a format similar to that of *Consumer Reports*. Each report would begin with an explanation of the standards against which a set of materials will be judged. Materials from different publishers could then be directly compared on the basis of these standards. Results would be summarized in a series of design diagrams (flip through an issue of *Consumer Reports* and note the use of graphics to communicate the evaluations). The combination of a user-friendly format with easy public access would greatly enhance the impact of the reviews.

This model would need the support of an organization with a ready made outlet to the audience. Two that come to mind are Phi Delta Kappa (PDK), the education fraternity, and the Association for Supervision and Curriculum Development (ASCD). PDK publishes the *Kappan*, and ASCD *Educational Leadership*. Both journals have gained the respect of a substantial practitioner and policy audience; both have published articles decrying the characteristics of instructional materials and the steps used by states and districts to select these materials. Both feature regular columns dealing with significant educational issues. Evaluations of specific instructional materials would seem to warrant some attention.

We are convinced that leadership from professional organizations could play an important role in supporting concepts such as the Instructional Support System. A reliance on design lenses would lend a coherence and logic to their work that could greatly enhance the impact, and their leadership could become crucial to any movements toward fundamental change.

Leadership from Universities and Colleges

Like professional organizations, university faculties are somewhat removed from the tyranny of practicalities and therefore are free to speculate, experiment, and advise. The specialized preparation of university researchers in observing, abstracting patterns, analyzing, and drawing implications places them in a unique position to study the present and make recommendations for the future. Universities and colleges also play a critical role in the preparation of teachers and administrators for the practice of schooling. Our reviews of the college textbooks for novice teachers suggest a discouraging prospect; the aim does not seem to be the development of a critical eye for analyzing instructional materials but, instead, instructions about how to follow the materials in a relatively unthoughtful manner. We know of only one program on textbook analysis – an ongoing series directed by Jeanne Chall and James Squire at Harvard – that prepares practitioners for critical consumption of instructional materials.

Goal designs/Review and try out   One of the most important roles that university researchers can play is to propose and test the fundamental underpinnings of innovations, to suggest design goals and put them to the empirical test through try outs. What *precisely* are the features in an Instructional Support System that promote student learning or that support competent teaching?

While the research record continues to grow, important considerations about writing style and curriculum and instructional characteristics remain unexplored, particularly those that encompass large systems spanning several years of school. It is far easier to conduct research on the comprehension of a 250-word passage than on the comprehensibility of an entire textbook or a series intended to cover the upper elementary grades. On the basis of their scholarship, however, educational researchers have many recommendations to offer. Even though some of these may appear contradictory because of contextual differences, they can help in solving parts of the puzzle.

Design lenses can be particularly useful in guiding empirical research. They have allowed the two of us to pull the bits and pieces of research conducted by different researchers at various institutions with a variety of purposes into a coherent whole, and speculate on the implications for entire Instructional Support Systems. Future research can focus on aspects of the system, considering large amounts of material intended to be used over long periods of time.

Similar to theories in other social and behavioral sciences, recommendations in education tend to be underdetermined. In other words, actual research support is insufficient to justify the conclusions. Recommendations from academia grow out of a combination of scholarship (Who else has made the same recommendation? How sensible do the ideas seem?), experience (what is the researcher's experience in real world classrooms, with actual publishers, or with state and district administrators?), and a shared body of carefully conducted research (reported in scholarly journals, at conferences, and across restaurant tables). All three of these sources are important. However, because of the researcher's training, conducting research, it seems to us, is the area in which an academician can assume the most leadership.

Institutions of higher education face a special challenge in connecting research with practice *at the institutional level*. As noted earlier, universities and colleges prepare practitioners. Research on instructional materials is seldom part of the curriculum for professional preparation. We see here a particular opportunity for advancing the research agenda while also improving practice. Many teachers and administrators will at various times in their career confront the task of deciding what materials to select and how to adapt them for their particular circumstances – an ideal task for learning about applied research methodologies!

Final steps: Dissemination   Educational researchers tend to communicate with one another, but are rather lackadaisical about the task of sharing their results with practitioners, including publishers. There is a tension here; researchers are often approached to become consultants or authors for a publishing firm. While the potential impact of a researcher's work may be enhanced through this arrangement, direct employment with a commercial firm means giving up some amount of objectivity. These circumstances pose two challenges in connecting research with practice. The first is that research does not reach the practitioner in the first place, and the second is that it influences practice only through individual idiosyncracies.

Despite these conditions, textbook reform does not currently lack for leadership in the academic community. The challenge, as depicted in figure 9.1, is for participants to assume leadership in different parts of the overall enterprise, relying on common design lenses to achieve coherence.

Collaboration Among Participants

Unfortunately, collaboration among participants barely exists. California invites publisher representatives to attend meetings to develop the curriculum frameworks that establish goals for textbook adoption. The representatives, from competing publishing firms, typically sit quietly through the meetings, reluctant to reveal their plans to one another. The 22 adoption states tend to go their separate ways, although California and Texas have announced plans to collaborate on some adoptions. Publishers mistrust states. States blame publishers. Districts in nonadoption states complain about the heavy influence of adoption states. Districts conduct independent selections, trusting no other analysis than their own.

Fundamental change from textbook series to Instructional Support Systems will require collaboration throughout the enterprise. Figure 9.1 depicts parties working together to establish goal designs, consider system design, conduct review and try out, and take final steps. Collaboration will require the separate collectives involved to begin to trust one another. We suspect that as collaboration develops, mutual respect will also increase.

Publishers will collaborate more cautiously than other participants. Publishers are competitors, and rightly so. We suggest that their competition can result in diversity among Instructional Support Systems. States and districts would have an array among which to choose systems that best fit their own situations. Despite the need of publishers to compete, we suggest several opportunities for them to collaborate as a group with the other collectives.

Goal Designs

All participants have something to gain from collaborating on goal designs. In the preceding section we suggested that professional organizations, states, districts, and university researchers could all take appropriate leadership in designing goals for Instructional Support Systems. By working together, theorists and practitioners alike will benefit from the other's perspective.

Without collaboration, their separate efforts will frequently either duplicate or contradict one another.

Publishers belong in the collaborative mix as well. Publishers do not want to be responsible for establishing goals, and we concur. Their primary expertise lies in system design. Nonetheless, they have a wealth of practical experience over time that they can use to judge what will work. Their contribution to goal design would bring a valuable practical perspective. The ultimate outcome would be a design that publishers could use to produce an Instructional Support System.

How could such collaboration be brought about? At this point, some of the participants are so suspicious of one another that it is difficult to imagine how they could work together to design goals. We suggest three conditions: (a) an analytic stance that relies heavily on design issues; (b) a perspective of mutual respect; and (c) a neutral venue.

Our suggestions grow out of personal experience. Early in our work with textbook publishers, we became impressed by the expertise and dedication of the editors and consultants with whom we talked. On their suggestion, we collaborated with the Association of American Publishers to bring editors-in-chief, vice presidents, and consultants from major textbook publishers to a symposium at a retreat center near Stanford University. During the symposium, our university staff shared many of the ideas in this book for feedback and critique. The lively give-and-take impressed us all. As one of the publisher participants said after the last session, "This was very valuable. And we are all competitors!"

The substance of the symposium focused on the design of Instructional Support Systems. We discussed elements, linkages, and themes without asking individual publishers to commit themselves on specifics. Publishers were candid about which ideas seemed workable. Publishers and university staff all came from a stance of mutual respect. We valued their expertise, and they responded positively to our desire to establish workable goals. The symposium took place in a venue that was not a "home base" for any of the collaborators. While our staff conducted the sessions, three of the editors worked with us to develop the agenda. Our experience could serve as a collaboration model that includes adopters, selectors, and those in professional organizations as well.

The most likely participants to spearhead the collaboration are university researchers and professional organizations. We imagine a scenario in which either develops a draft goal design and invites colleagues, major adoption states, several large districts, and editors from publishing firms to provide feedback and critique. The resulting design is then widely disseminated.

Our vision of collaboration is admittedly far-reaching, but collaboration among states is probably essential for fundamental change of the scope that we envision. Well-designed Instructional Support Systems will be impossible for publishers to produce if they continue to be given differing sets of goals from several different states.

Consider the history/social science adoption in California. The state developed a carefully specified (although perhaps less than well-designed) curriculum framework. Only one K–8 series was submitted for committee review, although a large handful of publishers submitted books for one or two grade levels. Publishers have explained to us that the California framework was so different from specifications in other parts of the country that they could not afford to participate. A prominent California official countered by placing the blame on the publishers. "If we could only get the publishers to do what we want them to do," she complained, "we could get the textbooks we want." Her understanding of the situation seems rather simplistic. Only if adoption states learn to collaborate on developing goals will transformational change be possible

It is less clear how one independent governmental entity can influence another. Certainly, quality work is likely to be persuasive. The framework or proclamation with a clear goal design should be more likely to attract the attention and support of other states and districts than specifications that are confusing, grandiose, or trivial. If California and Texas do attempt to work together on future adoptions, we propose that they might follow our design suggestions for successful collaboration.

Goal designs will be the engines that drive the development and selection of Instructional Support Systems. Consequently, the extent to which they are developed collaboratively will have a substantial influence on the entire enterprise.

System Design

We think that collaboration around this task is feasible. If publishers, states, and districts all accept the same goal designs, we can expect publishers to produce Instructional Support Systems that match the designs, and adopters and selectors to search for comparable elements, linkages, and themes as they make their selections. Because producers and consumers share goals, states and districts will not find themselves in the predicament of trying to analyze either poorly designed or mismatched materials. Their task will be far easier than the one faced by our fictitious district in chapter 7. Publishers will not be dangling out in front of most of the national market.

Since publishers and selection committees will speak the same language, they can be of great help to one another. A science consultant with one of the textbook publishers whose series was recently adopted by California bemoaned the strained relationship between his staff and the Instructional Materials Evaluation Panel (IMEP) members, who were evaluating the series. He suggested that editors and committee members collaborate during textbook adoption. Suppose, he mused, that every publishing firm were to have an 800 number to be used by IMEP members to ask design questions of editors. Committee members who talked to editors would understand the publisher's intent better and editors would have immediate feedback that they could consider for redesign. The consultant drew a useful distinction between the sales staff of a publisher (the group that typically has contact with IMEP members) and the editorial staff. Editors are far more knowledgeable about system design than sales staff and removed from the pressures to make a sale. Collaboration between adopters or selectors and editors could benefit both parties, he explained.

Review and Try Out

Reviews and try outs are typically given short shrift by adoption states and many districts. Publishers consider their own results to be proprietary and keep them as closely guarded secrets. University researchers, because they influence the market only indirectly, are usually brought into the loop too late to influence textbook design substantially. Carefully designed review and try out can be highly informative, and could distinguish successful from unsuccessful characteristics of Instructional Support Systems.

Suppose that parties shared outcomes with one another in a format that communicated clearly. For example, states and districts could share with publishers both their analyses of system design and outcomes from any piloting that they conducted. Publishers could use this feedback in the production of future Instructional Support Systems. James Squire has suggested that publishers could disseminate both pre-publication and post-publication market research, after materials have been on the market long enough to make the outcomes no longer of interest to competitors.[10] Results would be useful to all participants who are trying to improve instructional materials. University researchers could share research results directly with publishers, adopters, and selectors. Publishers could bring in university researchers in the early stages of materials production, when it is still possible to change the design.

Earlier, we proposed an alternate model to public review sessions based on the introduction of innovative computer technology. This model could support collaboration. Both the public body and the textbook publishers would be taking leadership in shaping the public discussion. A spirit of collaboration in which various participants valued one another's contributions would also be pervasive. Each collective would be given the chance to be heard in a thoughtful, carefully planned manner. State and district committees could share the design goals and pictures of the analysis at teacher workshops, public display centers, and public hearings, to shape the dialogue and influence decisions.

Final Steps

The final step for all participants is the placing of quality materials in the hands of students and teachers. Collaboration in planning this final step could create adoption and selection cycles that work well for everyone.

Editors and consultants have told us that rigid adoption cycles create conditions that actually make it too risky for them to develop series that are fundamentally different. Time is probably the most serious constraint, they explain. To replace traditional teacher manuals with teacher guides, for example, publishers would want to conduct several rounds of design–try out–redesign, a cycle that takes three to five years to complete. They would want to conduct similar cycles for the development of both valid, reliable assessment tools and comprehensible written material, computer software, laser disks, and so on that reflect the expert's lens. Adoption cycles that allow publishers two and three-fourths years at best to develop submissions provide too little time for publishers to complete these cycles competently. Furthermore, publishers are reluctant to spend the money to develop an entire series that may actually not sell very well.

Publishers explain that an attractive solution to both the time and money constraints is serial publication. Rather than producing an entire series at once, publishers would release series one grade level at a time, as soon as the grade level was ready rather than according to state adoption schedules. The production of each subsequent grade level could build on the experience that students and teachers were having with the earlier releases.

Adopters and selectors are less likely to be enthusiastic about serial publication than publishers. However, current trends suggest that a compromise may be reachable. Texas, for example, considers only some grade levels and some subject areas each year. California has legislated rolling adoption in which new materials can be submitted every two years in between the main seven-year cycle. Both of these systems suggest that moving from a rigid schedule to one that is more flexible to accommodate serial publishing may not be impossible even for large, influential adoption states. We would expect even more accommodation from districts in open market states.

Whether serial publication can actually become a reality, publishers and adopters/selectors must begin to collaborate on establishing adoption cycles and publication deadlines for fundamental change to occur. If publishers require a certain amount of time to develop instructional materials competently, then adopters and selectors must consider their timelines in establishing deadlines. If adopters/selectors require a regular cycle in order to convene and prepare evaluators who can complete their tasks competently, then publishers need to remain as efficient as possible to accommodate the cycle while still producing well-designed materials.

Concluding Thoughts

Change has already begun and will continue through the next decade. As we write, it will be technologically and economically feasible for every teacher in the United States to be on the World Wide Web in five to ten years. Teachers and their students will have access to vast amounts of multimedia, which will offer a potential for flexibility that was impossible with traditional textbooks. The tension between flexibility and coherence will grow ever greater as the banquet of possibilities expands. We have claimed that children's educational experiences – the materials they read, the instruction they are offered, and the curriculum that they encounter – have the potential to nurture their minds. These educational experiences can help children to see the world through the lens of the expert, if they are carefully designed. As teachers and children wander from web site to web site, for example, what will happen to the big ideas envisioned by Whitehead as providing order to the chaos of experience? Design rubrics could make the difference between education that is complete chaos and education that supports children as they construct for themselves important models, theories, and understandings.

In this book, we have laid out a vision that incorporates both the qualities of effective instructional materials and the characteristics of effective action. We have suggested where education might best go, how to get there, and how to recognize the destination once schools have reached it. This vision is demanding. It asks of the future that educational systems, including textbooks, genuinely nurture the minds of all children and effectively support teachers in reaching this goal.

Notes

1 Tyack and Cuban (1985).
2 Peters and Waterman (1982).
3 Stevenson and Stigler (1994).
4 Tyson-Bernstein (1988b), p. 198.
5 Farr, Tulley, and Powell (1987), p. 277.
6 Tyson-Bernstein (1988a), p. 76.
7 See, e.g., American Association for the Advancement of Science (1989) and National Center for Improving Science Education (1989, 1992).
8 International Reading Association and the National Council of Teachers of English (1996).
9 Tyson-Bernstein (1988a).
10 Squire (1987).

REFERENCES

Adoption Guidelines Project 1990: *A Guide to Selecting Basal Reading Programs*. Champaign: University of Illinois at Urbana-Champaign, Adoption Guidelines Project, Reading Research and Education Center, Center for the Study of Reading.

American Association for the Advancement of Science 1989: *Science for all Americans / A Project 2061 Report on Literacy Goals in Science, Mathematics, and Technology*. Washington, DC.

Anderson, L. M. 1993: Auxiliary materials that accompany textbooks: Can they promote "higher-order" learning? In B. K. Britton, A. Woodward, and M. Binkley (eds.), *Learning from Textbooks: Theory and Practice*. Hillsdale, NJ: Lawrence Erlbaum, 135–60.

Apple, M. W. 1985: The culture and commerce of the textbook. *Journal of Curriculum Studies*, 17, 147–62.

Apple, M. W. and Christian-Smith, L. K. 1991: The politics of the textbook. In M. W. Apple and L. K. Christian-Smith (eds.), *The Politics of the Textbook*. London: Routledge/New York: Chapman and Hall, 1–21.

Applebee, A. N. 1978: *The Child's Concept of Story*. Chicago: The University of Chicago Press.

Armbruster, B. B. and Anderson, T. H. 1985: Producing 'considerate' expository text: or Easy reading is damned hard writing. *Journal of Curriculum Studies*, 17, 181–94.

Armbruster, B. B., Osborn, J. H., and Davison, A. L. 1985: Readability formulas may be dangerous to your textbooks. *Educational Leadership*, 42, 18–20.

Avelar La Salle, R. 1991: The effect of metacognitive instruction on the transfer of expository comprehension skills: the inter-lingual and cross-lingual cases. Doctoral dissertation, Stanford University). *Dissertation Abstracts International*, 52, 3175.

Baumann, J. F. 1986: Effect of rewritten content textbook passages on middle grade students' comprehension of main ideas: Making the inconsiderate considerate. *Journal of Reading Behavior*, 18, 1–21.

Beck, I. L., McKeown, M. G., and Gromoll, E. W. 1989: Learning from social studies texts. *Cognition and Instruction*, 6, 99–158.

Beck, I. L., McKeown, M. G., Sinatra, G. M., and Loxterman, J. A. 1991: Revising social studies text from a text-processing perspective: Evidence of improved comprehensibility. *Reading Research Quarterly*, 26, 251–76.

Begley, S., Springen, K., Hager, M., Barrett, T., and Joseph, N. 1990: Rx for learning/ There's no secret about how to teach science. *Newsweek*, April 9, 55–64.

Bereiter, C. and Scardamalia, M. 1987: *The Psychology of Written Communication*. Hillsdale, NJ: Lawrence Erlbaum.

Berliner, D. C. and Biddle, B. J. 1996: *The Manufactured Crisis*. Reading, MA: Addison-Wesley.

Bernstein, H. T. 1985: The new politics of textbook adoption. *Phi Delta Kappan*, March, 463–466.

Bloom, B. S., Hastings, J. T., and Madaus, G. F. 1971: *Handbook on Formative and Summative Evaluation of Student Learning*. New York: McGraw-Hill.

Bransford, J. D. and Johnson, M. K. 1972: Contextual prerequisites for understanding: Some investigations of comprehension and recall. *Journal of Verbal Learning and Verbal Behavior*, 11, 717–26.

Brooks, C. and Warren, R. P. 1972: *Modern Rhetoric* (shorter 3rd edn). New York: Harcourt Brace Jovanovich.

Brown, A. L. 1997: Transforming schools into communities of thinking and learning about serious matters. *American Psychologist*, 52, 399–413.

Brown, A. L., Ash, D., Rutherford, M., Nakagawa, K., Gordon, A., and Campione, J. C. 1993: Distributed expertise in the classroom. In G. Solomon (ed.), *Distributed Cognitions: Psychological and Educational Considerations*. New York: Cambridge University Press, 188–228.

Brown, A. L., Armbruster, B., and Baker, L. 1986: The role of metacognition in reading and studying. In J. Oransanu (ed.), *Reading Comprehension: From Research to Practice*. Hillsdale, NJ: Lawrence Erlbaum, 49–75.

Calfee, R. C. 1981: Cognitive psychology and educational practice. In D. C. Berliner (ed.), *Review of Research in Education*. Washington, DC: American Educational Research Association.

Calfee, R. C. and Chambliss, M. J. 1987: The structural design features of large texts. *Educational Psychologist*, 22, 357–78.

Calfee, R. C. and Chambliss, M. J. 1988: The structure of social studies books: Where is the design? Paper presented at the annual meeting of the American Educational Research Association, New Orleans, April.

Calfee, R. C. and Curley, R. 1984: Structures of prose in the content areas. In J. Flood (ed.), *Understanding Reading Comprehension*. Newark, DE: International Reading Association, 161–80.

Calfee, R. C. and Patrick, C. L. 1995: *Teach our Children Well*. Stanford, CA: Stanford Alumni Association.

California Department of Education 1991: *The Invitation to Submit Basic Instructional Materials for Adoption in California/Science*. Sacramento, CA.

California State Board of Education 1988: *History–Social Science Framework for California Public Schools Kindergarten through Grade Twelve*. Sacramento, CA.

California State Board of Education 1990: *Science Framework for California Public Schools Kindergarten through Grade Twelve*. Sacramento, CA.

Canjemi, J. (ed.) 1987b: *Our World/Grade 6*. Orlando, FL: Holt, Rinehart, and Winston.

Carus, B. M. 1990: Using textbooks to improve the curriculum: Help or hindrance? Paper presented at the annual meeting of the Association for Supervision and Curriculum Development, San Antonio, TX, March 3.

Carus, B. M. 1987: California and textbook reform: Too little too late, too much too soon. Paper presented at the annual conference of the American Educational Research Association, Washington, DC, April.

Cazden, C. B. 1988: *Classroom Discourse: The Language of Teaching and Learning.* Portsmouth, NH: Heineman.

Center for Education Studies/American Textbook Council 1994: *History Textbooks/A Standard and Guide/1994–95 Edition.* New York.

Chall, J. S. 1988: The beginning years. In B. L. Zakaluk and S. J. Samuels (eds.), *Readability/Its Past, Present, and Future.* Newark, DE: The International Reading Association, 2–13.

Chall, J. S. and Dale, E. 1995: *Readability Revisited: The New Dale–Chall Readability Formula.* Cambridge, MA: Brookline.

Chall, J. S. and Squire, J. R. 1991: The publishing industry and textbooks. In R. Barr, M. L. Kamil, P. Mosenthal, and P. D. Pearson (eds.), *Handbook of Reading Research/Volume II.* White Plains, NY: Longman, 120–46.

Chambliss, M. J. 1993: Assessing instructional materials: How comprehensible are they? In C. J. Gordon, G. D. Labercane, and W. R. McEachern (eds.), *Elementary Reading Process and Practice* (2nd edn). Needham Heights, MA: Ginn.

Chambliss, M. J. 1995: Text cues and strategies successful readers use to construct the gist of lengthy written arguments. *Reading Research Quarterly,* 30, 778–807.

Chambliss, M. J. and Calfee, R. C. 1989: Designing science textbooks to enhance student understanding. *Educational Psychologist,* 24, 307–22.

Chambliss, M., Calfee, R., and Wong, I. 1990: Structure and content in science textbooks: Where is the design? Paper presented at the annual meeting of the American Educational Research Association, Boston, MA.

Cohen, M. R., Cooney, T. M., and Hawthorne, C. M. 1989: How does plate tectonics explain earthquakes and volcanoes? *Discover Science/Grade 6.* Glenview, IL: Scott, Foresman, 302–4.

College Entrance Examination Board 1986: *Academic Preparation in Social Studies/Teaching for Transition from High School to College.* New York.

Cook, L. K. and Mayer, R. E. 1988: Teaching readers about the structure of scientific text. *Journal of Educational Psychology,* 80, 448–56.

Cooper, E. K., Blackwood, P. E., and Boeschen, J. A. 1985a: Directing your body to move. *HBJ Science/Grade 5.* Orlando, FL: Harcourt Brace Jovanovich, 83–4.

Cooper, E. K., Blackwood, P. E., Boeschen, J. A. 1985b: Electricity: Energy from energy. *HBJ Science/Guide 6.* Orlando, FL: Harcourt Brace Jovanovich, 152.

Crabtree, C., Nash, G. B., Gagnon, P., and Waugh, S. 1992: *Lessons from History: Essential Understandings and Historical Perspectives Students should Acquire.* Los Angeles: The National Center for History in the Schools/A Cooperative UCLA/NEH Research Program.

Curley, R. G. 1990: Separable processes in reading comprehension: Assessment and instruction. Doctoral dissertation, Stanford University. *Dissertation Abstracts*

International, 51, 3685.

Dahl, R. 1961: *James and the Giant Peach*. New York: Penguin.

Davison, A. and Kantor, R. N. 1982: On the failure of readability formulas to define readable texts: A case study from adaptations. *Reading Research Quarterly*, 17, 187–209.

Dewey, J. 1902: *The Child and the Curriculum*. Chicago: University of Chicago Press.

Doctorow, M., Wittrock, M. C., and Marks, C. 1978: Generative processes in reading comprehension. *Journal of Educational Psychology*, 70, 109–18.

Dole, J., Rogers, T., and Osborn, J. 1989: *Improving the Textbook Selection Process: Case Studies of the Textbook Adoption Guidelines Project* (Technical Report No. 478). Champaign: University of Illinois at Urbana–Champaign, Center for the Study of Reading.

Drum, P. A. and Calfee, R. C. 1979: The compensatory reading survey. In R. C. Calfee and P. A. Drum (eds.), *Teaching Reading in Compensatory Classes*. Newark, DE: International Reading Association.

Education Development Center 1992: *Insights Elementary Science Program*. Newton, MA.

Elliott, D. L. 1990: Textbooks and curriculum: 1950–1980. In D. L. Elliott and A. Woodward (eds.), *Textbooks and Schooling in the United States: Eighty-Ninth Yearbook of the National Society for the Study of Education: Part I*. Chicago, IL: The University of Chicago Press, 42–55.

Englert, C. S. and Hiebert, E. H. 1984: Children's developing awareness of text structures in expository materials. *Journal of Educational Psychology*, 76, 65–74.

Farr, R. and Tulley, M. A. 1985: Do adoption committees perpetuate mediocre textbooks? *Phi Delta Kappan*, March, 467–71.

Farr, R., Tulley, M. A., and Powell, D. 1987: The evaluation and selection of basal readers. *The Elementary School Journal*, 87, 267–81.

Fiske, E. B. 1987: The push for smarter schoolbooks. *New York Times, Education Life*, August, 20–23.

Fraatz, J. M. B. 1987: *The Politics of Reading*. New York: Teachers College Press.

Freebody, P. and Anderson, R. C. 1983: Effects of vocabulary difficulty, text cohesion, and schema availability on reading comprehension. *Reading Research Quarterly*, 18, 277–94.

Freeman, D. J. and Porter, A. C. 1989: Do textbooks dictate the content of mathematics instruction in elementary school? *American Educational Research Journal*, 26, 403–21.

Fry, E. B. 1968: A readability formula that saves time. *Journal of Reading*, 11, 513–16.

Garner, R. 1987: *Metacognition and Reading Comprehension*. Norwood, NJ: Ablex.

Garner, R., Gillingham, M. G., and White, C. S. 1989: Effects of "seductive details" on macroprocessing and microprocessing in adults and children. *Cognition and Instruction*, 6, 41–57.

Goodman, K. 1986: *What's Whole in Whole Language?* Portsmouth, NH: Heinemann.

Graves, D. 1983: *Writing: Teachers and Children at Work*. Portsmouth, NH: Heinemann.

Graves, M. F., Prenn, M. C., Earle, J., Thompson, M., Johnson, V., and Slater, W. H. 1991: Commentary: Improving Instructional Text: Some Lessons Learned. *Reading Research Quarterly*, 26, 110–22.

Haley, A. 1976: *Roots/The Saga of an American Family*. New York: Dell.

Hare, V. C., Rabinowitz, M., and Schieble, K. M. 1989: Text effects on main idea comprehension. *Reading Research Quarterly*, 24, 72–88.

Hidi, S. and Baird, W. 1988: Strategies for increasing text-based interest and students' recall of expository texts. *Reading Research Quarterly*, 23, 465–83.

Hoffmann, J. V., McCarthey, S. J.. Abott, J., Christian, C., Corman, L., Curry, C., Dressman, M., Elliot, B., Matherne, D., and Stahle, D. 1994: So what's new in the new basals? *Journal of Reading Behaviour*, 26, 47–73.

Holden, C. 1987: Textbook controversy intensifies nationwide. *Science*, 235, 19–21.

Houghton Mifflin 1989a: *Houghton Mifflin Literary Readers/Book 4*. Boston.

Houghton Mifflin 1989b: *Houghton Mifflin Literary Readers/Selection Plans and Instructional Support/Book 4/Teacher's Guide*. Boston.

Houghton Mifflin 1991a: *Houghton Mifflin Social Studies/A Message of Ancient Days*. Boston.

Houghton Mifflin 1991b: *Houghton Mifflin Social Studies/Oh, California/Teacher's Edition*. Boston.

International Reading Association and the National Council of Teachers of English 1996: *Standards for the English Language Arts*. Newark, DE and Urbana, IL.

Kintsch, W. and Yarbrough, J. C. 1982: Role of rhetorical structure in text structure. *Journal of Educational Psychology*, 74, 828–34.

Klare, G. R. 1984: Readability. In P. D. Pearson (ed.), *Handbook of Reading Research*. New York: Longman, 681–744.

Klein, S. 1983: Table of contents. *Our United States/Grade 5*. Madison, NJ: Steck-Vaughn.

Komoski, K. 1985: Instructional materials will not improve until we change the system. *Educational Leadership*, 31–37.

Langer, J. A. 1986: *Children Reading and Writing*. Norwood, NJ: Ablex.

Lash, J. P. 1997: *Helen and Teacher*. New York: Addison-Wesley.

Lemon, R. S. 1955: The wonders of a feather. *All About Birds*. New York: Random House.

Linden, G. M., Brink, D. C., and Huntington, R. H. 1986: Table of contents. *Legacy of Freedom Volume I: United States History Through Reconstruction*. River Forest, IL: Laidlaw Brothers.

Lovitt, T. C., Horton, S. V., and Bergerud, O. 1987: Matching students with textbooks: An alternative to readability formulas and standardized tests. *British Columbia Journal of Special Education*, 11, 49–55.

Lukins, R. 1990: *A Critical Handbook of Children's Literature* (4th edn). Oxford, OH: Scott, Foresman.

Mallinson, G. G., Mallinson, J. B., and Smallwood, W. L. 1985a: How heat moves through solid matter: How does heat move through solids? *Silver Burdett Science/Grade 4*. Morristown, NJ: Silver Burdett, 139–41.

Mallinson, G. G., Mallinson, J. B., and Smallwood, W. L. 1985b: Reptiles: What are the main characteristics of reptiles? *Silver Burdett Science/Grade 5*. Morristown, NJ: Silver Burdett, 63–6.

McGuffey, W. H. 1867: *McGuffey's New 3rd Eclectic Reader for Young Learners*. Cincinnati, OH: Wilson, Hinkle, and Co.

McMurray, F. and Cronbach, L. J. 1955: The controversial past and present of the text. In L. Cronbach (ed.), *Text Materials in Modern Education*. Urbana, IL: University of Illinois Press.

Meyer, B. J. F. 1985: Prose analysis: Purposes, procedures, and problems, parts 1 and 2. In B. K. Britton and J. B. Black (eds.), *Understanding Expository Text*. Hillsdale, NJ: Lawrence Erlbaum, 11–64, 269–304.

Meyer, B. J. F. and Freedle, R. O. 1984: Effects of discourse type on recall. *American Educational Research Journal*, 21, 121–43.

Miller, G. A. 1956: The magical number seven, plus or minus two: some limits on our capacity for processing information. *Psychological Review*, 63, 81–97.

Miller, K. E., Nelson, J. E., and Naifeh, M. 1995: *Cross-state Compendium for the NAEP 1994 Grade 4 Reading Assessment*. Washington, DC: Office of Educational Research and Improvement.

Moore, D. W., Readence, J. C., and Rickelman, R. J. 1983: An historical exploration of content area reading instruction. *Reading Research Quarterly*, 18, 419–38.

National Center for Improving Science Education 1989: *Science and Technology Education for the Elementary Years: Frameworks for Curriculum and Instruction*. Andover, MA: The National Center for Improving Science Education, A Partnership of the Network, Inc. and the Biological Sciences Curriculum Study.

National Center for Improving Science Education 1992: *Building Scientific Literacy: A Blueprint for Science in the Middle Years*. Andover, MA: The National Center for Improving Science Education, A Partnership of the Network, Inc. and the Biological Sciences Curriculum Study.

National Council of Teachers of Mathematics 1991: *Professional Standards for Teaching Mathematics*. Reston, VA.

Newmann, F. M. 1988: Can depth replace coverage in high school curriculum? *Phi Delta Kappan*, January, 345–48.

Nickerson, R. S. 1985: Understanding understanding. *American Journal of Education*, 93, 201–39.

Orsolini, M. and DiGiacinto, P. D. 1996: Use of referential expressions in 4 year-old children's narratives: Invented versus recalled stories. In C. Pontecorvo, M. Orsolini, B. Burge, and L. B. Resnick (eds.), *Children's Early Text Construction*. Mahwah, NJ: Lawrence Erlbaum, 67–81.

Osborn, J. 1984: The purposes, uses and contents of workbooks and some guidelines for publishers. In R. C. Anderson, J. Osborn, and R. J. Tierney (eds.), *Learning to Read in American Schools: Basal Readers and Content Texts*. Hillsdale, NJ: Lawrence Erlbaum, 40–55.

Osborn, J. and Decker, K. 1993: Ancillary materials – What's out there? In B. K. Britton, A. Woodward, and M. Binkley, *Learning from Textbooks: Theory and Practice*. Hillsdale, NJ: Lawrence Erlbaum, 161–85.

Patterson, K. 1977: *Bridge to Terabithia*. New York: HarperCollins.

Peters, T. J. and Waterman, R. H., Jr. 1982: *In Search of Excellence*. New York: Harper & Row.

Piaget, J. 1970: *Science of Education and the Psychology of the Child*. New York: Viking.

Pressley, M. S. and Rankin, J. 1994: More about whole language methods of reading instruction for students at risk for early reading failure. *Learning Disabilities Research and Practice*, 9, 157–68.

Proett, P. and Gill, K. 1986: *The Writing Process in Action: A Handbook for Teachers*. Urbana, IL: National Council of Teachers of English.

Ravitch, D. 1985: *The Schools we Deserve: Reflections on the Educational Crises of our Times*. New York: Basic Books.

Rayner, K. and Pollatsek, A. 1989: *The Psychology of Reading*. Englewood Cliffs, NJ: Prentice Hall.

Resnick, L. B. 1987: *Education and Learning to Think*. Washington, DC: Academy Press.

Richgels, D. J., McGee, L. M., Lomax, R. G., and Sheard, C. 1987: Awareness of four text structures: Effects on recall of expository text. *Reading Research Quarterly*, 22, 177–96.

Sacks, H., Schegloff, E., and Jefferson, G. 1974): A simplest systematics for the organization of turn-taking for conversation. *Language*, 50, 696–735.

Schank, R. C. 1979: Interesting: Controlling inferences. *Artificial Intelligence*, 12, 273–97.

Schegloff, E. 1968: Sequencing in conversational openings. *American Anthropologist*, 70, 1075–95.

Schegloff, E. and Sacks, H. 1973: Opening up closings. *Semiotica*, 8, 289–327.

Schon, D. A. 1987: *Educating the Reflective Practitioner*. San Francisco: Jossey–Bass.

Schwab, J. J. 1978: Education and the structure of the disciplines. In I. Westbury and N. J. Wilkof (eds.), *Science, Curriculum, and Liberal Education: Selected Essays*. Chicago, IL: The University of Chicago Press, 229–72.

Silver Burdett 1986: *The World and its People/The United States and its Neighbors/ Annotated Teacher's Edition*. Morristown, NJ.

Silver Burdett & Ginn 1989: *Silver Secrets/Teacher Edition/Volume 1*. Needham Heights, NJ.

Simon, H. A. 1981: *The Sciences of the Artificial* (2nd edn). Cambridge, MA: MIT Press.

Squire, J. R. 1985: For better textbooks. *English Journal*, 74, 20–21.

Squire, J. R. 1987: Studies of textbooks: Are we asking the right questions? Paper presented at the Inaugural Conference of the Benton Center for Curriculum and Instruction, Chicago, IL, May.

Squire, J. R. and Morgan, R. T. 1990: The elementary and high school textbook market today. In D. L. Elliott and A. Woodward (eds.), *Textbooks and Schooling in the United States: Eighty-ninth Yearbook of the National Society for the Study of Education: Part I*. Chicago: The University of Chicago Press, 162–77.

State of New York 1847: *The Statues of the State of New York Relating to Common Schools*, Albany, NY.

Stevenson, H. W. and Stigler, J. W. 1994: *The Learning Gap: Why our Schools are Failing and What we can Learn from Japanese and Chinese Education*. New York: Simon & Schuster.

Stodolsky, S. 1989: Is teaching really by the book? In P. W. Jackson and S. Haroutunian-Gordon (eds.), *From Socrates to Software: The Teacher as Text and the Text as Teacher: Eighty-Eighth Yearbook of the National Society for the Study of Education: Part I*. Chicago: The University of Chicago Press, 159–84.

Taylor, M. 1976: *Roll of Thunder, Hear my Cry*. New York: Penguin.

Texas Education Agency 1991: *Proclamation of the State Board of Education Advertising for Bids on Textbooks/Proclamation 68*. Austin, TX.

Toulmin, S. E. 1958: *The Uses of Argument*. Cambridge: Cambridge University Press.

Trabasso, T. and Magliano, J. P. 1996: How do children understand what they read and what we can do to help them? In M. F. Graves, P. van den Broek and B. M. Taylor (eds.), *The First R: Every Child's Right to Read*. New York: Teachers College Press, 160–88.

Tufte, E. R. 1990: *Envisioning Information*. Chesire, CT: Graphics Press.

Tulley, M. and Farr, R. 1990: Textbook evaluation and selection. In D. L. Elliott and A. Woodward (eds.), *Textbooks and Schooling in the United States: Eighty-Ninth Yearbook of the National Society for the Study of Education: Part I*. Chicago: The University of Chicago Press, 162–77.

Tyack, D. and Cuban, L. 1995: *Tinkering Toward Utopia: A Century of Public School Reform*. Cambridge, MA: Harvard University Press.

Tyler, R. W. 1949: *Basic Principles of Curriculum and Instruction*. Chicago, IL: The University of Chicago Press.

Tyson, H. 1990: *Three Portraits: Texbook Adoption Policy Changes in North Carolina, Texas, California*. Washington, DC: The Institute for Educational Leadership, Inc.

Tyson, H. and Woodward, A. 1989: Why students aren't learning very much from textbooks. *Educational Leadership*, November, 14–17.

Tyson-Bernstein, H. 1988a: *A Conspiracy of Good Intentions: America's Textbook Fiasco*. Washington, DC: The Council for Basic Education.

Tyson-Bernstein, H. 1988b: The academy's contribution to the impoverishment of America's textbooks. *Phi Delta Kappan*, November, 193–8.

US Department of Education 1983: *A Nation at Risk*. Washington, DC.

van Dijk, T. A. and Kintsch, W. 1983: *Strategies of Discourse Comprehension*. New York: Academic Press.

Venezky, R. L. 1992: Textbooks in school and society. In P. W. Jackson (ed.), *Handbook of Research on Curriculum*. New York: Macmillan, 436–461.

Venezky, R. L. 1994: Literacy and the textbook of the future. In N. J. Ellsworth, C. N. Hedley, and A. N. Baratta (eds.), *Literacy: A redefinition*. Hillsdale, NJ: Lawrence Erlbaum, 39–54.

Viadero, D. 1990: History curricula stir controversy in largest states. *Education Week*, August 1, 33, 38.

Viadero, D. 1990: Panels in GA., N.C. reject controversial textbooks. *Education Week*, October 10, 13–14.

Vygotsky, L. Y. 1978: *Mind in Society: The Development of Higher Psychological Processes* (M. Cole, V. John-Steiner, S. Scribner, and E. Souberman, eds.). Cambridge, MA: Harvard University Press.

Wade, S. E. and Adams, R. B. 1990: Effects of importance and interest on recall of biographical text. *Journal of Reading Behavior*, 22, 331–353.

Walker, A. 1992: *The Color Purple* (10th anniversary edn). New York: Harcourt Brace Jovanovich.

Weaver, C. 1990: *Understanding Whole Language*. Portsmouth, NH: Heinmann.

Westbury, I. 1990: Textbooks, textbook publishers, and the quality of schooling. In D. L. Elliott and A. Woodward, *Textbooks and Schooling in the United States/Eighty-Ninth Yearbook of the National Society for the Study of Education*. Chicago: The University of Chicago Press, 1–22.

White, E. B. 1980: *Charlotte's Web*. New York: HarperCollins.

Whitehead, A. N. 1929: *The Aims of Education*. New York: Macmillan.

Whitehead, A. N. 1974: *The Organisation of Thought*. Westport, CN: Greenwood Press.

Whittaker, A. 1992: Constructing science knowledge from exposition: The effects of text structure training. Doctoral dissertation, Stanford University, 1992. *Dissertation Abstracts International*, 53, 3157A.

Wilson, S. M. 1990): *Mastodons, maps, and Michigan: Exploring Uncharted Territory while Teaching Elementary School Social Studies* (Elementary Subjects Center Series No. 24). East Lansing: Michigan State University, Institute for Research on Teaching.

Wojciechowska, M. 1964: *Shadow of a Bull*. New York: Aladdin Books/Macmillan.

Wong, I. B. 1991: The role of explanatory texts in students' learning of science concepts. Doctoral dissertation, Stanford University. *Dissertation Abstracts International*, 52, 3209.

Wong, I. and Calfee, R. C. 1988: Informational trade books: A viable alternative to textbooks. Paper presented at the annual meeting of The American Educational Research Association, New Orleans, LA, April.

Woodward, A. 1989: Learning by pictures: Comments on learning, literacy, and culture. *Social Education*, 101–2.

Woodward, A. and Elliott, D. L. 1990: Textbook use and teacher professionalism. In D. L. Elliott and A. Woodward (eds.), *Textbooks and Schooling in the United States/Eighty-Ninth Yearbook of the National Society for the Study of Education/Part I*. Chicago: The University of Chicago Press, 178–193.

Yager, R. E. 1983:. The importance of terminology in teaching K–12 science. *Journal of Research in Science Teaching*, 29, 577–88.

INDEX